# Liberation Theology and the Liberal Society

# Liberation Theology and the Liberal Society

EDITED BY

## Michael Novak

American Enterprise Institute for Public Policy Research
Washington, D.C.

Distributed by arrangement with

UPA, Inc.
4720 Boston Way
Lanham, MD 20706
3 Henrietta Street
London WC2E 8LU England

"Underdevelopment Revisted," by Peter L. Berger, is reprinted from *Commentary,* July 1984, by permission; all rights reserved.

"The Return of the Debt Crisis," by Tom Bethell, © 1985 by National Review, Inc., 150 East 35 Street, New York, N.Y. 10016. Reprinted with permission.

"Where the Latin American Loans Went," by Larry A. Sjaastad, © 1984 Time Inc. All rights reserved.

**Library of Congress Cataloging-in-Publication Data**

Liberation theology and the liberal society.

(Sym 86 B)
1. Liberation theology—Congresses. 2. Christianity
and politics—Congresses. 3. Economics—Religious
aspects—Christianity—Congresses. 4. North America—
Relations—South America—Congresses. 5. South America
—Relations—North America—Congresses. I. Novak,
Michael. II. Series: AEI symposia ; 86B.
BT83.57.L493 1987 261.8'098 87-11552

ISBN 0-8447-2263-4
ISBN 0-8447-2264-2 (pb K.)

AEI Symposia 86B

*Printed in the United States of America*

# Contents

# Foreword

The troubles of our neighbors in Latin America continue to vex citizens and policy makers in the United States. Of particular concern are the roles of religion and morality in our response. The ideals of liberation theology, Latin American style, and of the liberal society, North American style, are not identical. With the publication of this volume, the American Enterprise Institute continues to investigate the underpinnings and consequences of these two ideals.

AEI has always attempted to foster greater interaction among the various disciplines associated with public policy—economics, law, diplomacy, and the social sciences in general—in the belief that the competition of ideas is fundamental to a free society. The 1985 Summer Institute, from which this edited text derives, is the seventh sponsored by AEI's Center for Religion, Philosophy, and Public Policy since 1978. Held at Airlie House in Warrenton, Virginia, from August 4 to August 7, it brought together some forty persons from business, government, the church, and the academy of both Latin and North America.

Special thanks are due to Michael Novak, director of the center, and to Michael Jackson, Judy Shindel, and Scott Walter for planning and directing the proceedings.

CHRISTOPHER C. DeMUTH
President
American Enterprise Institute

# Contributors

Hugo Assmann teaches at the Universidad Metodista de Piracicaba in his native Brazil. He pursued his study of philosophy and sociology in Brazil and his study of theology at the Gregorian University in Rome. He has traveled and lectured throughout Europe and Latin America and has held teaching positions in Brazil, West Germany, Bolivia, Costa Rica, and Chile. One of today's leading liberation theologians, Dr. Assmann's professional activities and writings arc extensive. His *Teología de la liberación* was published in Montevideo in 1970, followed by *Opresión-liberación: Desafío a los Cristianos* and *Teología desde la praxis de la liberación*. His works available in English include *Theology for a Nomad Church, Practical Theology of Liberation,* and contributions to numerous anthologies of liberation theology.

Peter L. Berger is University Professor at Boston University and an adjunct scholar at AEI. He has traveled and lectured extensively and is a frequent contributor to *Commentary* magazine and many other publications. Professor Berger's eleven books include *Pyramids of Sacrifice, The Heretical Imperative,* and *The War over the Family* (with Brigitte Berger). AEI has issued a collection of essays by Berger and Michael Novak, entitled *Speaking to the Third World.* Professor Berger's latest book is *The Capitalist Revolution: Fifty Propositions about Prosperity, Equality, and Liberty.*

Dean C. Curry is chairman of the Department of History and Political Science at Messiah College in Grantham, Pennsylvania. He also serves on the board of advisers of the Institute on Religion and Democracy as well as the Peace, Freedom, and Security Studies Program at the National Association of Evangelicals. Mr. Curry received his M.A. from the University of Pennsylvania and his Ph.D. from the Claremont Graduate School. He has written for several academic and popular journals including *Orbis, Crisis,* and *Eternity.* He edited and contributed to *Evangelicals and the Bishops' Pastoral Letter* and is cowriting a book on the social ethics of war and peace in a nuclear age.

NICK EBERSTADT is a visiting fellow at the Harvard University Center for Population Studies, a visiting scholar at the American Enterprise Institute, and a doctoral candidate in political economy and government at the John F. Kennedy School of Government. Mr. Eberstadt is the author of *Poverty in China* and a forthcoming volume tentatively titled *State Power and Human Poverty under Communism*. He has written widely on population, nutrition, and economic policy problems in third world and Communist nations and has been a consultant to the World Bank and the Department of State on development issues. A contributing editor to the Rockefeller Foundation's *RF Illustrated,* Mr. Eberstadt is a member of the Council on Foreign Relations and the Committee for the Free World.

MARK FALCOFF is an international affairs fellow at the Council on Foreign Relations. He received his Ph.D. from Princeton University in 1970 and has taught at the Universities of Illinois, Oregon, and California (Los Angeles). A specialist on Latin America, he was a senior consultant to the Kissinger Commission and served as a professional staff member of the Senate Foreign Relations Committee during the Ninety-ninth Congress. His books include *Prologue to Perón: Argentina in Depression and War 1930–1943; The Spanish Civil War, 1936–1939: American Hemispheric Perspectives; Small Countries, Large Issues;* and most recently, *The Continuing Crisis: U.S. Policy in Central America and the Caribbean.*

ARTURO FONTAINE graduated in philosophy from the University of Chile and holds an M.A. and an M. Phil. from Columbia University. He teaches philosophy at the Universidad de Chile and Academia de Ciencias Pedagógicas in Santiago. Mr. Fontaine is the editor of *Estudios Públicos,* the quarterly interdisciplinary journal published by the Centro de Estudios Públicos. His essays and articles have appeared in *Economía y Sociedad, Aiesthesis, Realidad, Estudios Públicos,* and the *Wall Street Journal.* His poems have been selected for several anthologies of Chilean poetry.

WILLIAM P. GLADE, JR., is professor of economics at the University of Texas at Austin. His Ph.D. in economics is from the University of Texas, and he has served on numerous public committees and associations related to Latin America. His books include *The Political Economy of Mexico, The Latin American Economies: A Study of Their Institutional Evolution,* and *Latin America—U.S. Economic Interactions* (coeditor).

ARTHUR F. MCGOVERN, S.J., was born and raised in Columbus, Ohio. He graduated from Georgetown University in 1951 and entered the Detroit Province of the Society of Jesus in the same year. He obtained a master's degree in philosophy from Loyola University, Chicago, and an S.T.L. degree in theology from West Baden College, Indiana. His doctorate is from the University of Paris, where he did his dissertation under Raymond Aron on "The Young Marx on the State." Father McGovern taught three years at the Bellarmine School of Theology before going to the University of Detroit, where he has been since 1970. In 1980, he was promoted to professor and honored with the University of Detroit's President's Award for Excellence in Teaching and Research. His publications include *Marxism: An American Christian Perspective* and essays in *Demythologizing Marxism, American Business Values,* and *Three Worlds of Marxist-Christian Dialogue.* He has published articles and reviews in many periodicals and is working on a book dealing with large corporations. He has lectured in various parts of the country on Marxism, church social teachings, liberation theology, and related topics.

MICHAEL NOVAK holds the George Frederick Jewett Chair in Religion, Philosophy, and Public Policy at the American Enterprise Institute, where he serves as director of Social and Political Studies. He was appointed head of the U.S. delegation to the Experts' Meeting on Human Contacts of the Conference on Security and Cooperation in Europe and served as a presidential adviser to the Ford and Carter administrations. He is vice-chairman of the Lay Commission on the U.S. Economy and Catholic Social Teaching. Mr. Novak received his M.A. in the history and philosophy of religion from Harvard and has published numerous books including *The Spirit of Democratic Capitalism, Moral Clarity in the Nuclear Age, Confession of a Catholic,* and *Freedom with Justice: Catholic Social Thought and Liberal Institutions.* His most recent work is *Will It Liberate? Questions about Liberation Theology.*

ASHLEY J. TELLIS is a visiting reseacher at Georgetown University. He has published articles on third world theology, economic development, and national security in the Indian *Journal of American Studies, Indian Theological Studies, Strategic Review,* and *Comparative Strategies.*

GEORGE WEIGEL is president of the James Madison Foundation in Washington, D.C., and was a fellow of the Woodrow Wilson International Center for Scholars at the Smithsonian Institution, September

1984 through August 1985. His study, *Tranquillitas Ordinis: The Present Failure and Future Promise of American Catholic Thought on War and Peace,* was published by Oxford University Press in early 1987. Mr. Weigel was assistant professor of theology and assistant dean of studies in the graduate department of St. Thomas Seminary in Kenmore, Washington, before being named scholar-in-residence at the World without War Council of Greater Seattle, a position he held until 1984. His articles and essays have appeared in such publications as *Freedom at Issue, The National Catholic Register, The National Catholic Reporter, This World, Eternity, America, The Christian Century, Chicago Studies,* and the *Thomist.* He is a founding member of the editorial board of *Crisis* and has written a regular column for the archdiocesan newspaper in Seattle since 1979.

# Introduction

## Michael Novak

The purpose of the Summer Institute of 1985 was to open a public dialogue between the two forms of liberation theology in the Americas, the "liberation theology" of Latin America and the liberal society of North America. This has been a longstanding dream of the Center for Religion, Philosophy, and Public Policy at AEI. As a start, in 1981 we published a set of widely used essays, *Liberation South, Liberation North,* linking the two approaches to liberation.

Once again as he did for our 1984 conference, *Latin America: Dependency or Interdependence?* (AEI, 1985), Professor William Glade sets the stage with a fair-minded and generous paper on the current situation of political economy in the Americas. He offers criticism both of liberationists and of liberals, pointing out weaknesses of language and analysis in both. He also draws out several complicating factors in the dialogue, marks out some common ground, and in the end discerns an opening "for an unprecedented constructive dialogue between liberation's structuralism and liberal political economy, with more hope than ever before that both theory and policy—not to mention Latin Americans themselves—will benefit therefrom."

Hugo Assmann's paper fulfilled one of Glade's hopes directly; he set forth his case in terms that allow for a significant degree of empirical verification. When the debate between liberation theologians and those who support the liberal society is conducted with empirical reference, there are at least two good effects: first, one can be more certain whether both are speaking of the same concrete realities; second, one can try to establish which descriptions of reality are more correct. These are admirable gains.

Another critical gain was achieved by Dr. Assmann's emphasis upon democracy. Even more in his oral summary than in his paper, Dr. Assmann stressed the difference between the situation of the past fifteen years and today. Then there was domestic "repression" under dictatorships of various sorts (he himself had been exiled from Brazil for a dozen years). Today, in many countries in which the major libera-

1

tion theologians are working (for Gutiérrez in Peru, Assmann and Boff in Brazil, Sobrino in El Salvador, Segundo in Uruguay, etc.), democracy is returning. These democracies are fragile, to be sure, as Assmann stresses, but their existence both changes the field of action and brings to light tangible new values.

Less concerned about "repression," theologians have more reason to act to reduce poverty ("oppression"). Given the return to democracy, liberation theologians have reason to praise its values far beyond the suffering they have known under dictatorship. In this century, to be sure, the word *democracy* has been captured even by Marxist states (for example, the German Democratic Republic of East Germany). And Dr. Assmann did not spell out the institutional characteristics he intended by his use of the term. Nonetheless, that democracy should now become a point of dialogue between liberation theologians and those who love the liberal society is a happy turn of events. Dr. Assmann also shows how the new democratic realities of Latin America place liberation theology in a new situation, in which the opinions of theologians will be tested in the public forum.

Hugo Assmann also delineated the acute problems of the Latin American countries as they grapple with the ever-increasing burden of foreign debt. He stresses the potential effect of the debt on democratic development and democratic institutions. He speaks of defusing the debt crisis via a "new spirit of dialogue and negotiation."

Peter Berger then focuses attention on the successful economic development of the countries of East Asia, in order to propose several non-Western models that may be illuminating for Latin American pioneers. He shows how theories of dependency overlook such success stories. Berger's presentation—one part reprinted from *Commentary* (1984) and another recreated from notes taken during his remarks—is important for placing the discussion of liberation theology and the liberal society (in its economic dimension) in an international framework. It is also important for helping to diagnose key factors in successful development, especially in the order of culture and intellect.

Arthur McGovern, S.J., next tackles the history of "dependency theory" as used by liberation theologians in Latin America. No one else has mapped this terrain so clearly. Not himself a *dependencista,* Father McGovern nonetheless presents a sympathetic, moderate, and reasoned middle ground, saving what seems valid in dependency theory and correcting some of its weaknesses. This paper deserves to be a *locus classicus* for all such discussions in the future.

Arturo Fontaine, one of the brightest young lights among Chilean intellectuals, raises a different sort of issue, in part rhetorical, in part philosophical. He addresses what he takes to be severe problems of style in the writings of liberation theology. He bases his presentation and arguments on Father Ronaldo Muñoz's work, *Nueva Conciencia de la Iglesia en America Latina,* which articulates "the set of beliefs underlying the corpus of church documents" expressing the "new consciousness" of the liberation elites. Dr. Fontaine sifts through the underlying socioeconomic assumptions in liberation theology and offers a rational and cool analysis of their probable consequences.

The final paper, by Latin American specialist Mark Falcoff, a resident fellow at the American Enterprise Institute, describes the tensions in Latin American culture concerning ideals of political economy—"a combination of statism and populism"—in the face of nearly universal demands for rapid economic growth. Marxism has limited appeal for Latin Americans, he argues, and there are several serious social obstacles to any popular acceptance of democratic capitalism. His analysis effectively ties together many of the observations discussed in the preceding papers.

Together, these essays offer new ground for the discussion of political and economic change in Latin America. They define the debate of the future.

Meanwhile, the discussion periods following each presentation were unusually fruitful. One could often sense how participants were changing their minds, or seeing things in a new light. Face-to-face, partisans of different views were able to seek clarifications, definitions, and responses to objections on the spot, in ways that might have taken months or years through the mere exchange of published papers. The motto of Cardinal Newman—*Cor ad cor loquitur* (Person speaks to person)—was well exemplified. The transcription of highlights from the discussion in cold type can scarcely convey the sense of one another's presence actually achieved. We hope, though, that at least a little of the mutual enjoyment of the occasion may be vicariously shared by readers.

All participants were invited to submit brief written comments after the event, and several chose to do so. These, too, have been reprinted at those places in the argument to which they addressed themselves.

In addition, since the discussion of Latin American debt loomed large in the proceedings, the editor has reprinted two articles that appeared in the public press—Tom Bethell's "The Return of The Debt Crisis" in *National Review* (August 1985) and "Where the Latin American Loans Went," by Larry A. Sjaastad of the University of Chicago and the Institute of International Studies in Geneva, from *Fortune* (November 26, 1984).

# A Dialectic between Liberationism and Liberalism

*William P. Glade, Jr.*

This is not the place for yet another gloss on the texts of liberation theology, nor would I be the person to offer such even if it were appropriate. One needs to recognize at the outset though that, in contemporary Latin America, perspectives having strong affinity with that viewpoint have already inspired several major streams of critical writing. These span a spectrum from variations of neo-Marxian and structuralist economics to literary and art criticism to philosophy of religion. Relations among the elements in this intellectual mélange are far from reciprocal.

Some liberation theologians, for example, see themselves as rounding out the Marxism that constitutes the bedrock of this system of thought—or as complementing the structuralism that is an abbreviated and considerably modified form of the Marxian critique. Other liberationists, however, relativize the Christian element, redefining it in terms wholly subordinate to Marxist categories. A group calling itself Cuban Christians for Socialism in Cuba illustrates this reductionism in its claim that "it makes no sense to talk about a specifically Christian contribution within the concrete context of the Cuban revolutionary process . . . something qualitatively distinct and supplementary within the overall revolutionary project." "Worship" is redefined by this group as an interest in increased national productivity, technological advance, and defense of the revolution. Traditional modalities of religious expression are dismissed as "idols" or "alien gods." A Christian, they argue, must be an atheist; and it turns out, not surprisingly, that the only "authentic God" is revolution.[1]

Interesting in this respect are recent developments in Central America. There liberationists have made much of the involvement of clergy and parish-level organizations of the laity in the Sandinist revolution, claiming a formative contribution to the process. In fact, many churchly visitors to Nicaragua have returned fired with enthusiasm for the work of both clerical politicians and the humble faithful in allegedly christianizing the new social order. From the perspective of the secular Left, however, what some might call the Potemkin priests of Nicaragua and their followers are often not even remarked for their decorative value. They simply disappear as irrelevant or are mentioned as "backward religious and reformist elements" among the working population.[2] In the event, liberationism, especially in sacralizing violence, clearly has far greater need of and draws far more heavily on Marxism and structuralism than vice versa. So far as is known, neither of the latter has yet rushed to the baptismal font.

Differing among themselves in several respects, the varieties of critical thinking linked with liberationism nevertheless have in common that they are loaded with political meaning. So, too, for that matter, are most expressions of liberal political economy, the transparency of its pretensions to technocratic neutrality and impartiality having long since been exposed. As almost everyone recognizes nowadays, at least outside the confines of a few economics departments, neoclassical marginalism involves a particular social definition of reality no less than does liberationism in any of its several guises. One major difference is that in the latter the political content is there by intent and design, whereas in the former the political norms are most often bootlegged in, disguised as assumptions.

Another major difference between the two schools begins with the process of concept formation. Thanks to a referentiality based on social categories or groups generally derived from class structure,[3] liberationism operates at what one might, for the moment, call the molecular level. As such, it risks losing sight of the constituents of the social molecules or institutions. For its part, the essentially atomistic frame of reference of liberal political economy is no less flawed from an analytical point of view by its difficulty in recognizing and mapping the operations of any institutions other than those of government and firms. By virtue of its individualistic focus, it is ordinarily innocent of or blind to the constraining influences of the very social categories and structures that constitute the stock-in-trade of the liberationist family of analytical approaches, except insofar as such influences get swept together into the notion of "market imperfections." The difference in view, moreover, applies to interpretations of phenomena at the international level no less than at the national level. Nowhere, in fact, is this divergence of perspective more sharply highlighted than in the contrasting understandings of the implications of world market operations. Whereas liberalism talks in terms of interdependence, specialization and division of labor, and reciprocally rewarding trade, the other rings the changes on dependence, exploitation, and monopoly—to say nothing of imperialism. The regional disparities that are simply uneven development in liberalism become internal colonialism in liberationism. Where one speaks of participation in a trading system, the other almost invariably alludes to countries being "inserted" into a global system driven by capitalism. The distinction between participation and insertion is revealing.

At a minimum, this seems to be yet another instance of communications bypass. Clearly, discourse is being frustrated because the parties to the conversation are working at different levels of observation, if not speaking altogether different languages. Although the problems are actually more complex than this, there is, as I shall show, reason to be hopeful that humanity may someday reach a synthesis in conceptual vocabulary that will at least further the discussion.

## Complications in the Dialogue

The communications chasm is partly a matter of age and style, for one difficulty afflicts liberationism that is almost completely absent from liberalism. Being fresher and not so fully formed as an idea system, liberationism is more susceptible to the distortion induced by enthusiasms, whether youthful or otherwise. The declaration of Marxism/structuralism that a particular social order may not work to the advantage of a great many people can hardly come as a revelation to those who have had to live with the ill effects of Latin America's institutional shortcomings or to the downtrodden elsewhere in the world who have now begun to take up liberationist cudgels. But among those of the system's beneficiaries who find liberationism titillating, the intellectual response and social activism this disclosure has prompted have frequently been rashly indiscriminate. What parades as analysis seems, with distressing frequency, lacking in conceptual rigor and refinement. Yet, there is no mistaking the instrumental value of liberationist slogans for engaging the emotions and energizing the comfortably discontented. To be sure, the richly textured humanistic scholarship of the major liberationist works is awesome for its erudition, but "applied liberationism," if one may call it that, is an altogether different matter. At its best evocative and moving but often scarcely more than a jeremiad, the genre is perhaps more properly assessed for its prophetic values than for its scientific insights, despite the pretensions of the dialectical materialism on which it draws.

By contrast, liberal political economy, with its denatured methodology, has left far behind the stage in which it had the capacity to stir the juices and ignite the imagination. "The magic of the market place" somehow just does not do the trick. Some, in fact, would say that in general neoclassical marginalism suffers from a notable staleness, notwithstanding the innovative work of such scholars as Gary Becker, Anthony Downs, Harry Johnson, and Thomas Sowell, who have imaginatively trained the sights of the neoclassical paradigm on a variety of new subjects. Certainly, compared with the galvanizing insights of its youth, latter-day liberal political economy has often seemed to combine a fancy technical virtuosity with underlying substantive aridity. Against the exuberance of liberationism, its expressive poverty is extreme.

To no small extent, this contrast comes from the way the theorizing process itself is conceived. Here the phenomenological cast of liberation philosophy stands in sharp opposition to the analytic cast of applied symbolic logic and the philosophical tradition behind neoclassical economics. Whereas liberal political economy emphasizes abstraction and speculation, becoming increasingly mathematical and nonverbal, liberationism proclaims openly that it involves analysis for commitment, invoking metaphor, authority, and other rhetorical means of persuasion in the process.

Basically, then, the distance between the two approaches is methodological. They differ radically, also, in the way in which they state and solve problems. The difference between Marxism/structuralism and liberal political economy is rooted in contrasting perceptions of how economic experience is related to other social and cultural phenomena and turns in part on the degree to which the institutional matrix of economic processes is admitted into the analysis. This latter point, in turn, serves as a reminder of the usefulness of Wesley Clair Mitchell's observation that systems of economic thought and analysis spring from a reflection on objective economic conditions. Just as the classicism of Hume, Smith, and Mill represented an effort to understand an economic reality defined by early capitalist development, the more refined musings of the neoclassical tradition have taken the institutional structure of a mature capitalism for granted and looked at various aspects of the allocation problem within that framework. With some lag, changes in institutional structure have shown up as theoretical refinements: for example, theories of imperfect competition or, more boldly, Keynes's confrontation with the problem of capitalist instability. By the same token, just as the economic reality with which Marx wrestled was the underside of capitalism, that with which the structuralists of the United Nations Economic Commission on Latin America (ECLA) have tried to come to grips is the distinctive form capitalism has taken as it has spread throughout the world, particularly during the 1930s, 1940s, and 1950s. The institutional context that neoclassical marginalism takes as a point of departure thus gets reintroduced—in the liberationist amalgam of Marxism, structuralism, and *dependencia*—as the very core of the *problématique*.[4] Yet, notwithstanding their profound dissimilarities, the

7

two paths into social analysis may in the long run be more complementary than opposed if we remind ourselves that every theory is simply a way of seeing and that every way of seeing is also a way of not seeing. Under the best of circumstances, the two should help illuminate more of the social territory that we all need to see more clearly, whatever our political preference.

There is, however, a further source of difference between liberationism and liberal political economy that could be troublesome even if a common conceptual vocabulary were eventually worked out. Though ownership of the means of production is certainly a major point at issue, the distinction between their preferred forms of economic organization—communitarian socialism and capitalism—may be overly crude labels for cultural differences that are much deeper and more pervasive than the issue of who owns the means of production.[5] To get at this difference, one needs to keep in mind that systems of analysis and intellectual perspectives are cultural products no less than, say, family structure or ethnic identity and as such are strongly conditioned by cultural patterns and norms. This being the case, what colloquially is called the long shadow of the past comes into play. The point is the same as that of the more elegantly stated anthropological maxim *omnia cultura ex cultura*. On these grounds one may hypothesize that liberalism has taken a very different tack from that posited by liberation theology because of the contrasting cultural progressions of Northern Europe (and North America), on the one hand, and Iberia (and Latin America), on the other. A differentiated exposure to the Renaissance of the fifteenth and sixteenth centuries, the Reformation, the Enlightenment, and the later encounter with urban industrialism have shaped the world views that inform their respective schemes of value, commonsense traditions, and even the lexicon of development. Denis Goulet captures these historical resonances succinctly when he notes that "at stake, therefore, is something more than a war over words; the battle lines are drawn between two conflicting interpretations of historical reality, two competing principles of social organization."[6]

Both schemes of social analysis reflect cultural and historical coordinates peculiar to the societies that were reaching for new critical metaphors at the time the theories were devised. Thus it is not really surprising that the ancient norms of a bureaucratic centralism, enshrined in both civil and ecclesial traditions, still shine through in the proposals of today's liberationist illuminati as they seek a new state-engineered order, one that sails under the banner of Marxian socialism. This is not, it should be noted, just a matter of abstract discussion. In all of the concrete instances of social change with which liberationists appear to feel much affinity, a centralizing bureaucracy seems to be just as dominant, and a pluralist sensibility just as absent, as ever. There are, to be sure, differences between the imperial centralism at the core of the Iberian institutional tradition and the new socialist society the liberationists seek. There are, however, striking parallels, too. First is their common reliance on a comprehensive scheme of administrative regulation and guidance.[7] As for the predilection for ideological conformity, one of the chief proponents of liberationism airily passes over the Draconian repression of dissent that has typified the so-called socialist bloc because "political radicalization tends to lead to united— and impassioned—positions and because the kind of activity which develops does not allow for entirely free expression of ideas."[8] On account of these circumstances, he comments, the kind of catholic action that historically brought together Christians with different political preferences is no longer viable. This inhospitability to pluralism, in fact, was a main objection raised by the Chilean episcopate in its rebuke of the "Christians for Socialism" organization.[9] What is more, throughout liberaticnism runs a zeal for conforming people to some envisioned model of "new man"—a sure sign of what lies ahead for those who may harbor different inclinations. One does not, of course, have to reach very far back into history to observe the consequences of official zealotry: the inquisitors of old were mere pikers by comparison with their twentieth-century counterparts.

In the traces of its institutional ancestry, liberationism displays more than a slight penchant for something very much like caesaro-papism, a neoclericalism that reinserts religious/ideological functionaries squarely into the realm of secular affairs. Explicitly repudiating what has been termed the "distinction of planes" model in which clergy and laity keep to their respective social missions, liberationists appear to favor an amalgamation of matters temporal with matters spiritual (or ideological). What this mixture means in practice is not altogether clear. On the one hand, it might lead to priests and nuns frolicking on the playing fields of revolution or disporting themselves in public office, as did the clergy on behalf of the Spanish crown. On the other, it could eventuate in subjugation. Neither Gutiérrez nor other liberationists appear much concerned by the fate of the church in Cuba where ecclesiastical activity has shriveled to the forlorn inconsequentiality that characterizes the orthodox hierarchy in the Soviet bloc. In either case, liberationism shows no reluctance to harness professional shapers of ideology to the service of the bureaucratic state, in this respect carrying forward an institutional tradition of remarkable longevity.

By the same token, liberalism has its own historically conditioned institutional proclivities. Save for acknowledging assorted market imperfections, liberal political economics remains, analytically speaking, oblivious to exactly the phenomena that are of central concern for liberationists—private constellations of power and their interdigitation with the state. Such macrosocietal power relations are ostensibly put outside the purview of conventional economic analysis to get on with the business of making a scientific inquiry into the economy. Yet, as structuralism makes plain, behavioral relations in the economy, at both micro and macro levels, are constrained by the overarching institutional architecture. Both the special social validity claimed for the price system and the notion of Pareto optimality are, consequently, severely limited by this fact. To its lasting credit, the Marxian/structuralist critique used by liberationism serves as an effective antidote to the neoclassical tendency to confuse revealed preference with revealed truth.

The capitalist institutional architecture has unmistakably feudal features. When the barons at Runnymede had their showdown with King John, they did not, of course, obliterate the coercive exercise of power; they merely reapportioned it to suit their own purposes, asserting in the process an essentially feudal constitutionalism. For all the vaunted connection between the Magna Carta and liberal society, only in comparatively recent history did many people begin to realize that baronial entitlements could themselves be parceled out to other categories of people in an essentially political process. The Petition of Right, the Bill of Rights, the Emancipation Proclamation, Women's Suffrage, and so on followed in due course as additional social categories were cut in on feudal privilege.

The market had precious little to do with this redistributional process until it was discovered that market-based power distributions would admirably serve the aims of yet another set of people determined to take matters into their own hands. At this point, such prophets of social reconstruction as Hume, Smith, and Mill came into their own, deputizing property holders in their various social representations (saver, investor, capitalist, proprietor) as the new peers of the realm. In due course, elegant theories were crafted to provide ideological support for an allocative system, baptised as consumer sovereignty, that for all practical purposes was designed to cater to the interests of the rich. So much has been written over the years about the social naiveté of this analytical framework, and of the plutocracy it upholds, that I need not dwell further on it. Not even the increasingly baroque theoretical constructions of contemporary economics can conceal that a notion of limited enfranchisement—an attenuated feudalism, as it were—remains rooted in its basic suppositions.

A related and more positive feature, however, sharply distinguishes the liberal scheme of social organization from that implied by liberationism: the polycentrism that provides the structural link with liberalism's historical roots in medieval subsidiarity. Nothing else since feudalism, in fact, has provided quite the same degree of decentralization in decision making. In this the basis of liberal political economy differs markedly from the older institutional pedigree of liberationism, in which the dominating sensibility is that of a bureaucratically centralized order, leavened at best by benevolence. The contrast is not unlike the eternal dialectic between improvisation and system, with the more supple organizational matrix of the market providing a relatively fertile seedbed for innovation. Compared with a large bureaucratically directed economy, the market is, in fact, much like the versatile structure that in organization theory is called a matrix organization. False consciousness is the label Marxism would probably apply to the liberal order's perception of its own intellectual organization; but, if this a priori characterization be laid aside, by any other standards liberal society would be distinguished by its tolerance of pluralism in beliefs and ideas, a function in turn, of the discretionary social space it provides to its constituent units.

To be sure, the differentiation just drawn between the liberationist social model and that of liberal political economy is in practice more implicit than explicit—and is masked by the vocabulary in which liberation doctrines usually find expression: for example, cultural action for freedom, the new man and the new world, and conscientization. But whether we are dealing with the present phase of social struggle or with the posited postrevolutionary setting, the institutional exigencies of the liberation movement seem to call for a social system in which power flows from office, with office in turn roosting in credal affirmation and ideological orthodoxy. Extirpating the mind set of capitalist developmentalism (social modernization, political reform, economic growth) and rescripting dialogue in terms of domination, dependency, and internal colonialism do not come out of the blue. Ideological mobilization and political activation on behalf of social revolution are not matters of spontaneous combustion, least of all when much attention is given to ensuring the niceties of doctrinal correctness. For that matter, the socialist society that is awaited in the aftermath of a radical transformation of the present regime can hardly get along without a considerable managerial apparatus. In short, the tasks inherent in the liberationist project call for mechanisms of conversion, for doctrinal maintenance, for mass mobilization, for planning and implementation of the new marching orders, and, finally, for large-scale administration.

Doubtless a visionary, vanguardist bureaucracy most fits the need in all this, but it is a bureaucratic elite nonetheless. Significantly, the framework of liberationism almost invariably postulates this dichotomy between an animating—and, later, a planning and administering—elite on the one hand and the so-called popular masses (a favorite, though probably redundant, term), on the other. Whereas liberal political economy poses as an ideal a great multiplicity of decision-making centers and, hence, a dispersion of learning-by-doing opportunities for human resource development, the liberationist paradigm appears implicitly to emphasize the social experience of following directives handed down by a mandarin class.

Lest this view be construed as entirely too lopsided, two qualifications need to be added before I move on. First, the effectiveness of a broadly distributed decisional process for human resource development partly depends on access to resources, including those of information and knowledge. Substantial resource deprivation, therefore, largely nullifies the potential advantage of the system in this respect. (For this reason, the market economy failed to harness more of the productive potential in Latin America up to the 1930s, when it was largely abandoned.) Second, although liberationism seems to relegate the large majority of human resources to an essentially passive role in the production process, it may well enjoy certain advantages when it comes to effecting large-scale deployments of these and other resources to bring about rapid structural alterations.

## Unbundling for Synthesis

However much some devotees of liberal political economy would argue that the market economy and a liberal political order are virtually inseparable, Oskar Lange many years ago developed a persuasive case for the possibility of market socialism (and, hence, the usefulness of the conventional tools of marginal analysis for socialist economics). Indeed, this may have been one of the early instances of unbundling in international transactions: an analytical technology was, in effect, divorced from the organizational trademark with which it was historically linked. By the same token, it should be no less possible to extract from the customary ideological packaging various parts of the analytical instrumentation of liberationism, which is to say, the concepts from Marxian theory and Latin American structuralism that most clearly have some empirical referent. Very likely this selective technology transfer invites invective from both sides. I propose, however, that the combined insights of both schools of thought make for a richer understanding of today's complex reality in Latin America than is available from either one singly. Further, I suggest that changes that have taken place in economic and social conditions have gradually laid the basis in objective reality for a productive synthesis of the two.

In excoriating the traditional social order of Latin America, as this was modified by its contact with world capitalism, liberationism invites our attention to the operations of systems of inequality at both national and international levels. Rather than highlighting the mutuality of benefit and the play of growth-conducive equilibrating tendencies in a market context, it brings into sharp focus the imperfections, market rigidities, and instances of market failure that hamper mobility of resources and heighten intergroup disparities in the benefits derived from participation in market processes. The effects of large-scale landownership on small-holder agriculture and on rural labor markets where few or no alternative employment opportunities exist, the impact of class structure on social investment patterns, discrimination in the allocation of bank credit between those "of the house" and customers off-the-street, entry barriers (both economic and noneconomic) to various lines of production, rent-seeking behavior by those enjoying (thanks to family and class) privileged access to the policy machinery of the state—such are only a few of the baleful institutional features that have fueled the drive for economic rectification. Structural and Marxian analyses commonly state these problems in a language that differs from that which most orthodox economists would use; but in many instances one can translate the concepts from one frame of reference to the other. The Marxist/structuralist view of dualism, for instance, can be restated in terms of labor market relations and employment options, so that the depressed level of productivity and income in the traditional sector is shown to be functional to modern export activity in that it holds down the returns to labor in alternative uses and thus restrains the rise of wages in the enclave sector—to the benefit, of course, of profits. This is true even of some concepts that might require a modest amount of innovative reworking. The scheme of institutionalized oppression that draws the ire of liberationist critics can, for example, be recast as a set of social relations (with associated patterns of income and wealth distribution) that runs counter to the preferences of all but the elite. The set of social relations and income/wealth distributions desired by the majority, in turn, can be construed as a public or collective good the production of which is blocked by the existing political system.

At the international level, in which the conceptual mapping of counterproductive institutional territory is less clearly drawn, one can nevertheless translate some of the major economic maladies from liberationese into standard economics. Conventional references to the monopoly power less developed countries (LDCs) confront in their relations with the industrial center may, for example, seem hard to square with reality since the incidence of monopoly, in the usual sense, is rare in the international market. The complaint, however, can be

13

restated in a form that is much more comprehensible and persuasive. Joseph Schumpeter, who was hardly a radical, spoke at length of the monopoly profits that accrue temporarily to firms that innovate. If we recognize that the stream of technological and organizational innovation continually being generated in industrially advanced economies surpasses by far that emanating from the LDCs, it follows that the advanced countries *as a group* are receiving a stream of monopoly profits that has practically no counterpart in the export earnings of the LDCs. In this Schumpeterian sense, then, there is merit to the liberationist contention that in a dichotomized world economy, the distribution of gains from trade is skewed by a structural element of monopoly.[10] The pattern simply reflects the geographical-institutional concentration of technological innovation and, behind that, scientific prowess.

Mainstream economic analysis can also be employed to explicate a further structural source of liberationist dissatisfaction with the world economic order. Formulated originally on the basis of a dubious analysis of the terms of trade, the liberationist critique was elaborated by Prebisch, Singer, and others to take account of such factors as differential productivity gains, elements of imperfect competition in market structures, different elasticities of demand, and interproduct substitution. A more basic situation, however, constrains the world market's operations in a manner adverse to developing countries' needs: namely, the highly unequal distribution of purchasing power among countries and regions. Because of this inequality, the whole structure of prices, the use of resources, and the composition of output are preponderantly determined by the preference schedules of the affluent economies, much as, domestically, the principle of consumer sovereignty enthrones some consumers' desires while leaving others virtually unacknowledged.

Examples of this feature have been remarked so frequently, and abound all around us, that we take them as part of the natural order. A recent issue of the Austin, Texas, *American Statesman,* for instance, carried the usual reports on African famine and related the difficulties of moving food into and starving people out of the most seriously affected region. No transport problems were reported, however, in bringing some six dozen manicurists to town for the 1985 Southwest Annual Nail Show, an event billed as a national competition. There the winning "senior nail technician" in only 2½ hours decorated the ends of ten fingers with "paintings" of bluebonnets, a cherry tree, and other "nature scenes." Can it be wondered that liberationists harbor such misgivings about the effects of marginal valuations in the market on resource allocation, or that they are unwilling to draw back from judging these valuational outcomes, muttering, as neoclassical economists do, comments about the impossibility of making interpersonal comparisons of utility functions?

There is no need to go point by point over the whole of Marxian and structural interpretations of Latin American conditions. The foregoing observations are offered merely to suggest, first, that much therein needs to be taken seriously by anyone trying to understand the economic process in Latin America and, second, that conventional economics offers a powerful means of refining Marxian/structural analysis. The conceptual instruments thereof that are scientifically valid can be greatly sharpened, while propositions grounded solely in ideology can be winnowed away: for example, the claim that capitalist economic growth has almost invariably deepened the impoverishment of the masses. None of this necessitates buying into the liberal predilection for capitalism any more than recognizing the intellectual contributions of structuralism leads to an embrace of socialism.

## Policy Implications

If the inception of capitalism spawned an intellectual offshoot in the guise of liberal political economy and the contradictions of peripheral capitalism gave rise to structuralism and neo-Marxism, changes in economic organization in contemporary Latin America may well call for yet another modification of the analytical framework. The standard *dependencia* reading of the record, with which liberationism is essentially congruent, is that "dependent peripheral capitalism" perpetuates "underdevelopment"—that is, a scheme in which the center continues a four-centuries-old exploitation of the periphery by extracting its surplus and leaving it in conditions of poverty and inequality.[11] The only way out of this trap, presumably, is through the installation of socialism, though this conclusion follows more from the ideological premises than from the empirical analysis.

Painted in such broad strokes, of course, the theory is not particularly helpful for elucidating the profound differences that exist in the historical experiences of Latin American countries, to say nothing of the East Asian countries that have exhibited such dynamism in recent decades. But if we abandon this empirically untenable position, while retaining the sensitivity to structural complications that liberationism emphasizes (and marginalism overlooks), a reassessment of the past century leads to an appreciation of policy nuances that are obscured by a doctrinaire embrace of either point of view in its extreme form. The forces of the market, for example, considerably transformed the economic structure in the River Plate region and southern Brazil by the end of the 1920s but altered the structures in, say, Chile or Colombia somewhat less. For all the dynamism of the external sector of Mexico or Peru in the five decades that ended in 1929, vast portions of economic life remained enthralled to earlier forms of organization and operations, as did even more of the national economies of Guatemala, Ecuador, and Bolivia or the major regional economy of northeastern Brazil. By the Great Depression, Uruguay, Argentina, Brazil, and Mexico had begun industrialization and tertiary-sector elaboration. This was in large measure attributable to the working out of new market relations, though in Mexico massive state intervention had been unleashed after 1910 by a revolutionary change of regime. Owing to the persistence of more archaic organizational elements, however, the pace and extent of change were notably less in most of the rest of Latin America. Not only does the standard *dependencia* treatment prove insufficiently discriminating to capture the significant differentiation among countries that developed during this period, it also misleads. Since insertion of a country into the international market is presented as a mechanism for foreign appropriation of the national surplus, one might expect the economies most engaged in world trade to be the worst off. Such was not, of course, the experience in Latin America. Further, any accurate diagnosis of the problems that beset Latin America today would have to recognize that many of them have their roots in development successes, not in a failure of development to occur at all.

The half-century following 1929–1930, *dependencia* interpretations notwithstanding, has completely redrawn the economic and social map of the region so far as concerns the major countries and even some of the lesser ones, a significant discontinuity that liberationism tends to overlook. Partly this change can be attributed to the cumulative effects of market-based influences, but a strong case can be made that the widespread wave of interventionary policies hastened structural realignment. While many mistakes were made along the way and the notion of "second-best" solutions may convey more of what was happening than optimization concepts, without doubt the recontextualization of public policy in a manner wildly at variance with the classical norms of liberal political economics greatly influenced the course events have taken—for better and for worse. Whatever one may think of what has taken place in the region, there is no gainsaying that the alterations have been structural, by any reasonable definition of the term, and not merely marginal.

In consequence, the possibilities for production, except in the most backward areas of the continent, today look quite unlike what they did, say, only three decades ago. A much less constricted range of production options is now spread before decision makers in both public and private sectors, thanks in no small part to the vastly enriched organizational infrastructure that now, with the substantially upgraded human resources, makes up so much of the overhead capital of the region. Further, in pursuing social integration, policy makers have often opted correctly in assessing the trade-offs between macro-level stability and micro-level inefficiency. The Central American experience demonstrates only too well how systemic productivity and efficiency can be disastrously affected by environmental turbulence. Though many interventionist measures of the past half-century have been faulted for reducing micro-level efficiency, their contribution to building political consensus and hence stabilizing the broader dimensions of economic strategy have made for an overall policy coherence that is easily overlooked if the social and political aspects of policy making are disregarded.

This is not to argue a Panglossian view of the hemisphere. Far from it. Just to our south, a short oil boom enabled corruption to soar to a positively African scale and the mismanagement of public finance to reach appalling proportions. Further, despite all the economic travail of the past few years and the country's demonstrated pragmatism, there is a danger that Mexican policy may yet freeze into a totemistic pattern. Over much of Central America, the exodus of capital has been substantial, and the established political systems are clearly unraveling. In Brazil, as in Peru, it remains to be seen whether Aaron can successfully follow Moses' lead and move his flock across the political and economic Jordan, though in the latter case there is still quite a bit of wilderness that remains to be traversed even before the crossing. In Argentina, where the last vestiges of predictability may have vanished years ago, and still too much indecision exists in high places, perhaps one can at least now cautiously hope that Péron will not stage quite so many come-backs as Banquo did. Elsewhere, too, there are plenty of grounds for worry, if not on account of political complications then because of problems of external financing, which may now have become long-term rather than episodic. Structural change, in other words, may be a necessary condition for growth, but it is plainly not a sufficient one; and in some parts of the hemisphere, even the stage-setting intervention of the state has yet to be carried out to provide the infrastructure and externalities on which modern economic growth depends.

The point at issue, however, is whether in the major countries, or most of the region, there has been much structural change. In this connection abundant statistical series describe far-reaching changes that have reshaped objective reality to the extent that the liberationist

17

thinking prompted by earlier conditions no longer seems to correspond to the circumstances of today. Material conditions, in other words, appear to support a new synthesis of structuralism and marginalism.

More specifically, the combined impact of rapid urbanization, accelerated industrialization, and the patterns of public investment and regulation associated therewith, along with a whole set of other sociocultural changes, have created conditions for turning to microeconomic analysis and to the more nuanced policies that neoclassical analysis can provide. Key parameters having been shifted by the structuralist policy strategies of the past few decades, many productivity gains in the period ahead are thus likely to come from relatively greater reliance on the market-based policy prescriptions of liberal political economics. Supporting this analytical and policy shift is the fact that nowadays the production environment of Latin America is, on the whole, much better endowed than formerly with social and economic overhead capital and, therefore, much richer in the externalities which, through the mediation of the market, firms use in orchestrating resources and opportunities. In the days when this institutional seedbed for growth was far less fertile, state action was undoubtedly helpful as a means of compensating for market failure by virtue of government's ability to internalize the externalities in its planning and allocations. Today, however, the case for continued intervention of the sort and on the scale practiced heretofore would seem to rest on a very narrow view, or even an obsolete one, of the situation.[12]

The greater economic versatility that prevails today in the large and middle-sized economies—including Colombia, Venezuela, and Chile (and, more arguably, Peru) alongside the Big Three (Brazil, Mexico, and Argentina) and Uruguay—is in considerable measure still latent rather than fully realized; but there is no mistaking that supply elasticities are greatly different from what they were formerly, that new forms have evolved for exploiting existing comparative advantages, and that new areas have been created in which other comparative advantages can eventually be developed. It would be going too far to say that the infant industries have reached maturity, but many have almost certainly attained adolescence and are well along the respective learning curves of labor, management, and entrepreneurship. The same, for that matter, can be said of the policy community in many of the republics.

We need not subscribe to the extravagant claims of those who, observing the vitality of the so-called underground economies, see full-blown capitalist prosperity just around the corner if only the state would get out of the way. A tremendous need for social investment continues in most countries, and in many a strong case can still be made for major structural alternations—though this need not mean re-concentrating excessive private power in bureaucratic hands. Over most of the continent, however, the time has come to adopt more realistic price structures, to discipline the parastatal sector, and to dismantle much of a rococo regulatory apparatus that mainly provides jobs for functionaries and encourages counterproductive behavior by everyone else. In short, the way seems open for an unprecedented constructive dialogue between liberation's structuralism and liberal political economy, with more hope than ever before that both theory and policy—not to mention the Latin Americans themselves—will benefit therefrom.

# Notes

1. See John Eagleson, ed., *Christians and Socialism* (Maryknoll, N.Y.: Orbis Books, 1975), pp. 136–40.
2. See the chapter on Nicaragua in Ronaldo Munch, *Revolutionary Trends in Latin America* (Montreal: McGill University, Centre for Developing Area Studies, 1984).
3. Structuralism employs sectoral groupings along with class analysis.
4. It is also instructive to compare and contrast the social gospel movement with liberation theology for the differing ways in which each responded to and reflected the institutional milieu of its day.
5. For a particularly strong argument from the liberationist side, see José Porfirio Miranda, *Marx and the Bible* (Maryknoll, N.Y.: Orbis Books, 1974). Miranda uses a remarkable interweaving of biblical, theological, and Marxian analysis to develop his arguments.
6. Denis Goulet, "'Development' . . . or Liberation," in Thomas E. Quigley, ed., *Freedom and Unfreedom in the Americas* (N.Y.: IDOC, 1971).
7. Since interventionism is a basic fact of life throughout most of the Third World, we are not claiming here that it is solely culturally determined. In large measure it appears to spring from the circumstances of "peripheral capitalist development." But if structure (i.e., the objective economic situation and its exigencies) creates the "demand" for interventionist policy, culture comes in to shape or supply the policy response.
8. Gustavo Gutiérrez, *A Theology of Liberation* (Maryknoll, N.Y.: Orbis Books, 1973), pp. 103–104.
9. See John Eagleson, *Christians and Socialism*, pp. 179–228.
10. Analytically speaking, the structuralist center-periphery model is used very much like the familiar two-country model of neoclassical economics: that is, for its heuristic value in clarifying certain relations. The two-product dimension of the standard version is simply redefined as two broad product categories, manufactures (from the center) and primary commodities (from the periphery).
11. That this internationalized version of the "increasing misery of the

proletariat" proposition has had virtually no confirmation in the evidence has not stopped it from being used as a cornerstone in an argument somewhat quixotically styles "the development of underdevelopment."

12. This is not to deny the existence in particular instances of suitable places for state action: for example, Brazil's current agrarian reform.

# Discussion

ANTHONY DOWNS, Brookings Institution: Please give us some examples of the kind of structural changes that you have described that have had these positive effects.

MR. GLADE: Examples of these changes would be the great rise in the manufacturing sector, the change in industry as a source of GNP or GDP, and the distribution of the labor force, which is radically different from what it was, say, fifty years ago. Many of these changes have been, in a sense, artificially induced as a result of import-substitution and industrialization policies. But we can see—perhaps preeminently in the case of Brazil but in other countries, too—the learning by doing that has occurred in the manufacturing sectors as industries have been able to enter international markets competitively with nontraditional exports. It is this sort of structural shift that I am referring to.

PAUL SIGMUND, Woodrow Wilson Center: Please clarify your point about the indifferences among cultural responses to liberationism. If I understood your point, we would be very unlikely to develop a liberation theology in this country; yet in fact we did in the 1960s.

In the summer of 1963, a number of my students at Princeton went to the South, where they experienced a lot of very unpleasant things—the FBI, the police beating them up, black children being killed, and the like. They came back as liberationists. They believed that there was something structurally wrong with a society that would permit this kind of thing. What we have been told about American liberalism is a myth, and it is false. We have seen it, and it is demonstrably false in the South. This was long before Gustavo Gutiérrez coined the word "liberation." After that came the SDS, black liberationists, and women's liberation, well before the formal liberation movements in the late 1960s. Gutiérrez, who was writing around 1969, was translated into English in 1972. Therefore, the idea of liberation was not borrowed from the Latins at all.

I am arguing that it was a response to a situation in which social ills could be corrected only by changing the structure of society itself. I am attacking the notion that the predilection for liberationism is largely

21

culturally determined. I believe that we would have a lot more advocates of liberation theology in the United States today, if a number of things had not happened—if the Vietnam War had not ended, for instance, or the racial situation had not improved.

Michael Novak implied that liberationism was a product of Iberian culture and that liberalism was a product of Anglo-Saxon culture. I would argue that that is not enough of an explanation. In fact, cultural differences are central. More central is that liberationism is a response to structural rigidity and to the nonconformity of ideology with reality.

Second, don't you think it is important to make distinctions among liberation doctrines, rather than grouping them all together?

Your discussion of "vanguard orthodoxy" and of a "penchant for bureaucratic centralism" is true for some of them. But what about the very strong movement toward decentralized, participatory, community-oriented arrangements that everybody associates with liberation theology? This is a very strong thrust and has little to do with an ideological orthodoxy imposed by a centralized, unified state.

MR. GLADE: I agree that there are variations in anything as large, broad, and involved with as many people as liberation theology. Certainly the Brazilian expressions tend to be less statist than some of the other expressions of that point of view.

These Spanish-American varieties, perhaps, are somewhat more state oriented—if not explicitly, then implicitly. Sooner or later advocates of this form of liberationism support state-centered social reform or social restructuring, in which, if the world looks the way it is presented in those versions of liberation theology, a state-engineered program is not unreasonable.

RAY PAGAN, Nestlé Coordination Center for Nutrition: My question pertains to the timing of liberationism in Iberian culture, tradition, and history. In the 1930s when very strong attempts were made to change the social structure in Latin America, where was the church? Where were the liberationists then? Where were they after World War II or in the 1950s and early 1960s? My question is, Why has the church failed to sense the times and react when changes occurred?

MR. GLADE: In some research that I was doing some years ago on cyclical labor movements in Latin America, it did appear that the church was involved in social issues relatively early. In the 1920s and certainly in the 1930s, Catholic social action doctrine was present to some degree in most of the major countries. There were even notable speakers who were trying to relate the message of the Roman Catholic church to the need for social reform.

22

These reforms were, in almost all cases, I think, strongly influenced at the time by European norms. Not surprisingly, the vocabulary and the ideas of all that early Catholic social action were essentially Euro-centric.

A critical turning point for Latin American liberation theology came with the formation of the Latin American Bishops Organization. For the first time, bishops from a particular part of the world met to address what seemed to them their distinctive regional problems. Before that, the social agenda had all tended to come from Rome, which is to say, from European thinkers, with some adaptations for local conditions. But here, for the first time perhaps, it was possible for people from a region to get together and in their own frame of reference to develop the terms of discussion and criticism.

Of course, parallel to this, the social science community in Latin America was looking at the historical experience and rethinking it critically. These two social phenomena thus tended to converge. The social scientists were developing an apparatus for critical analysis that was useful then to the Latin American clergy, who now wanted to analyze their own problems.

The response of the church certainly did lag behind the events, but I think that in terms of the organizational history, it makes sense that the response came about when it did.

ARTHUR MCGOVERN, Department of Theology, University of Detroit: You mentioned that liberationism seems to be associated with statism, with an inclination toward centralism. Yet at the same time, you mentioned that one of the great breakthroughs in Latin America probably occurred because of state intervention.

I find myself critical of people who reject state intervention because they associate it with Marxism or liberationism or socialism. State intervention is a Latin American phenomenon, from what I can read. Such intervention occurs, not because a certain group in Latin America favors statism, but because that is the way—whether you are right wing or left wing—you move, if you are a Latin American. That is the cultural difference.

MR. GLADE: I would agree with you entirely that statism is nothing new in Latin America. In fact, the hiatus for more liberal policy was simply that. In the late nineteenth or early twentieth century there was never as complete a hiatus as has sometimes been claimed. In any case, there were essentially state-organized, state-directed societies from the beginning. The state has been a key institutional feature as much given to indirect intervention, surely, as to direct intervention. Although by some conventional economic measurements Latin America would not

23

look very state centered, when all of the indirect interventionary measures by which the state structures the price system and influences price decisions and the like are taken into account, it is, and has been almost all along, strongly state centered.

And as you quite correctly point out, it does not really matter much whether the government has a left or a right political leaning, as long as it is nationalist, it tends to be heavily interventionist.

LESLIE LENKOWSKY, Institute for Educational Affairs: To me, the interesting question has already been stated: why the failure of liberation theology to catch up to the times?

As your analysis has it, it is precisely at this point that the structural conditions that justify the critique of the liberation theologians are melting away and that now is a time to examine some of the microeconomic approaches. Furthermore, some political basis might nurture the growth of liberation theology even as conditions that give it a rationale wane.

Liberalism as an ideology, you say, serves certain interests—namely, the interests of the rich, the capitalists, or the owners. I did not note in your paper any discussion of who benefits from liberation theology.

Could you comment a bit on that, particularly in light of the well-known phenomenon in which rising expectations for political power take on a life of their own and those expectations become institutionalized? Earlier comments on the growing liberation among women, blacks, students, and other groups proved to me that this is precisely what is happening in the real world: changes were already occurring that, indeed, undercut some of the grievances that were later expressed politically. Is not something similar happening behind liberation theology in Latin America?

MR. GLADE: We can ask who has benefited from the structurally inspired policies of the past several decades in Latin America. In fact, particular social groups have benefited: national industrialists but, to some extent, foreign investors too, insofar as they have invested behind the tariff barrier and have protected national markets in which to operate.

The industrial labor force, particularly, has benefited and more generally broad segments of the middle class. Many urban middle-class people, professionals, have benefited from the state policy design of the past few decades. It is not out of the blue, then, that these policies come about; they respond to real interests. Moreover, some of the older, more entrenched or traditional interests were severely weakened by the Great Depression, World War II, and evolutionary changes taking place in the larger, more advanced Latin American societies.

Here, then, as in the case of the liberal economy, one can identify economic interest groups who benefit from these policies. By the same token, we can identify the groups who pay the price for these policies, which often turn out to be the rural sector and the poor, whether urban or rural.

ROD GRUBB, Department of Political Science, St. Olaf College: You commented that the infrastructure has made a good beginning in much of Latin America. By that, I assume that you mean an infrastructure for liberal economic development. And you can quote all kinds of statistics to show the gross national product is up, for example.

But I wonder if, in a relative sense, the infrastructure in comparison with advanced societies may be in a worse situation now than it was twenty or thirty years ago, for a variety of reasons. A lot more people are now excluded from the land than before because of a rise in population. The advent of TV has generated a lot of rising expectations, and these societies are now competing with highly advanced technological ones.

Might not these countries be, as a matter of fact, in a relatively worse position than they might have been?

MR. GLADE: In some cases, that may be true. But some recent World Bank statistics developed on the subject show that two-thirds to three-fourths of the people live in countries with a better endowment of infrastructure than they had in the 1960s and 1970s. This improvement does not mean that their social problems are solved or that they don't have acute social problems. It simply means that statistically they have been catching up with the United States.

In other countries, however, there has been a notable lag. Peru, Argentina, and some other countries have fallen behind and are now farther behind the United States than they were, say, twenty to twenty-five years ago.

Although there is a variation among countries in that respect, about two-thirds to three-fourths of the total population of Latin America have, in fact, narrowed the gap.

MR. GRUBB: The gross national product can be a very misleading statistic, because a country can advance greatly in gross national product and the poor may remain where they always were. Do we need a better indicator?

MR. GLADE: We have better indicators. And I certainly think that we cannot put all the weight on gross national product per capita, although I do not think that we can discount those figures as much as you appear to suggest either. They do mean something, and they are the products of large aggregates. Many people are involved in the production of the aggregates that come into the gross national product in income accounts.

The kinds of changes in some of the social indicators over a twenty-year period, however, in literacy, life expectancy, and infant mortality, for example, will not occur without broadly distributed gains.

This in no way means that these gains have been egalitarian in their distribution. Obviously, some people have reaped the lion's share and others rather little. At the same time, though, these broad social indicators do not advance as they have without reasonably broad distribution of some of the benefits and gains.

DAVID BECKMAN, World Bank: I appreciate what you are trying to do in pulling out reliable insights from both liberation theology and liberalism. But your paper would be stronger if you would do more to bring it up to date. In a certain sense, it does not address the debt crisis much at all, which has had a tremendous structural impact on Latin America. And it says very little about the process of democratization. Would you reflect a bit on those two current realities?

To what extent do they fit with the preconceptions of liberation theology or liberalism, and to what extent do they affect your thesis that some sort of synthesis might be possible or that social conditions are now conducive to synthesis?

MR. GLADE: Democratization is a challenging but very difficult issue to deal with. We can certainly say that now, as compared with fifteen years ago, there are far more people in Latin America living under civilian elected regimes. Peru, for example, just had its first transition from one elected regime to another in about forty years. In fact, in Peru, Argentina, Brazil, and others—the majority of people in Latin America—are now living under some sort of a civilian regime as opposed to a military or a militarily installed regime.

Whether this means democratization in any sense is another question and one, I think, that we could probably spend a lot of time on. But maybe it is one of the forms of democratization. Whether it has any long-term meaning remains to be seen. This is not the first time that Latin America has had a majority of countries under civilian rule. It has happened before, and these regimes were shuffled out by the military or

26

others in one country after another. Whether this is in any sense an enduring or a more enduring democratization, or whether our democracy has to some degree taken root, is for us to discuss.

Certainly, one of the tests of this will be whether these regimes can survive the economic crunch in which they have been thrown by the debt crisis and other complications associated with it.

I think that they have been doing a surprisingly good job so far. This does not mean that three or four years from now, all of these regimes will still be in office, or will have given way to duly elected regimes. That is very difficult to foretell.

I don't think that we really understand fully the political dynamics of the present set of circumstances in Latin America. But we can, at least, take heart in the fact that these governments have tried.

In the Brazilian case, the elected regime has been going fairly well, and even in Colombia and Venezuela. We can see a real basis for optimism that some of these civilian governments will reach the end of their terms of office and hand their power to their elected successors.

The economic crunch remains, and I think that there will be many difficult problems ahead for various reasons—not least if the United States moves into its next recession any time soon.

A recession in the United States would do some damage to some of the countries, not all. On the other hand, the economic recovery of the other OECD countries, which looks reasonably well assured for the foreseeable future, on some modest scale, will be of benefit to the Latin American countries.

Probably with the rescheduling of some of the major debts, or likely rescheduling for some of them—notwithstanding Mr. Garcia's threat to do something more drastic in Peru and perhaps a few other cases—I think the worst of the financial adjustment problem is behind Latin America. Although I see no prospect for the region to resume the level of growth that it had in the 1960s and 1970s, the projections available from the World Bank seem to suggest positive growth in most of the major countries for the next five or six years, and even some positive or modest growth in per capita product.

EDWARD LYNCH, National Forum Foundation: To return to our earlier discussion concerning state intervention, I have several related points that I would like you to comment on.

Both the liberationists, or the liberation theologians, and those who have actually been in power in most of Latin America seem to favor state intervention in one form or another. As you pointed out, most Latin American economies include a great deal of state interven-

27

tion, and those who believe in liberation theology also, for the most part, advocate this. Please comment on the type of state intervention that we are talking about and on the differences among these types.

Liberation theologians disparage the current structures, which include state intervention, yet in many cases they say that what they are criticizing is capitalism. Perhaps, then, capitalism as practiced in North America or Western Europe is something that has not really been tried in Latin America. And if this is the case, are liberation theologians chasing a shadow?

MR. GLADE: You quite rightly point out that there are different types of state intervention as well as different aims of state intervention, and this is why so many people in Latin America have favored one sort or another of state intervention.

As I tried to suggest, the state plays a very prominent role in at least the major economies. Maybe there are some smaller ones in which the state is less consequential. But when we look at the largest of all, Brazil, the state sector is really quite large; the major enterprises are in large measure offshoots of state initiatives.

The same is true in almost all Latin American countries. The largest enterprises are parastatals. The private sector in Latin America has had a very ambivalent view of all this. On the one hand, from time to time it objects to certain kinds of state intervention. But it has strongly favored other types of state intervention, including even direct intervention because, after all, the parastatals are themselves large markets for the output of certain privately owned industries in Latin America. They represent ensured customers for some of the major private firms in those countries.

That kind of mixed economy is a style of economic organization that has commanded very broad support. The criticism that comes from the liberationist camp is that Latin America has a mixed economy, which they insist on calling capitalism. We need not get into, at least for the moment, whether it is or is not capitalism. What clearly is a mixed economy may or may not be capitalistic in basic inspiration, according to one's point of view. The criticism has been that the operative system is not socialism. The aim of some of the most prominent liberation theologians and their associated social critics is the installation of some variant of socialism that presumably entails not only an amplification of state intervention, but also perhaps an increased emphasis on re-distributive goals.

I see that as the major difference. In a sense, then, the mainstream of the policy community in Latin America favors intervention. And liberationists do, too. Liberationists want to go much beyond the mixed system that they charge supports newly established vested interests and works to the disadvantage then of so-called popular masses, the lower socioeconomic brackets.

JIM WEAVER, Department of Economics, American University: A point made earlier about the dichotomy you set up between liberation theology growing out of Iberian culture and liberal theory growing out of European culture troubles me. I believe that the point of liberation theology is essentially to say that theology can be slanted toward the interests of the oppressors or of the oppressed: God is either on the side of the powerful or the weak. Traditional theology in Latin America, therefore, has supported the interests of a ruling class and a ruling world system.

That very same theology is being developed in this country. Feminist theologians Phyllis Tribble and Rosemary Ruether are arguing exactly that same position. In her book *The Color Purple*—a fantastic book of liberation theology—Alice Walker argues that God is not the old white man that we have been taught he is. Furthermore, she says we have got to get this God out of our minds before we can really be liberated, be free ourselves.

In contrast to your view, I see the two strains of liberation theology as identical. I don't see any distinction at all.

My second quarrel with your paper is that while you very rightly point out the success of the structural transformation that has taken place in Latin America, you leave unsaid all the structural transformations that are still needed. You imply that what we need to do now is to tidy up around the edges with traditional neoclassical microeconomics.

I do not see the situation in quite such a hopeful way as you do. As Peter Berger points out, there are three criteria for successful development: one is growth; two is equitable distribution; and three is no gross violations of human rights.

Almost no country in Latin America meets those criteria of successful development. Costa Rica, perhaps, is one. I see those structures as still grossly unjust, however. Moreover, those countries face enormous problems today—debt problems, declining per capita incomes, and a net capital outflow from the region. The people at the bottom of the heap are suffering enormously today. For all the decisions that the elites made to borrow, it is the poor who are experiencing the belt tightening.

I think that you are a little too optimistic about the structural transformation that has been taking place. I think the theologians' points are still very valid.

MR. GLADE: I must confess to ignorance of the literature that you cite. It may well be that people in this country are working along somewhat similar lines. If their work is very much like Latin American liberation theology, I suppose it is also based on class analysis, because the Latin American work is.

As for your point about structural change, quite clearly Latin America is experiencing continuing structural change. It follows, then, that structural change has not ended. Whether we see the situation from a Marxian point of view or from a neoclassical point of view, we must suppose that structural changes will continue; that is in the nature of the case. Certainly, as you rightly point out, a great many structural changes that will surely come about are very much needed and desirable for creating more humane economic systems. A lot of people have, in fact, been unable to participate in the progress that has taken place or to enjoy the fruits of this unequally distributed progress. I wonder if the kind of vast inequality that has characterized so much of Latin America is really productive from any point of view.

At the same time, however, I think one can fault liberation thinking for not being sufficiently precise and attentive to what exactly is involved in structural change. Advocates of liberation theology should perhaps look at the costs as well as the benefits of structural change and should try to consider alternatives to bring about a range of policy options.

Let me cite just one case, which I think indicates the crucial importance of this. In 1968 when Mr. Belaunde first left office in Peru, that time involuntarily, a regime came to power that was fairly committed to structural change and by Peruvian standards (or almost any other standards in Latin America) introduced very far-reaching reforms of a revolutionary nature in many cases. Some very basic economic structures were shaken up.

Looking at that experience in retrospect, however, I think that we have to appreciate how difficult structural change is in every sense. First, in spite of the frankly redistributive orientation of the Peruvian government rather a small amount of real redistribution of income and wealth actually took place. There was some; it was measurable. But it worked within broad categories and did not reach the people who are presumably of greatest concern to, say, the liberationists. The poor, then, remained more or less where they were.

Perhaps in some sense they were even in worse shape, because the reforms that were implemented not only had only a marginal effect in redistributing income but also in many cases seemed closely related to diminishing productivity. The Peruvian economy had little cushion of productivity to begin with. Peru is one of the cases where the per capita income is actually lower today than it was in 1970. Even under fairly optimistic assumptions, the most that can be hoped for in the Peruvian case is that per capita income by 1990, for example, will regain or just barely surpass what it was in 1970. Immense damage was in fact inflicted on the Peruvian economy by some of the structural experiments of that period.

Now, in many cases the reforms were long overdue. Some reforms were widely applauded; some reforms were certainly inspired by good intentions. But the fact of the matter is that they had limited benefits and very severe costs, so that the cost-benefit calculation would have suggested that some other route might have been more efficacious in the long run.

I don't want for a moment to suggest that the problems with the Peruvian economy can all be laid on the doorstep of the Belaunde government, or even the successor governments, because that would be a gross oversimplification of the case. Natural disasters and a lot of other things happening in the world markets have affected the country adversely. But those reforms, those deliberate structural changes, were certainly part of the problem and would be very hard to overlook.

I hope that liberationism in its various guises can be used as a means of sensitizing people to the need for continuing structural change and for trying to influence it in a desirable way. But also I hope that we would always want to consider both the costs and the benefits of changes and try to assess what options are, practically speaking, possible. In the long run, if the reforms not only failed to benefit the poor in Peru directly, but also undermined the economy, then the poor were even damaged by those reforms in the long run.

JEAN ANDERSON, School of Business Administration, University of San Diego: The bottom line is still inequality in the distribution of wealth. Latin America cannot move forward in any kind of real development until we find a way to solve that basic distribution problem. I do not think that capitalism or a free market economy can really succeed with that level of inequality, given the extremes.

As for Peru's failure, we should learn from that what it did wrong. That failure does not mean that there are not ways of working through. Of course, redistribution is not pleasant. Somebody will always lose; it will always have tremendous costs and always cause disruption in the economy in the early stages. There are probably no ways around those things.

This extreme inequality is really the critical element of the problem and is probably the basis of our debate.

MR. NOVAK: Are you really talking about inequalities, or are you talking about raising the bottom base? It seemed to me that you were concerned not so much about inequality as about the problem that there are so many people below a minimal level.

Ms. ANDERSON: Yes, I am worried not nearly as much about the extreme rich as I am about the extreme poor.

When you mentioned the relative figures, I thought that it was probably more relevant to look at what has happened to the bottom 40 percent rather than at the per capita incomes. When those are compared, they are not as favorable. Moreover, when the bottom 40 percent is not even within the market structure, market economies, capitalism, and democracy cannot really operate.

MR. GLADE: Certainly we would do well when we get to the point of discussing practical policies and strategies to focus on that target population. It was suggested long ago that the object of economic development was to alleviate mass poverty, to try to reduce its dimensions. That is as good an object to strive for as any. When we discuss the actual strategies and policies, that seems as good a criterion for judging them as we could possibly come up with. What effect, ultimately, will particular policies have on the reduction of mass poverty?

Fairly impressive development such as Latin America has, in fact, had can take place, however, amid horrendously distributed income. The inequalities are certainly great, and yet, notwithstanding that, many though not all of the countries managed an impressive rate of development until the recent crisis set in.

We need to keep in mind that development can occur without much alleviation of the highly unequal distribution of income. It is fair to look at the rich as well as the poor. I think the consumption patterns that characterize the rich in Latin America are simply too garish and are inappropriate for a society in which so many live the way they do. We should look at both sides, without suffering the illusion that if the extreme wealth of the rich were redistributed, it would go far toward helping the poor: it simply would not.

Latin America will have continuing economic development, albeit for reasons quite unrelated to income distribution. Its development probably will not be as rapid in the future as it has been for most of the past several decades.

From a human point of view, perhaps from a democratic point of view, we would like to think that some policies could be found that could distribute the fruits of this development somewhat more broadly. I think that we can agree on that anyway.

COMMENT: Economics and performance may be the bottom line, and even if we meet to think about liberation theology, we should not get hung up in theological or terminological dimensions.

I was impressed by the earlier comment on expectations. Perhaps our later discussions will address that issue.

Furthermore, I think as we evaluate recent performance we might do well to take Deng Xiaoping's comments on cats seriously. He says that while Maoist Communism is one kind of cat and his Marxism is another kind of cat, they are both cats. His economy achieved a goal broadly shared, I am sure, around this table. The Chinese economy grew by about 15 percent last year and also greatly benefited the people with the lowest per capita income in China—those in the agricultural sector.

The old Maoist-Marxist argument still followed in East Germany and other places is to keep food prices low for everyone and to keep incentives down. The "new kind of cat" in China is one that, if it could be followed, might help the lowest economic groups there.

LEON KLENICKI, Jewish Anti-Defamation League: I cannot understand the liberal attitude and philosophy that would bring the Industrial Revolution to Latin America and change the structure of societies that are between the Middle Ages and the French Revolution. Nor can I understand the attraction of movements like the theology of liberation, which uses a terminology and methodology based on Lacan, Althusser, and other French writers to analyze a whole continent that is not yet in the capitalist system. I see a basic confusion there, and I hate seeing so much time wasted in this enterprise. Perhaps we are paying too much attention to this theology and not paying enough attention to other developments. Why don't we examine, for example, the theology of development or the ideas of Jacques Maritain, who was so influential in Latin America until this new Romanticism came on the scene?

Perhaps we should pay more attention to other Christian groups who are trying to bring certain changes, like that organization called Opus Dei. The very name makes us tremble. In Spain it was that group that went from Franco to the Industrial Revolution. It is doing something similar in Venezuela. Why not pay attention to those movements that really bring a change of structure to a country?

MR. GLADE: Your remarks call to our attention that there is not just one current of thinking in Latin America that monopolizes the whole scene. Liberation theology has received the most publicity and has been the most stimulating, perhaps, in terms of its reverberations elsewhere.

It would be ideal, of course, to know more about what else is going on in Latin America. And the fact that so many conferences have been held on liberation theology in recent times may be a sure sign that it is on the way out and that we really ought to be looking at something else.

Among the many other currents of thought in Latin America is the development of Protestant fundamentalist groups in Guatemala, of all places. It is a fairly important religious development.

Whether these be Calvinistic in their inspiration or not, I don't know. Any change might help the Guatemalans, whether Calvinism or whatever. How do you get a Calvinist conversion in Latin America at this point? I don't know myself, but I think that it probably would help.

QUESTION: Didn't someone make the point that Latin America has not really entered a capitalist age?

MR. GLADE: I disagree. A form of capitalism—a mixed economy with capitalist dimensions—is certainly very much installed in a number of the countries, some more than others perhaps. And before we say that they have not really tried capitalism, maybe we need to clarify what variations of capitalism still qualify under that label. Their economic systems may look noncapitalistic when compared with that of the United States or with that of pre-Mitterrand France, for example, or indeed, with that of many of the continental economies.

Many institutions of capitalism, if not all, are working there, amid a great many imperfections to be sure, in most cases.

MR. SIGMUND: One thing that we have not really been discussing is liberalism and liberationism. What I thought was actually the most positive, interesting, and provocative part of your paper was the suggestion that the vocabularies of one approach can be converted and used to translate the rhetoric of the other—and what does that tell us?

Rephrasing the liberationist critique in liberal terms gave some insights, and it still remains a critique of liberal society. Conversely, stating liberal philosophy in liberationist terms and analyzing it using liberal terminology helps evaluate some of the assertions of liberation theology.

What I did not see in the paper is anything about democracy. If we are talking about the convergence of liberationism with liberalism, I think that this is one area on which there can be genuine agreement. And if some have criticized liberation theology for not paying enough attention to democracy, I think that now both the Catholic left and the Marxist left are much more aware of its importance, having seen what happens when democracy goes. Contemporary writers on socialism now contend that socialism turns out to be democracy. Socialism does not turn out to be statism or nationalization or any of these other things: it turns out to be genuine democracy—economic democracy, political democracy, participatory democracy.

Similarly, throughout the history of liberalism, democracy has been very important. If we are looking for areas of common concern and common commitment between what appear to be opposing schools of thought, democracy is a large area of common commitment. Of course, it is also an area of disagreement. For instance, what are the appropriate areas for democracy? Is economics one?

BARRY LEVINE, Florida International University: Earlier, we discussed the issue of distribution and whether we should look at the rich as well as the poor. It always seemed to me odd that the same people who would like to take from the rich also lament the lack of a development of a national bourgeoisie. At some point, we should discuss that.

Another topic is how to define capitalism. Max Weber had a very simple way. He made a distinction between capitalism and modern capitalism. He said that "capitalism" exists when anybody is involved in a private enterprise. Modern capitalism exists when capitalism is systematic, methodological, and is taken to its logical extremes: when you try to develop in long-term, planned ways as if you will be around in the future.

Capitalism in Latin America reminds me of real estate in Miami. It is venture capitalism, it is taking a chance, it is trying to make a killing whether you are speculating in marijuana or coffee. You do it, and you try to get out of it.

I take issue, then, over the extent of capitalism in Latin America.

FATHER MCGOVERN: Despite Michael Novak's conviction that capitalism and democracy grew hand-in-hand, other writers say exactly the opposite; in Latin America, they claim, economic liberalism was used as a force to crush democracy or democratic liberalism. That observation seems worth looking at.

MR. GLADE: I did not get much into the whole question of democracy, which I assumed other papers would do. Just as a matter of product differentiation, if you like, I left that aside and tried to focus on other matters.

I particularly like the question of the much-criticized rich in Latin America. Are they necessary for the development of more productive systems—the national bourgeoisie in the historical sense, which can transform the economy and install a capitalistic economy?

Maybe the question, however, could be rephrased, and we could ask more diagnostically, How, in fact, do the rich behave in Latin America, and why do they behave that way? That might lead us into a more constructive understanding of the situation. Clearly, the rich in

35

Latin America do not behave the way the Calvinist rich in the historical legend were supposed to behave. They are not brutal, thrifty, and given to wholehearted capital formation. But having said that, we really do not know very much more. The more interesting question is why?

If we ask why they exhibit the behavior that they do, we see that many of them are really quite rational. Then perhaps we have a better understanding of the situation—for instance why they export so much of their capital. They do not invest it at home, thereby contributing to national capital formation. If we look at the answers to that question, then they lead us to an understanding of erroneous exchange rates and the like.

We could focus on the behavior of the rich as an interesting diagnostic tool. We could start our discussion by asking why those who control a very large share of the private sector's capital do not contribute very much to national capital formation. And I think that then we can really track down some of the problems that afflict the society.

In a sense, this would demythologize the rich—whether we call them the national bourgeoisie or the exploiters or the capitalist heroes for that matter—and really understand the workings of those societies and see what the real problems are.

Mr. Novak: I wish to comment on why liberation theology is so well known and why we don't pay equivalent attention to movements that might be much larger. In my recent trips to Latin America I was constantly told that I was overestimating the strength of liberation theology. You could drive many miles, I was told, without seeing anyone who knows anything about liberation theology, or cares. The explanation may lie in the question raised at the very beginning: in the 1960s, particularly in West Germany and here, people were searching eagerly for examples of liberation, and if you are from Latin America, you can only be published in the United States, if you are a liberation theologian. It is very hard to find the books of nonliberation theologians translated into English. And I think that the same thing is true in Western Europe. We are thus getting a picture of theology in Latin America that is not representative of theology in Latin America as a whole.

# The Improvement of Democracy in Latin America and the Debt Crisis

*Hugo Assmann*

### Introduction

In focusing on the matter indicated in the title, my paper will (1) show the essential link between the solution of the debt crisis and the advance of redemocratization in many Latin American countries and (2) suggest that the fundamental problems of humanity have arrived at such a crucial point that a decisive shift must be made from the spirit of confrontation to a new spirit of negotiation, on all levels. This purpose makes clear that I harbor no polemic intentions; rather I am interested in urgently needed practical results.

I do not confine myself to theories. Macro-level problems, first, are more and more essentially practical and, second, are constantly and profoundly related to practical micro-problems, and vice versa. I would much prefer to discuss concrete problems tied to day-to-day grass-roots work. As a militant of a workers' party, as a sociologist concerned with new forms of organization required by a "grass-roots democracy," and especially as a liberation theologian, I have as my immediate commitment grass-roots demands. In spite of this preference, I have for two reasons concentrated on the problem headlined above (which touches both macro- and micro-levels): (1) its extreme urgency and (2) the kind of forum in which I have the opportunity to introduce the debate on this issue. I hope that this theme will, at the same time, allow us to exercise a dialogue in which polemic exacerbation and ideological radicalism should be viewed as obstacles.

Allow me some additional remarks on how the theology of liberation is related to micro- and macro-level problems. This relation is tied to the question of why liberation theology is seen by some powers as highly dangerous[1] and why presently it is the target of a symptomatic and harsh offensive. Liberation theology obviously does not pretend to be an economic theory, although it implies a series of economic re-evaluations. It is essentially a strong movement of spirituality growing out of faith experiences in the grass roots; and, as it is partially projected in writings, it is constantly concerned with the grass roots. Perhaps the greatest innovation of liberation theology is precisely this: it has ample and congeneric grass-roots constituencies, profoundly influences many experiences in popular education, supports new forms of popular organization (thus the importance of the wide penetration of liberation theology in the ecclesial base communities, which only in Brazil number more than 100,000), helps overcome the antipopular fallacies of the traditional Left, foments self-reliant solidarity and creative forms of survival at grass-roots levels, in addition to inspiring, to a great extent, in the numerous groups that work with human rights, the shift in focus from problems of repression to problems of oppression.

As is well known, liberation theology conceives of itself as a movement against idolatry: the faith in the God of Life versus the antilife idols.[2] The generating matrix for the basic criteria of faith in practice refers to the affirmation of life, understood as concrete means for living, and living with joy and with the tenderness of participating in the fullness of life for all. This nucleus of criteria revolutionizes completely the technocratic view of "basic needs," as table 1 shows:

TABLE 1
PRODUCTION AND REPRODUCTION OF LIFE

| Principle of Organization | Historical Agents | Concrete Mediations | Basic Needs |
|---|---|---|---|
| The affirmation of life-means for living | The logic of the majority: the poor/ the impoverished/ the oppressed classes | The right to: —work/employment —freedom for participation/levels of organization —transformed human relations in day-to-day life | food shelter health education joy of living (feast/tenderness) |

SOURCE: Author.

This redefinition of basic needs certainly implies a radical challenge both for capitalism and for the majority of existing socialist models. The socialist models are challenged especially through the insistence on participation and on the transformation of human relations in everyday life (for example, sex, race, party). Capitalism is challenged to take seriously its democratic promises, placing priority on their social content. The predominant institutions of advanced capitalism are not labor intensive and therefore contrast brutally with the employment demand, especially in the underdeveloped countries.[3] In Brazil, for example, the parallel economy or submerged economy—in which the unemployed or underemployed exercise their incredible creative capacity—represents a quantum, not officially quantified, equivalent of one-third of the gross domestic product (GDP).

In a recent meeting of Latin American theologians, I was strongly affected by a colleague's formulation, which stated the following: (1) Since the beginning of capitalism there was only one alternative proposal, the radically anticapitalist, Marxist one. Now capitalism is attacked a second time by liberation theology, but in an innovative form that challenges at the same time the socialist models on crucial points. (2) Not anti-Marxist, liberation theology is nonetheless not altogether Marxist, although it incorporates elements of Marxism. Different from Marxism, liberation theology is not cold or elitist, and it is linked with the grass roots through religion. (3) Liberation theology challenges capitalism in a new and profound way, in aspects in which traditional Marxism is weak. Precisely for this reason the challenge of liberation theology is also significant for some socialist models that are thus forced to rethink crucial aspects of their ideology. The churches in the socialist countries are finally challenged to assume the political dimension of the practice of faith. If liberation theology truly represents all this, even still in an embryonic form, it is perfectly understandable why it is being opposed from many sides.

### The Debt Crisis as an Obstacle to Democracy

I will deal with the debt crisis with special reference to Latin America, although all considerations could be extended to the other indebted countries of the third world. Emphasis will be placed on the link between the debt crisis and the improvement of democracy. I cannot analyze here several other aspects of the problem such as the origin of the debt, imprudent risks taken by creditors and debtors, and irregularities and false priorities in the application of these loans. These aspects are also important. But the crucial point at which the debt crisis has arrived and the urgency of a needed solution permits me to state that the identification of causes is not always sufficient for the discovery of solutions.

The debt crisis has a long history. But it started deteriorating with accelerating speed in 1982, when several Latin American countries found themselves unable to pay not only the principal of the debt but also the interest. The success of some countries in obtaining a commercial surplus to continue paying the interest on the debt—through strong import restrictions and other clearly recessionary measures, with tremendous social consequences—led their economies to an impasse. The possibility of continuing this path no longer exists. A more profound solution must be found.

None of us ignore that this discussion is on the table. Henry Kissinger, Fidel Castro, and Senator Richard Lugar in recent trips through Latin America; a Latin American congress of union leaders; a meeting of the Group of 77 (in reality, already about 130) underdeveloped countries in New Delhi at the end of July, an emergency meeting of twenty-five state governors called by President Sarney of Brazil on July 17, 1985—all seem to agree on the absolute urgency of a solution. In my country, Brazil, the external debt question has become an internal debate on all levels. In the extremely condensed style I must use in what follows, my intention is not to obscure the complexity of the matter.

**The Debt That Can No Longer Be Paid.** That the debt cannot be paid is a mathematically demonstrable fact. The problem no longer resides in the full amount, or the so-called principal of the debt, which in any way has become unpayable. Even the bankers are not interested in killing the goose that laid the golden eggs. It is the interest of the debt, as it is currently calculated, that can no longer be paid. Those countries that continue in their efforts to pay this part of the debt service find their minimal economic growth, which is necessary to avoid the genocide now in practice, threatened.

The February 1985 figures of the UN Economic Commission for Latin America are already outdated in several cases and are therefore conservative. They exemplify the debt amounts as follows (in millions of dollars):

| | | | |
|---|---|---|---|
| Brazil | 101,800 | Peru | 13,500 |
| Mexico | 95,900 | Colombia | 10,800 |
| Argentina | 48,000 | Costa Rica | 4,050 |
| Venezuela | 34,000 | Panama | 3,550 |
| Chile | 18,440 | Uruguay | 4,700 |

The totality of Latin America has an accumulated debt of more than $360 billion, and the debt of the third world is coming near to $1 trillion. That the largest portion is in short- or medium-term loans alone implies a constant need to reschedule the principal of the debt and issue new bridge loans while the rescheduling is being negotiated. On one hand, the rescheduling of the principal often includes a mechanism for needed new money that increases the debt. On the other hand, almost all of the debt is tied either to high interest rates, plus high spread, or to the high fluctuating interest rates of the financial market, plus high spread.

To offer some examples of what this means, the service of the debt (almost always only interest, without amortizing the principal) represented in 1984 the following percentages of gross exports: Brazil 36.5 percent, Argentina 52 percent, Bolivia 57 percent, Mexico 36.5 percent, Peru 35.5 percent, Chile 45.5 percent. These kinds of deceptive figures are often used to demonstrate that, although paying the debt means a heavy burden, it is possible once domestic economies are adjusted. Why do these figures mask reality? Because one needs only to subtract the imports, heavily controlled and restricted, to discover that, even in the cases with substantial surplus as Brazil, almost 100 percent of the remaining surplus is absorbed by the interest on the debt. The number of countries for which this amount is more than 100 percent is increasing, making new loans necessary simply to pay the interest on the debt. From a teller one receives new money only to hand it immediately to another teller to pay overdue interest. This bad situation is exacerbated by the terrible problem of domestic economies that are conditioned to export the maximum, with the prices of their products at the 1930s level (which means that they must export 40 percent more than in the 1950s to obtain the same amount of dollars); with irrational subsidies for exports (because to produce one kilogram of tin costs sixteen dollars, while its market price is only five dollars; in several products the relation is 3 to 1); with the consequences of uncontrollable money issuance, increased public debt and inflation, decreased wages, and ruined domestic markets. The impositions of the International Monetary Fund (IMF) (rigid control of money issuance, reduction of public spending, control of the budget deficit, combating of inflation, increase of exportation) are like demanding more milk production while killing the cow.

Brazil, within the deep recession from 1980 through the second half of 1984, monitored by the IMF since 1982, made a fantastic effort to increase the surplus of its commercial balance, which jumped from $3.6 billion to $12.9 billion from 1983 to 1984. This performance was praised by the IMF and by the international bankers. But the service of the debt was $11.6 billion in 1984, and it swallowed practically all of the surplus. In 1982 Brazil had exported $20,172 million and imported $19,395 million, thus paying the interest on the debt with new debt. In 1984 Brazil exported $26,960 million, imported only $14,360 million, and had a substantial surplus. Thus Brazil was able to pay the interest on the debt without borrowing new money but had lost more and more control over the public debt, the issuance of money, and inflation. Brazil has arrived at a point at which it simply cannot adjust to the demands of the IMF without provoking a new recession and impairing a minimal growth rate. This is the impasse that the new government faces. The schedules and the interest rates of $45.3 billion urgently need to be renegotiated to continue in the same diabolic logic: do one's best to obtain the maximum commercial surplus to pay off the interest on the debt. Without renegotiation not even this payment on the interest is feasible. I give details of my country because it exemplifies "good performance." Countries like Bolivia do not have the smallest chance of continuing to pay the interest on their debt without becoming further indebted.

Another aspect of the problem is also worth remembering. According to a document of the National Conference of Brazilian Bishops (CNBB), 86 million of the 130 million inhabitants of the country survive on less than 2,200 calories per day. When responding to the question, "Why is there hunger in Brazil?" the bishops state: "Brazil deceives itself thinking that it will resolve its social problems by paying the external debt. We produce food exports to send to superfed countries and not for the feeding of Brazilians."[4] Brazil is already the largest exporter of citric juices, the third largest exporter of chicken, and one of the largest exporters of beef. A country with cattle that never saw people, and people that never saw meat.

In several Latin American countries the GDP is suffering a reduction in absolute terms. From 1981 to 1984, for example, the GDP decreased in the following countries: Uruguay, −13.9 percent; Argentina, −6 percent; Chile, −5.4 percent; Venezuela, −6.1 percent. But the reduction of GDP per capita from 1981 to 1984 is much more significant: Bolivia, −24.6 percent; Argentina, −11.2 percent; Chile, −11.2 percent; Venezuela, −16.2 percent; Uruguay, −16.2 percent; Costa Rica, −14.1 percent. As one can see, not only the quality of life is affected but also the productivity of our domestic economies.

**Indebted Countries That Are Capital Exporters.** We have arrived at a strange situation: many of the countries that no longer can pay their debt become, partly by the very mechanism of the debt, really net capital exporters. According to a recent study by the World Bank of 104 indebted countries of the third world, these countries taken as a block (although not in all individual cases) have become exporters of net capital to the rich countries. In 1984 they paid the rich countries $92 billion, having received $85 billion, including new loans, financial or speculative capital flow, and new investments. The twelve countries with the largest debts without exception became capital exporters (among them Brazil, Argentina, Mexico, Venezuela, and even Chile). In Latin America the figures are proportionally more shocking. The commercial surplus increased 28 percent totaling $37.6 billion. The service of the debt was $37.3 billion. Subtracting the modest input of new capital, Latin America exported nothing less than $26.7 billion in capital, just in 1984. If one adds the figures in 1983 and 1984, the amount increases to $56.7 billion.

Do these data mean that the underdeveloped countries help to finance, with an impressive amount of money, the growth of rich countries? This type of reasoning sounds immediately polemic, because it could be misinterpreted to imply that advanced economies are not self-reliant. Useless polemics do not favor mutual understanding. For this reason one should not rush to aggressive conclusions from isolated elements. Clearly the foreign debt is not an independent variable in the context of all the other determining factors of international commerce. By now one can arrive at two conclusions: (1) the foreign debt has become a mechanism for extracting net capital from indebted countries, and (2) this capital flees forever and cannot possibly return.

The net capital outflow situation from underdeveloped countries to the rich world becomes much more dramatic if one includes other forms of capital drainage. I mention only the major factors, all of them intimately intertwined. First there is the famous deterioration of terms of trade: that is, the prices of the products Latin America exports have increasingly declined over the past decades, and the prices of imports from the rich world have constantly increased. The regulating bodies of this trade (for example, GATT) are controlled by the rich countries and obviously do not simply obey the rules of the "free market." Second, the international financial system is more and more based on the dollar (the original Bretton Woods agreement is no longer operative) and the overvaluation of the dollar in the past few years has been accentuated (approximately 40 percent since 1978, which signifies that $1 borrowed now costs $1.40). Third, interest rates have been prohibitive, in contrast with the historic interest that was maintained for more than half a century (more or less 6 percent a year). Fourth, private capital of the third world has subsequently flowed out toward more lucrative financial markets. Fifth, the rich world has released on the market, or "dumped," those same products that were traditionally exported by the underdeveloped countries (as currently occurs with sugar and is beginning with stocked beef). Sixth, the establishment of rigid exportation quotas for primary products and the protection of certain manufactured products render practically impossible the medium- and long-range planning of lucrative export and thus force the underdeveloped countries to recycle their export products constantly. Seventh, money in royalties and patent rights flows outward. Eighth, the earnings of transnational corporations have been repatriated.

43

Taking into account only four of these factors, Latin American economists have arrived at the following conservative conclusions: in 1984 alone Latin America lost $20 billion because of deteriorating terms of trade; $10 billion because of excessive interests; $10 billion because of capital outflow; $5 billion because of the overvalued dollar. If one adds to this the service of the debt, recalculated at the historic interest levels (approximately $25 billion), one arrives at a total of around $70 billion, of which $50 billion is in cash. Therefore, the debt crisis, although it should be dealt with directly with urgently needed solutions, clearly cannot be conceived as an issue isolated from the overall search for a new international economic order. The existing world economy is totally biased toward the interests of the industrialized giants.

Abraham Lincoln said, "You cannot fool all the people all the time." The underdeveloped countries are forced to maintain commercial surpluses and restrict their budget deficit. The United States took 205 years to arrive in 1981 at an accumulated public debt of $1 trillion. But it took only four years (from 1981 to 1984) to amass an accumulated additional $650 billion. The second trillion will most likely be reached during 1986. The commercial deficit of the United States has also been accumulating at an impressive rate. In 1984 alone the commercial deficit was on the order of $123 billion, and it promises to be much larger in 1985 (more than $50 billion just in the second trimester). Why is anyone surprised when many begin to understand that the situation is artificially maintained through the extracting of money from the rest of the world via monetary and financial policies that "normalize" the capital flow to the United States?

**A Debt Bomb Explosion.** This is a war that has been going on for years, and the number of human victims of this war is almost impossible to calculate. Many, nonetheless, predict that, unless urgent solutions are found, a big explosion will occur around 1988, and the situation will become uncontrollable. The capitalism of today is much different from the capitalism of the crisis of the 1930s. Now productive capital is being increasingly surpassed by the more lucrative financial capital. We are sliding into the purest metaphysics of artificial figures. It is urgent to return to realism of production of wealth. The palliative solutions and intermediate formulas are increasingly losing their plausibility.

A simple mathematical exercise will demonstrate the impossibility of paying the debt through four hypotheses, always supposing something improbable: that this debt will not surpass current levels.

Hypothesis 1: Latin America would have a ten-year grace period, without amortization of the principal; it would pay only interest during these ten years and then would have another ten years to pay off the principal with interest never higher than 10 percent. According to this hypothesis, Latin America would pay $400 billion in the next ten years, without having amortized anything of the principal, and then pay $558 billion in the other ten years. In twenty years Latin America would have transferred $958 billion to its creditors. This hypothesis implies a global and immediate renegotiation of the schedules and interest rates, which is not probable. Suppose that the other factors of capital outflow are maintained; without a new international economic order there will be an unacceptable bleeding.

Hypothesis 2: Latin America would pay no more than 20 percent of its export earnings per year, the interest on the current amount of the debt would be fixed at 10 percent, and the nonpayable interest along with the 20 percent of export earnings would automatically be integrated into the principal. The export earnings of Latin America do not yet total $100 billion per year, but suppose that they could arrive at that figure shortly. Suppose that the global debt had been renegotiated on that basis for a period of twenty years. What would happen? The Latin American countries would pay $20 billion dollars in interest per year, requiring a very serious effort. At the end of twenty years they would have paid $400 billion, but their debt would have increased three times to a total of $1,161,850,000,000. Having arrived at such a fantastic figure, someone might have to invent more sophisticated hypotheses, because even under favorable conditions, the other variables untouched, our countries would have their development impaired.

Hypothesis 3: Latin America would have ten years paying absolutely nothing, no interest or amortization. Then it would have ten years to amortize the debt with interest of only 10 percent. In this hypothesis the alleviating effects of this ten-year period of grace could translate into a certain degree of development, even if the other aforementioned adverse factors were maintained. It would even be possible to accumulate a certain amount of domestic savings. But during the second ten years it would be necessary to pay $1,447,310,000,000. And this is practically impossible to imagine without a new international economic order.

Hypothesis 4: There would be an immediate reduction of interest to 6 percent (the historical rate) and ten years without paying anything, no interest or amortization, and ten more years to pay the amortization and the interest. In this hypothesis Latin America would have the same advantages as in the previous hypothesis and with a slighter accumulation of old interest. Even so, if the global debt were renegotiated immediately under this benign formula and for a period of twenty years, during the second decade Latin America would have to pay $857,471,000,000.[5]

This simple mathematical exercise then reveals the slight viability even of the more benign intermediate formulas. If the other current variables of international commerce are maintained, the payment of the debt presents itself as an economic impossibility, that is unless one is willing to accept genocide as a "necessary sacrifice." At no time do I accept the thesis that the simple cancellation of the debt would signify the full solution to Latin America's problems. The domestic distortions of our economic models and the acquired bad habits demand a specific analysis and should be faced seriously. But it is practically impossible to do so without an urgent solution of the debt crisis, since this is a determining factor in relation to the other aspects of our economic, political, and social crisis.

Is it possible to find an acceptable solution to the debt crisis without provoking virtual chaos in the international financial system? Everything indicates that chaos has already been created. Precisely for this reason, new measures, other than the simple solution of the debt crisis, are needed to create an international order more favorable to peace, justice, and development. It is worth remembering, nonetheless, that the global debt of the third world has not yet reached $1 trillion. Just in the past ten years the rich countries have already paid around an additional $1 trillion, because of increases in the price of the petroleum they import, without impairing their earnings and prosperity. A further comparison: if one calculates 10 percent of the defense budget of the United States in the past ten years, one arrives at a similar figure. If one takes 10 percent of the probable defense budgets over the next ten years, one will arrive at an amount probably much larger than the entire debt of the third world. These are public budgets. Is it not possible to imagine available resources, tied to public budgets, to alleviate the losses of private banks in the case of a benign solution to the debt crisis?

**The Vulnerability of Redemocratization in Latin America.** I do not intend to provoke here a debate on all of the ideal aspects of democracy. Neither do I find it appropriate here to discuss the thesis, evidently as ideological as all others, that the democratic ideal is essentially tied to a society with absolute predominance of free enterprise, in the style of huge corporations as we know them today. Even within traditional liberal thought serious objections to this thesis exist. In synthesis, I would like to suggest that our debate start on a more modest and realistic level that would permit us to arrive at a minimum consensus in relation to the following: in the concrete reality of Latin America today, the question of democracy must be considered, first of all, in terms of transition to democracy or redemocratization, or, in the best of cases, as preservation of fragile democracies. In such a situation we cannot afford ideological warfare. A serious and profound debate on incontestable priorities is needed. Perhaps it is even important to state that, in the short run, the question of democracy is essentially linked to the fundamental problems of survival of threatened human beings. In this sense, the question is neither capitalism nor socialism. First of all, in almost all Latin American countries, no socialism exists presently or around the corner. What does exist is an absolutely savage and inhuman form of "capitalism."

As a committed Christian, I cannot deny that it would please me to insist on a more explicit definition of democracy, along the lines of what the bishops of my church maintain.

> Democracy, today a reference of national consensus, in countries like Brazil, marked by such unacceptable forms of social inequity, doesn't consist only in the preservation of political liberties. It consists also in a process of incorporation of the large masses into higher forms of education and capacitation, a better level of living and full participation in public decision making. Political democracy is a form and a prerequisite, whose very definition and destination is social democracy.[6]

But, in the short term, we must content ourselves with a more modest concept regarding the transition to democracy, as in the case of Brazil, after having experienced more than two decades of military rule. What does this transition mean to us? First, it means choosing a type of economic development that emphasizes social goals fundamentally tied to the satisfaction of basic needs, at least guaranteeing the "vital minimum" for the majority of the population. Second, this option for economic development and the minimal participation in the means for living demand social stability, which will always be threatened as long as just one-third of the population monopolizes the wealth resulting from the labor of all. Third, this process of transition to democracy cannot easily be consolidated if the economic problems directly resulting from the foreign debt are not resolved.

In other words, one cannot think of political and social stability, necessary to the consolidation of a democratic process, in countries submitted to such extortionistic drainage. From where comes the threat? The threat of new military coups no longer predominates because, in many countries, the military no longer feels capable of administering the crisis. Neither does the threat come from the radical Left because, in practically all of Latin America, the groups and parties of

47

the Left have learned much from their own mistakes and thus realize that they must now reestablish their organic relation to the popular majorities, which never understood their abstract revolutionism. For this reason many of them have begun to understand that democratic values are revolutionary values.

We must be very clear about this: the real threat to our fragile democratic processes comes from those who, both on the international and on the domestic levels, refuse to understand that our impoverished masses demand their right to life and to the means of living. The United States is committing many serious mistakes in relation to Latin America. I have heard from many people, even from the grass roots, that the U.S. government does not seem to realize that it is "exporting revolution." Either we resolve the debt crisis and overcome the economic crisis linked to it, or social explosions in Latin America are inevitable.

If it were not tragic, it would be comic to remember an event that occurred twenty-four years ago: President John F. Kennedy, concerned with possible social convulsions in Latin America, proposed to supply, through the "Alliance for Progress," a sum of $20 billion over a period of ten to fifteen years. As is well known, this modest reform failed. The proposed amount of aid earmarked for the period of ten to fifteen years was less than the net capital Latin America now exports annuallly. Today, with double the population of the early 1960s and with more than double the social problems, Latin America finds itself forced to hand over, during the period contemplated in Kennedy's project, twenty times the dollars intended to prevent revolutions. But today the real revolutionaries have learned to value democratic participation and the authentically popular movements. For this reason they are no longer interested in chaotic social explosions, which frequently result from despair and extreme poverty.

Another important element is that Latin American countries have reached a greater maturity. Now a larger sense of identity and solidarity exists among the Latin American countries. The Malvinas war was certainly an important test for this Latin American solidarity. The adventurism of the Argentinean generals, already debilitated in power, was not exactly a catalyzing element. Notwithstanding, the support the United States offered England against the overriding sovereignty issue of the Continent, without having previously consulted its neighbors, hurt Latin American sensibilities. I bring up the fact simply to underline that many things, little understood by the United States, have happened since then. It is not an overstatement to point out that the current economic crisis and the debt problem are increasingly uniting the countries and the region.

The new Latin American leaders are agreeing more and more on three issues. (1) They are not willing to have the people suffer the consequences of the foreign debt with survival-related sacrifices. Tancredo Neves said: "The debt you pay with money and not with the hunger of the people." (2) They no longer accept imposed recessionary policies, according to the intrinsically contradictory formula of the IMF. (3) They begin to make clear that they are willing to defend reasonable rates of economic growth. These leaders do not always have sure answers about ways to implement these policies, but one must recognize that they express basic elements of a common democratic process that counts upon popular support, overriding radicalized ideological positions.

Recently high-level talks among Latin American governments began in order to define converging positions with regard to the external debt issue.

## On the Spirit of Negotiation in Extreme Situations

The payment of the debt has become economically impossible. Therefore the solution of the debt crisis demands resolute political and ethical decisions. I would like to make some additional remarks about the new spirit of dialogue and negotiation that this and other fundamental questions of our world today demand of us.

**The Ethical Immaturity of Humanity in the Face of Planetary Problems.** At times I have the impression that the end of the twentieth century will be characterized by a great rigidity in the power relations and by serious impasses in the creation of a minimal consensus about the fundamental interests of all human beings. Human evolution has arrived at a crucial point: the great problems (preservation of peace, survival of humanity, extermination of hunger and poverty) have acquired planetary dimensions, but the structures of power operate with "security" concepts that hinder the consensus on the most elementary common interests. All of this happens as though humanity were unable to perceive and implement effectively its own interests.

Mankind possesses the conditions for self-destruction and does not seem to be horrified with itself. Human destructiveness has installed itself within the conscience, which displays insensitivity regarding the annual genocide of about 40 million lives, due, in the majority of cases, to historically determined and resolvable causes. No religion to date has been able to elaborate "theories of sacrifice" so cruel as those embodied in the economic, political, and military strategies that are

49

applied, with cold logic, in our world today. In terms of destroyed lives, every year we have a devastation equal to that of the Second World War, which had a duration of five years.

When dealing with these facts, liberation theologists normally find strong resistance. We are accused of emotional blackmail, psychological terrorism, and creation of artificial culpability. I insist that sick culpability is an obstacle to ethical maturity.

The current crisis of mankind is not like any other experienced in history. The difference lies in the following aspects: the increasing speed of the destruction, the number of destroyed lives, and the difficulty of negotiating and putting into practice technically possible solutions, which are hindered by ideological and political motivations. The operational relevance of certain traditional concepts—such as "mutual understanding" and "consensus about interests common to all," which are the basis of the democratic ideal—is seriously threatened because we are unable to apply the concepts to planetwide strategies: those concepts still function, to some extent, at the level of small groups, social classes, and nations but do not yet operate as a basis for worldwide consensus. Humanity has not been able to shed its "territorial imperatives" that determined its earlier evolutionary stages (those stages were characterized by violence, which was always manageable in interterritorial terms, while the current violence is of a planetary nature). The national, group, and class interests are still, tragically, the only kinds of interests that people are capable of feeling and experiencing in a more or less coherent fashion. The general concerns of humanity are still perceived as abstract and distant. We remain territorial and preplanetarian beings, but we are perfectly capable of creating worldwide crises. We are ethically immature creatures in relation both to the crises we have historically created as well as to the technology we have developed, capable of resolving problems or creating new ones.

The fundamental question is to ask ourselves why the formidable mystical, prophetical, and revolutionary potential of past great thinkers has not yet been incorporated in our ethical-political "know-how" when related to planetwide concerns. Why, instead of enhancing fraternity, did we consolidate "institutionalized violence" on a world scale? This is a question that the world religions also must ask themselves.

**The Need for Negotiation.** Perhaps I have reached the moment that requires frankness. Let people not continue to deceive or delude themselves, as though everyone desired the same thing and only lacked consensus on how to put it into practice. Even on the most fundamental interests of humanity and on the priorities among so many problems, one can no longer suppose a previous, automatic consensus by all. It is necessary to rediscover the language and priorities of the nucleus of basic criteria, which may come to reflect real consensus. What do all people really want at a minimum? Further, how can people put it into practice together?

What I am saying may seem shocking. Let me make a short test. All desire peace, and nobody wishes nuclear holocaust. But what does this desire for peace signify in terms of practical consensus at the negotiation table? Perhaps all agree with the generic meaning of the phrase "The problems of international peace are far more important than any internal problem of an individual country." But what concessions will be made on domestic problems? The urgent relocation of all workers of the arms industry? Immediate restructuring of an economy, in which a great part of its research and development and its capital interests function in accordance with a heavily militarized economic model?

The necessary negotiations to resolve the debt crisis have a lot to do with threatened lives. All people wish to see poverty eliminated from the world so that we would no longer have millions of deaths from hunger and undernourishment. But ideological resistances appear as soon as one tries to explain that most of this misery is due to historical causes rather than simply to natural catastrophies. Mohandas K. Gandhi said: "Poverty is the worst form of violence." The temptation is to ask, "Who is responsible for this violence?" Why do we accept so often this misleading question? Because speaking of historical causes means for idealistic anthropology that one must find the guilty agents. And when one arrives at this point, not only is the dialogue stalled, but the very analysis begins to be distorted by emotionalism. The reason is simple: Almost all language about the involvement of human agents in the historical processes supposes, or even mentions explicitly, intentionalities calculatedly virtuous or perverse. This is precisely the classic Manichaeism that survives in people when speaking of human agents: divinization or demonization. For example, the language of certain leftist circles on imperialism is extremely moralizing and Manichaean. That is to say, the words as well as the actions continue to function within dualistic rather than dialectic fashions. People need to learn a new language that, without losing the capability for analysis, can speak both about personal responsibility and about its involvement in power structures, which function according to their own laws and take over persons with a low level of social consciousness.

People need to learn to negotiate. We have no other choice. But what does negotiating mean? There exists a purely pragmatic view of the process of negotiation, which, precisely because it is pragmatic sounds strongly realistic. In this conception, to negotiate means the

51

intelligent use of bargaining power from all sides, starting with the interests of each of the parts to guarantee the preservation of the largest number of particular interests. According to this conception, the fundamental objective of the negotiation would be the preservation, as far as possible, of one's own interests in their historical configuration. The concessions to the other part would take place on the strict bargaining of quotas of power from each side. Unfortunately, this is the predominant conception of negotiation. Negotiations normally take place at the level of counterbalancing of existing powers and under the command of particular interests. A common basis of interest appears when concessions on both sides become inevitable because the power of the other side has to be taken into account. It is naive, then, to expect as a previous position a more generous concept of negotiation.

In relation to its fundamental problems, mankind has reached the tragic point at which it has with great difficulty to relearn the spirit of negotiation *in extremis,* that is, when negotiation becomes inevitable. This spirit implies that one favors negotiation above all other recourses to power, is always willing to negotiate, and never breaks off this process. Unfortunately not even this spirit of negotiation in extreme conditions is entirely accepted by the great powers in the face of such fundamental questions as international peace, human survival, and the right of all to possess the means of living. This situation must be changed, because to deny this spirit in face of such fundamental problems, means to deny the fundamental character of these questions. In other words, it means to ignore their absolute priority and still to consider them secondary in relation to particular interests.

For this reason liberation theologists and all those in the third world concerned with these problems reaffirm the need to relearn even this basic spirit. This relearning process signifies concretely the following: to learn that there are no other options other than recognizing that the debt crisis has reached a situation *in extremis* and that the defense of any particular interest, opposed to a general consensus about the urgency of a solution, is illusory. To accept this position means to have arrived at an understanding that in this problem common interests are at stake. There can no longer be winners—for if one side wins, all will be losers.

Theologically, all divinities invoked to legitimize the sacrifice of peace or of human survival or to concede that the sacrifice of so many human lives is justifiable must be denounced as idols. There are ideological streams within Christianity that arrive at the point of admitting, in a display of great cynicism, that some forms of sacrifice at the level of these fundamental questions may even have a salvific character before gods angry with the sins of the world. Such trends are idolatrous, because idols, in the biblical sense, are the gods of oppression that demand the sacrifice of human life.

In a world of so much misery and in which so many perish from hunger, to produce wealth means two things: to produce material goods for survival and to strengthen, at the same time, the forces of life as opposed to the forces of death: that is, to produce energy opposed to human destructiveness.

Human fraternity begins, today, in a spirit of openness to negotiate minimal consensus in that which interests all and when refusing to negotiate means something wholly irrational. This spirit must be learned and intensely exercised in grass-roots organizations, popular movements, and in all other institutions of civil society, so that the powerful can no longer hold back the pressure of this collective consciousness.

# Notes

1. For instance, explicitly, in resolution 3 of the famous "Santa Fé Document," favoring the Reagan campaign, August 1980; in the publications of "religious ideologists" supporting the Reagan administration; and in the Vatican's strong offensive against liberation theology.

2. This emphasis has become stronger in liberation theology in the past five years. See Gustavo Gutiérrez, *El Dios de la Vida* (Lima: Pontifica Universidad Católica, 1981); Victoria Araya, Hugo Assmann, et al., *The Idols of Death and the God of Life* (Maryknoll, N.Y.: Orbis Books, 1983). This kind of language is present in many official documents of the Brazilian bishops.

3. See C. Fred Bergsten, Thomas Horst, and Theodore H. Moran, *American Multinationals and American Interests* (Washington, D.C.: Brookings Institution, 1978), p. 367:

> Majority-owned affiliates of American-based manufacturing firms employed approximately 525,000 workers in developing countries in 1966, a number which probably rose to between 1 million and 1.5 million in 1975. A hypothetical increase in labor intensity of 50 percent would add "only" 500,000 to 750,000 jobs, compared with more than 100 million workers estimated to be unemployed or underemployed in the developing countries (excluding China) in 1970. Should one view the glass as 1/100 full or 99/100 empty?

Theodore H. Moran, "Multinational Corporations and Third World Investment," in Michael Novak and Michael P. Jackson, eds., *Latin America: Dependency or Interdependence?* (Washington, D.C.: American Enterprise Institute, 1984), p. 21:

> In 1979, MNCs supplied work for approximately 4 million persons in the third world. An increase of labor intensity in local operations by one-half would still produce no more than about 2 million additional

jobs in the entire less-developed world, in which the United Nations estimates there are 680 million people who need work.

4. Conferencia Nacional dos Bispas do Brasil, *Pão para quem quem tem fome,* Campanha da Fraternidade 1985. Edições Paulinas, São Paulo, 1985, p. 6.

5. Data mentioned throughout the paper were collected from several works concerning the debt crisis. I am especially indebted to Joelmir Beting, *Os juros subversivos* [*The Subversive Interest Rates*], (São Paulo, Editora Brasiliense, 1985).

6. CNBB, *Reflexão Cristã sobre a Conjuntura Politica.* Edições Paulinas, 1981, p. 10.

# Discussion

MR. NOVAK: Dr. Assmann has fulfilled admirably what we had asked of him because he has brought us a state-of-the-art discussion of liberation theology at the present moment. His paper has some historical importance, which I want to underline. I believe that it is the fullest statement of a commitment to democracy, which he recognizes as very new but developing, that I know of in a liberation theology text. Second, the paper, more than most other liberation theology texts, presents mostly propositions that are empirically testable. That is, Mr. Assmann has presented a lot more on the economic side than one normally encounters. In these two respects, he has considerably advanced the argument, and I am grateful to him for that.

BARRY LEVINE, Florida International University: The overwhelming presentation of data in the paper makes me feel as though the sky is falling. The paper is presented simply, in an extraordinarily pessimistic way.

What we have to look for are optimistic signs, and I can find at least two. One sign is that ten years ago people were pessimistically discussing the fate of Latin America using a concept of dependency that they no longer use. We can hope that in ten years people will no longer be speaking about the debt crisis and the debt bomb and they will be onto another set of concepts, perhaps equally pessimistic, but at least there will be some change. The other sign is in the presentation of the data.

In the presentation of the total debt of the Latin American countries, Colombia is said to be the seventh country in terms of its total debt but third in terms of population. In some sense, therefore, Colombia must be doing something right. If Colombia is doing something right, we cannot talk simply in terms of all of Latin America's being in some kind of global mess.

Whatever the reason, not all of Latin America is caught equally in the same morass. Therefore, we have to look for the places in which some things have been going right, rather than simply concluding that everything has been going wrong all the time.

Tony Downs, Brookings Institution: First, if liberation theology has even one-half the implications Dr. Assmann suggests, it is a profound movement.

Second, I agree that the debt crisis represents an unjust imposition of costs on Latin American countries by the developed countries, particularly the United States. The U.S. position on its own internal deficit, which is part of the debt problem because it stimulates high interest rates and other things that aggravate the problem, is morally bankrupt. We are becoming the largest debtor in the world and importing capital throughout the world even though we are the richest nation.

There really is no excuse for holding that position. We impose tremendous costs on the Latin American countries and others through that policy. Latin American countries would be justified in getting together and insisting on a more equitable settlement of interest.

One must distinguish between the original borrowing by these countries, at terms into which they entered voluntarily and for which they are therefore responsible, and the subsequent aggravation of their problem by international credit developments caused by policy in the West. These parts of the problem are difficult to separate because of the accumulation of interest caused by the higher interest rates generated by the Western policy. But after all, the Latin American countries did enter into these engagements voluntarily, and therefore they have some responsibility for dealing with that debt.

In the last part of the paper Dr. Assmann calls essentially for a forgiveness of the debt. He does not quite say that; but he points out that the debt is a trillion dollars, that we did without a trillion dollars during the oil embargo, and that we could cut our defense 10 percent. In essence he says that the debt problem cannot be separated from the worldwide North/South problem, which seems to me again to imply that we ought to allow Latin America not to pay off much of this debt—not to pay the interest—as a means of redistributing wealth and of establishing justice between North and South. I think that he implies that even if he did not quite say it.

It seems to me that one could advance that argument, and in the last part of his paper he talks about ethical maturity and the necessity for viewing problems on a worldwide basis. But by ethical maturity he means a renunciation of the debt by the rich countries but not a renunciation of privileges within Latin American countries.

If we renounced or substantially cut the interest payments on our debts, most of our large banks would be bankrupt. I am sure the Federal Reserve would not allow those banks to go bankrupt—it would intervene at a large cost to the taxpayers. Such a stand is calling for an imposition of costs on our country.

Some argument can be made for that imposition; but if Dr.

Assmann is asking the United States to absorb such costs, what about doing the same within Brazil? Where is his example of dealing with poverty within Brazil by a similar ethical view of the situation by the wealthy and the middle class in Brazil? Brazil would be in a much stronger position to ask for U.S. moral rectitude if it exhibited more itself.

The New Testament even has a passage to that effect, about what is in one's eye and in one's neighbor's eye, I recall.

I wonder how Dr. Assmann would respond to that?

MR. ASSMANN: I really do not think about forgiveness of the debt. In the paper I use the word "moratorium." I want to make clear, to underline, that not only I personally, but many, many of my political colleagues do not agree with Castro's proposal of a general moratorium or of complete forgiveness.

Perhaps the action of the Peruvian government has to be studied as a specific case, because about half of the Peruvian debt is not to bankers. Much more than other countries, Peru has loans from world import agencies or multilateral agencies such as the World Bank and the Inter-American Development Bank.

But Peru has a de facto moratorium as does Bolivia. Neither country can pay the amount they are supposed to pay over the semester or over the year. A de facto moratorium now begins to be a kind of credit-expressed moratorium as when Alan Garcia says we will pay only 10 percent of the earnings of the exports. This is the beginning of the open moratorium declaration. From Brazil, and even from Mexico, Venezuela and Argentina one will not see a moratorium declaration. Therefore I must clarify my position. It is not for forgiveness of the debt. If I bring up the comparison of $1.8 trillion for petroleum imports and of 10 percent of the defense budget, I do it only to make a clear point that perhaps solutions could be arranged so that the private banks alone would not suffer all the consequences.

I also do not support redistribution of existing wealth in the world. On that point, I agree with Michael Novak, that world production is an essential issue. But what does producing wealth mean?

I have a short section at the end of my paper about wealth production. As a Christian—perhaps a bit utopian—I say that, in a world of such misery where so many perish from hunger, to produce wealth means two things: to produce material goods for survival and at the same time inspire the forces of life as opposed to the forces of death, that is, to produce energy opposed to human destructiveness. This is a new conception of the production of wealth. As a movement producing energy as opposed to human destructiveness, even in its influence on leftist parties, liberation theology has produced much wealth. And as

57

the possibility of organizing people to be more in solidarity, it has produced much wealth. So the issue for me is the production of wealth.

The last point is the strongest. I stated in my exposition that insofar as the debt crisis becomes an internal issue for discussion on all levels in Brazil, it means discussion of the participation of civil society, of the people at all levels, in controlling state power. The economy in Brazil is statist. Around 60 percent of our economy is controlled by the state, but not only by the Brazilian state; there are strange relations between the government and the multinationals.

My last point is about the internal privileges in Latin American countries. What does the debt crisis mean as a political challenge in the internal discussions about the interrelations between the multinationals and the state and between multinationals and the internal bourgeoisie and the possibility for microenterprises to survive in Brazil? Now there will be new legislation about microenterprise in Brazil. It is very difficult to be a microfarmer in the United States, and it is very difficult to be a microentrepreneur in Brazil.

PAUL SIGMUND, Woodrow Wilson Center: I want to pick up on the mention of liberation theology as an alternative to capitalism other than Marxism.

I am trying to get a somewhat clearer idea of what the nature of that alternative is. I have been watching Latin America for twenty-five years. When I first looked at Latin America, I saw a tendency to look for a third alternative—neither capitalism nor socialism nor communism. I saw that in the question of democratic writings and policies, in the populist parties, and in the Peruvian General Valasco. And then at a certain point in the late 1960s around the time that liberation theology was born, there seemed to be no middle way; there was a radical dichotomization of social thought in Latin America. One had to declare which side he was on—socialist or capitalist. That kind of dualism or dichotomy did have some effect on the writing and the thinking of liberation theologians.

So my question is whether or not that dichotomy remains or whether it has become a trichotomy.

I saw some sense of that three-way approach in Dr. Assmann's paper and presentation, when he talked about the socialists as masochists and as not enjoying life and insufficiently concerned with democracy, particularly grass-roots democracy. The emphasis in his paper is not on anticapitalism but on grass-roots democracy.

My question is whether that emphasis indicates a shift in his thinking, and more generally in liberation theology, away from a militant anticapitalism to a deepened concern with the poor through participation and genuine democracy.

Is that shift occurring in the thinking of liberation theologians. If it is, it is important, and it opens the way for a possible diminution in the radicalism of liberation theology.

Democracy is not radical in the sense that I am talking about regarding liberationism and liberalism. A liberal would accept the notion that there is not enough participation, that grass-roots democracy is important, that race and sex are excuses for blocking opportunities. That statement raises a question about methods.

Liberation theology has been seen as revolutionary, and a whole debate about violence exists. Every time I have heard a liberation theologian speak in the United States, the first question is about violence.

Where does Dr. Assmann stand on violence? That did not come up at all in his paper. If liberation theology is shifting or the emphasis on the notion of grass-roots democracy and the basic needs of the poor is becoming greater, does the shift mean that the anticapitalist thrust is lessening to the point at which one might consider a mixed economy in which market forces are important?

Suppose one can find a form of capitalism, welfare capitalism basically, that has a productive economy because it is a market economy but that also has a social concern for redistribution and for opening up opportunities to the poor and eliminating discrimination against the poor in a way that moves liberationism very close to liberalism. Where does Dr. Assmann stand on capitalism and on revolution at this point, if his fundamental thrust is on grass-roots democracy and preferential option for the poor?

MR. ASSMANN: What Mr. Sigmund is saying is very important. It is true that liberation theology, insofar as it appears in writings, was strongly conditioned by the dichotomy of capitalism versus socialism. In the beginning, dependency theory was conditioned by that also. The dichotomy is, in a certain sense, really an original sin of liberation theology that must be overcome. At the same time, the situation out of which liberation theology merged was not academic discussion, was not at the beginning as it became later. One must consider the large, grass-roots experiences since the 1950s and the 1960s, not just a discussion about dependency, to explain why the theology of liberation emerged.

Mr. Sigmund has asked whether or not we are losing or lessening radicalization? For me democracy is a radical issue, not in terms of revolutionism, but in terms of participation. Democracy with a social content is a very radical issue.

The general secretary of my party, Francisco Lafour, is one of the famous dependentists, and he insists that democracy understood as the participation by all is a radical, revolutionary issue. I think this also. Does this position bring us back to an alliance, or a common base, with the liberal thought? I guess, yes. Why not? What kind of liberal thought?

Frankly, I am really not prepared to elaborate on this issue. I feel that we have to return to some original proposals of liberal thought to find out whether or not capitalism is essentially linked to a certain, specific concept of profit. I am beginning to doubt the Marxist principle that capitalism is always linked to pure profit.

One always needs incentives; therefore, one needs also the possibility of profit. If a person works, he has the right to have something out of his work. If one puts energy and money—the results of effort in investment—one has the right to a return. In this sense, profit is important.

In the socialist countries, insofar as they did not take into account that material incentives are necessary, the economic proposals of Che Guevara were completely utopian.

MR. NOVAK: I would like to make three comments. First, Dr. Assmann seems to see a more single-handed agency of decision making in developed countries than those who live in liberal societies know to be the case. Perhaps Latin Americans, accustomed to being governed by elites over which they have little or no control, do not readily make the distinctions among centers of power and decision making that seem obvious to North Americans. Let me mention but two examples: the independence of the Federal Reserve Board of Governors from the U.S. president and the large gap between the interests of private bankers and those of the U.S. government. Conservatives such as Tom Bethell fiercely resist having the government "bail out" the banks.

Second, there are several points at which one might take issue with figures adduced by Dr. Assmann. At one point, he argues that the worldwide indebtedness of third world countries (counting interest payments) is close to a trillion dollars and suggests that "10 percent" of the money the United States spent for arms during the past ten years would cover it. As I recall, during the ten years from 1975 to 1984, total U.S. defense spending (including salaries, pensions, and administrative costs) came to $1.2 trillion. Ten percent of that would come to about $120 billion. That comes close to the foreign assets held by private citizens in Argentina, Brazil, and Mexico.

Third, two "slogans" in Dr. Assmann's presentation are of special poignancy. Speaking of large ranches dedicated to exporting meat, he cites a saying about poor Brazilians: "People who never eat meat and cows that never see people." In the United States, farmers and ranchers constitute only about 2 percent of the total civilian labor force. Still, this 2 percent produces food and meat in superabundance. It is difficult for citizens of the United States to comprehend why immense and fertile Brazil does not feed itself lavishly. The second slogan, glimpsed by Dr. Assmann written on a wall in Peru, is: "The rights of the poor are also human rights." For citizens of the United States, the principles of "equality before the law" and "a government of laws, not men" make this very point. What is difficult for U.S. citizens to understand is why so large a proportion of Brazil's relatively small population of 135 million remains propertyless, in a country of such vast territories. The Homestead Act, so taken for granted in the United States, has virtually no parallel in Brazil.

This is not the place for extended discussion of each of these points. But they may suggest fruitful investigation in the future.

LEON KLENICKI, Jewish Anti-Defamation League: I want to share with you a biblical reflection.

When I read Gutiérrez's book on the theology of liberation, I was very excited about it, because here was what we in Hebrew call a midrash, a literal explanation and expounding of a text to arrive at a meaning for the present.

But I also realize that the theology of liberation is less generous to the Jews than the Church Fathers were. The Church Fathers finished with us in the year 70 A.D. when Rome destroyed the temple of Jerusalem, but not the people of Israel. The people then went all through the land of Israel, later creating the Jerusalem Talmud.

In chapter 19 of *Exodus,* we left Egypt, liberated by God, not by the trade unions, to go into the promised land via the Sinai. We celebrate that liberation and the giving of the Ten Commandments in our liturgy at the Passover. To be truly liberated, however, one has to be liberated from the outside and from the inside.

What is lacking, perhaps, in the theology of liberation is an understanding that after we Jews left Egypt, it took us a generation in the desert to reach Mt. Sinai. We had many problems, and some rebelled: Korah, and then Balak, who wanted to curse the Jewish people. The point is, the people had to go through an inner transformation to reach God and the promised land.

This sense of the necessity for inner transformation is what I don't find in your paper or in those of other theologians of liberation. This

61

discipline in which people stop thinking in terms of manecheism in turn, and think in their own good. We can talk about the debt the democracies have inherited from the dictatorships, but if there is not good, essential change in structure, *plus la change, plus la même chose*. There won't be any difference between the generals of Argentina and Mr. Alfonsin, if the people are unchanged.

Perhaps as we consider that discipline of the spirit, we should pay attention to Moses's words in *Exodus,* that salvation means something, that redemption means something. Perhaps, then, we should not place the guilt for all our sins on banks and American companies or corporations. We have our own sins.

Of course, I would love to put all the blame on the Americans, because for many years we Jews have had to pay for being the scapegoats. When I was a student in Argentina, one of my teachers was a firm believer in translating Lexion Française into action: he said that Jews were the agents of Moscow. When I went back to Argentina in 1967 as a rabbi, I heard another thing: that Jews were now the agents of Wall Street. (I prefer the second because the dollar is better than the ruble.)

The question, though, is that we have an obligation to illustrate otherwise to our people. We are continuing a very bad practice that started in the church with Constantine. We are paying for that sin, and you are still paying for that sin.

I also call for some realism in responding to Mr. Castro's talk about not paying the debt. The comrades in the Kremlin must be very uneasy, because what if his arguments discourage Poland, Yugoslavia, or Romania from paying their debts to the Soviet Union? We could reverse the whole thing: I don't find that possibility in your paper, and I would like to see that. Not all the sins are the West's; there are also Eastern sins that should be demonstrated to the world.

I suggest to you, Dr. Assmann, that perhaps especially in Latin America, we should speak less romantically and more realistically. We should ask our theologians to be less Lord Byron and more William James. Otherwise, we suffer the disease of Victor Hugo, *le malaise de siècle,* that romanticism in which we put all the guilt on the big corporations but don't see our own problems.

We Americans should also become less romantic. We must go back to the good, old pragmatic way of our tradition. Indeed, I shiver when I read certain theologians of liberation, but I also shiver when I read some of the papers of the bishops or the eternally rosy language of the National Council of Churches.

A lesson for us lies in contemplating the Hebrew language of the Bible: the language is very poor in adjectives, but very rich in nouns, a solid, pragmatic element which is missing in our approach to the world.

# Commentary

## Nick Eberstadt

I commend Professor Assmann for his integrity and moral courage in presenting these arguments and opinions before this predominantly North American audience. To face a conference that, without undue imagination, could be expected to be unsympathetic to one's outlook and yet not to shrink from prosecuting one's case directly and forcefully is an act of forthrightness that merits respect.

There are issues—rather, there is an issue—on which I find myself in total agreement with Professor Assmann. This is protectionism. Protectionist trade policies, and other actions that unnaturally restrict commercial and financial contacts between rich and poor countries, create needless economic hardships. Such protectionism reduces the opportunities for income generation in less-developed nations, thus affecting earnings, output, employment, and economic efficiency. At the same time, barriers against entry and competition in the domestic markets of the more affluent nations punish consumers in those countries by reducing diversity of selection and supporting unnecessarily high prices. Higher prices in turn mean higher costs of production, reduced competitiveness, constricted output, and unnecessarily low employment. The protectionist measures adopted by developed nations have an additional, and ironic, effect of making it more difficult for less-developed nations to earn the foreign currency they need to make good on their sizable debts to private and public institutions in the West. (Of course, the adverse consequences of protectionism arise regardless of whether the state imposing it is "developed" or "developing"; lest we forget, the array of protectionist devices employed by indebted and comparatively poor nations to prevent competition in their local markets is far-reaching, and their impact is consequential.)

Apart from protectionism, I disagree with Professor Assmann over virtually all the substantive areas touched upon in his discourse. Although the differences that separate us may center upon our contrasting philosophical perspectives, they include interpretations of fact, and even issues of fact themselves. If Professor Assmann will bear with me,

63

I will attempt to elucidate our differences, so that we may perhaps see where our points of disagreement lie.

Professor Assmann seems to cast Fidel Castro in the role of "tough cop" in the current confrontation over external debt in Latin America. Schematically, it seems that any government or actor adopting a posture even fractionally less hostile to Western creditor institutions than Castro's own are thus cast as "nice cops." Such actors can then be described as "moderate" or "pragmatic," not by the actual merits of their arguments, but by their location on a spectrum of negotiating stances artificially extended by the inclusion of Castro's proposals within the realm of serious discussion.

There is little reason to accord Fidel Castro either attention or authority on the questions of economic independence or financial self-reliance. Fidel Castro's Cuba is a more dependent country today than when he came to power. Economically, Cuba is more a one-crop country in 1985 than it was in 1958. Although it is difficult to measure real output and trade for economies where prices reflect neither scarcity nor articulated demand, but instead reveal imposed governmental preferences, it appears that Cuba today derives something like four-fifths of its export revenues from its sugar harvest. In 1958, the fraction from sugar was about three-fifths—so much for the great talk of "diversification."

But Cuba's sugar harvest alone, and even the totality of Cuba's exports, is insufficient to pay for everything that the Cuban government must currently import simply to continue its existence. Simply to function, Cuba today relies upon large and steady subsidies from the U.S.S.R. The size of these annual contributions should give pause to any advocate of "economic independence." Although, as I have mentioned, the precise magnitude of economic flows is difficult to determine when the prices of goods and services are set at the command of the regime in power, there is little doubt that gifts and loans from the COMECON bloc finance about a third of Cuba's current economic consumption. Put another way, direct donations and lines of credit advanced by other Communist nations allow contemporary Cuba to live on half again as much as it could if it had to purchase everything it consumes today on the basis of its own production.

No other country in this hemisphere is so heavily dependent on foreign largesse. Nor is any other nation in this hemisphere so beholden to her creditors. The Soviet Union is neither forbearing nor shy toward those regimes under its financial obligation. And Cuba's ruble indebtedness, now running into the tens of billions and mounting by several billion each year, is a lever that Moscow does not hesitate to use. We can recall the spectacle of Fidel Castro, self-proclaimed exponent of nonalignment and national independence, warmly endorsing the Soviet invasion of Czechoslovakia shortly after Soviet energy supplies to his island were "accidentally" interrupted. Cuba depends far more on the Soviet economic system today than it did in 1968, and what is required of it in return is commensurately greater. Tens of thousands of Cubans have been sent to the labor-scarce regions of Eastern Europe and the U.S.S.R. as a sort of human amortization on the Cuban national debt. These men and women toil at artificially reduced wages so that their government can make a partial payment to its Warsaw Pact allies on the enormous financial debt it owes them. But Cuba's effort to redeem its government debt through traffic in its own citizens is not limited to *bracero* socialism. Cuba's youth today is shedding its lifeblood in Angola and Ethiopia; this, too, is a *direct* response to their government's enormous ruble obligations. If Professor Assmann wishes to find a vivid illustration of the violence forced upon a local population by international indebtedness, he need search no farther.

But this is not the violence Professor Assmann sees. Professor Assmann argues instead that the international system of commercial finance and trade in which Western nations play so great a part is wreaking extraordinary destruction in the less-developed countries. As he portrays the arrangement, it is actually murderous. By his account, the current international system can be connected with what he says are 40 million needless, even unnatural, deaths in the third world every year.

It is necessary to inject some facts into this discussion. One of my own areas of interest is demography and population studies, and there is a considerable literature on world population trends. Conditioned by some uncertainty, demographic estimates pertaining to less-developed countries are generally least reliable for precisely those areas where poverty is greatest and mortality is highest. As a best guess, however, the number of deaths for the entirety of the human race currently comes to somewhere around 50 million a year. (The World Bank's 1985 *World Development Report,* whose figures generally reflect the received wisdom in the development business, would place the total number of deaths in the world in 1983 at 48.3 million, although the margins of error suggested by such a precise estimate are obviously unwarranted.)

Let us say, for the sake of argument, that the actual number of deaths is higher—say, a global total of 60 million a year. To say that 40 million of those deaths are unnecessary would be to say that at least two-thirds of the people in the world who die each year should not do so.

The point at issue here is not ethics, but arithmetic. To presume that upwards of two-thirds of the deaths in the world each year are unnecessary is, in effect, to posit a "natural" lifespan for human beings of 120 years, or even greater. It would be impossible to reduce the annual toll of death on earth by 40 million without raising the current expectation of life at birth for the planet as a whole to at least 120 years. While a life expectancy at birth of this order, and the good health that would presumably accompany it, may currently be desired by many national populations, these are within the grasp of none. The healthiest nation of the earth is now Japan; its life expectancy falls short of this target by more than forty years. It serves neither practical nor ethical purposes to treat the ethereal desideratum of a 120-year lifespan as a feasible norm.

For what it is worth, the *World Development Report 1985* places the total number of deaths for Africa, Latin America and the Caribbean, and Asia (minus Japan and the U.S.S.R.) at under 39 million. Under such conditions, reducing the annual toll of deaths in these regions by 40 million would be an imposing task.

A nation's life expectancy is an important indicator of a population's well-being. As best can be told, the gap in life expectancy between the United States and Canada and the rest of the hemisphere, taken as a whole, is now close to a decade. This gap speaks to meaningful and important differences in a variety of life chances. It is well to remember, however, that the gap in lifespans between North America and Latin America was much larger in the recent past. For the early 1950s, for example, it is thought that the difference in life expectancy between the two regions was about two decades. Thus, this most significant of material inequalities has been narrowing, not widening, and it has narrowed substantially in recent decades. And the narrowing is not just a trick of averages. The data that I have had a chance to review show that overall levels of life expectancy in every Latin American society with reliable statistics has been increasing over recent decades.

Moreover, no data suggest that national life expectancy has fallen *anywhere* in Latin America in the years since the onset of the so-called financial crisis. In Argentina, where such data may be regarded as reasonably reliable, infant mortality is down. This is also true in Venezuela. In Chile infant mortality dropped sharply in the early 1980s. We can be less confident about Mexico, since death registration there is incomplete, but the tentative indications are that infant mortality has dropped, not risen, in the period since September 1982. While infant mortality figures for Brazil are somewhat conjectural, owing to the poor registration of both births and deaths, no statistical evidence suggests that the nation's slow but steady improvements in overall health have been arrested or reversed. In short, if the argument that current international economic arrangements are contributing to the "murder" of great numbers of people in Latin America is to be treated as a verifiable proposition, it appears to be demonstrably false.

There has been much discussion of the causes of Latin America's current debt problems. One school of thought, which might be called "structuralist," seeks explanations for the current problem of Latin America's nonperforming loans. Such talk fastens upon, for example, the ratio of external debt to GNP, or the ratio of service payments to export earnings. While these comparisons can highlight economic trends, they do not speak to the fundamental causes of financial difficulties. A more fruitful way to pursue the issue is to consider the rate of return being earned by borrowed money in comparison with the rate of interest that must be paid back on it.

Not all third world nations with substantial international financial obligations now find themselves in financial difficulty. The example of South Korea immediately comes to mind. Korea's foreign debt today approaches $50 billion; yet it seems to meet its payments of interest and principal on time and has not found it necessary to enter into rescheduling negotiations. Why is this? The answer is that, to date, the government has managed to earn a higher rate of return on the foreign money it is putting to use than it is obliged to pay back in interest.

To my way of thinking, any discussion of a debt crisis in Latin America must ineluctably lead us to consider the ways in which borrowed funds were spent. What is the cause of what must obviously have been low rates of return on the enormous quantity of money borrowed? Understanding Latin America's current difficulties requires us to address this question directly and honestly.

Some claim that vast amounts of money have been lost to theft and corruption in Latin America over the past decade. I am not in a position to judge the accuracy of those claims. It is my inclination, however, to suspect that theft and corruption are not the main explanation for Latin America's current financial difficulties. From an arithmetic standpoint, the case does not look plausible. Simply put, it would be difficult for any person or group to steal the sum of money required to drive rates of return on borrowed funds down to the level that was reached by some of Latin America's debtor nations.

The explanation for these low rates of return, it seems to me, is largely to be found in a systematically unproductive application of public funds. Faced with easy access to credit from Western banks in the wake of the OPEC oil price increases, many governments seem to have adjusted their policies toward less, rather than more, productive uses of capital. This seems not solely to have been a question of pursuing ill-advised or mismanaged investment programs on the public account. In many nations much of the borrowed money appears to have been used to maintain unsustainably high levels of consumption for the general population through a complex and ambitious array of subsidies. Common rhetoric notwithstanding, these subsidies conferred immediate benefit on very broad portions of the populations in question. Indeed, their broad incidence was precisely the reason for their widespread popularity.

A chorus of voices is raised to insist that Latin America's debts to Western institutions are too large to repay. Professor Assmann seems to concur with these voices. His paper and his talk assert that it is quite impossible as a practical matter to make good on these debts.

If this point is pursued as a proposition in arithmetic, rather than ideology, it is not convincing. In most of the Latin American nations where the "rescheduling" of debts is under way, the public sector owns 40, 50, or even 60 percent of the country's industrial base. It is highly illogical to state, on the one hand, that a government owns half or more of a country's industrial base and to assert, on the other, that it has no assets that might be sold to help repay its various international obligations. Many Latin American governments, not just Brazil and Argentina, also possess large tracts of public land that could also be sold if there were a serious intention to make good on contracted debts. I have not, to date, heard any discussion of such measures. There is a distinction between inability and unwillingness to pay a debt, and it must not be obscured in the present context.

Indeed, the policy changes that would enable Latin America nations to pay their debts more easily are not inconsistent with improved welfare of the masses, particularly of the poorest fractions of those populations. Far from it: the same policies that led to low rates of return on foreign debt also depressed exports, discouraged cost management in private and public enterprises, and restricted the opportunities of the less privileged segments of society for increased earnings and employment. Pursuit of less manifestly uneconomic and restrictive trade regimens and domestic policies would perhaps increase the capability to generate not only export revenues, but also domestic output, demand for labor, and, ultimately, purchasing power for the poor.

Professor Assmann suggests that pressing the debt issue will jeopardize the prospects for democratization in Latin America. My perspective is quite different. It seems to me that assuming full responsibility for the debt would promote democratization, not endanger it, in the nations in question.

Two things that separate democracies from dictatorships are liberty and responsibility, secured by law. To qualify or reject one's obligation to repay contracted debts, even though broad portions of a nation benefited from the money borrowed, is necessarily to raise serious questions about both responsibilities and individual rights. Western nations, it is sometimes said, are dangerously strong. Western banks are often accused of having unfair bargaining power in their negotiations with debtor nations. Let us take such rhetoric at its face value for the moment. If the rights of the strong can be summarily repealed and dismissed, what does this portend for the weak? If a government feels it acceptable to renege on its obligations to other sovereign states, what does this suggest about its attitude toward those individuals who live under its administration? If law can be interpreted to allow violation of the rights of the influential at the pleasure of the state, what protections can the poor and the defenseless expect as their inalienable right? The poor and the weak are always more vulnerable to the abuse of power than the privileged. To deny protection or absolve responsibility for one segment of society is a perilous business, for it exposes all to risk. Repudiating the debt, thus, would seem to me to lead Latin American nations away from true democracy, not toward it.

As a final point, I have great personal difficulty with Professor Assmann's use of the word "genocide." To my way of thinking, "genocide" recalls the destruction of European Jewry between 1939 and 1945. The horrible details of that episode of modern history do not need to be rehearsed. I might simply mention that the life expectancy of Jews in Europe dropped rather dramatically during the Nazi effort to achieve their complete extermination. Neither Brazil nor any other Latin American countries for which reliable data can be found have seen life expectancy fall in recent decades, or in recent years. To the contrary: as I have already mentioned, life expectancy in Latin America and the Caribbean has been steadily and significantly improving.

"Genocide" is not a term to be used frivolously. To do so not only denigrates the memory of the dead, but also degrades the value of life for the living. To muddle the meaning of "genocide" is, in my view, to assault both the sanctity of individual lives and the universality of human worth. Casual use of the term "genocide" does not sit well with Professor Assmann's frequent references to a "logic of the majority." However humanitarian its intention may be, such thinking can be expected to contribute little to the "liberation" of man and may do much to excuse or even sanction his oppression.

## Hugo Assmann

The use of the word "genocide" is verbally aggressive, but in reality one has to decide for oneself about the use of statistics. When one cites figures of 28 million children say from birth to five years dying every year in the world, predominantly because of historical causes, and children over five years, one comes near to 40 million deaths a year.

Now, I am really surprised by Mr. Eberstadt's observation that he cannot see a link between the debt crisis, its social implications, and life expectancy. If one considers only northeast Brazil during the five-year drought, the statistics presented by the Conference of Bishops show that about 7 million people died. Statistics presented by other institutions show around 5 million people. That is a lot of people.

Life expectancy is an issue that cannot be used in the same form as per capita distribution; to use it so is completely absurd. Life expectancy in northeast Brazil is one problem, and life expectancy in the center of the big São Paulo capital is another. Depending on the context, the problem is completely different. In the regions around São Paulo, the death rate of children in the first year of life is near 250 per 1,000, if the statistics of the Archdiocese of São Paulo are right.

So I have to make a choice as to what kind of statistics I will believe. I am deeply convinced that the statistics of many international groups studying populations are completely false or ideologically distorted. They do not take into account many variables that must be taken into account because the issue is complex. There are many, many social implications of this situation.

As a political militant, I am really more interested in discussing, not the economic issue, but the political consequences of the economic issue. What does the issue really mean for our internal discussion of privileges or differences of income?

Well, paying off the principal of the debt is possible. It is possible, but we have to sell off our country. In Brazil, one topic of discussion is why the government spent the loans in such a wrong way, in the fantastic, big planning of useless things. (Other expenditures—such as energy—are not so useless.)

Mr. Eberstadt says that the infrastructure and the capital goods are there with which to pay the debt. Denationalization of our economy is already so great, that if you ask for more denationalization . . . I ask him please to understand why nationalism is now a very complex political issue.

I can think of a general in the Brazilian military who publishes newspaper articles developed by his advisers on the debt crisis, and he is an extreme nationalist from the right. For me nationalism is a dangerous issue, because I think about a world in which territorial imperatives have to be overcome. If the rights of the strongest, the big are impaired, what about the rights of the individuals, of the poor, of the lower classes?

If one thinks that the possibility of improving the right of the poor is essentially linked to the historically established power of the powerful, he really is thinking in circles. One must attack at some point the so-called right of the powerful, the dominant classes, or the privileged. If one never puts the finger on that issue, he cannot really speak about democracy. There is no possibility of improving the rights of all, especially of most of the poor, if one does not change anything of the established or acquired rights of the powerful.

## George Weigel

It would indeed be an important development if liberation theologians were to bring notions of participatory, democratic politics more directly into their reflections and if the various theologies of liberation were to begin using non-Marxist forms of social analysis. I am inevitably reminded here of Barbara Tuchman's description of Sidney and Beatrice Webb: "What the Fabian Society wanted was Socialism without Marx or revolution, something like 'Macbeth' without murder." If participatory democracy were added to, and Marxist social analysis subtracted from, theologies of liberation, one might then wonder about the distinctiveness of this school of thought: would it still be liberation theology, or something rather resembling classic twentieth-century Catholic social theory, particularly as that has been worked out in the United States? But questions of taxonomy can be deferred until we learn a bit more about these purported, and potentially decisive, shifts in the winds blowing from Latin America.

Since liberation theologians pride themselves on their attention to *praxis,* it should not be too much to ask that a "reformed" liberation theology pay close attention to the institutionalization of human freedom. Those who enjoy the blessings of living under liberal institutions fully understand the wisdom of Walter Lippmann when he wrote: "Liberty is not the natural state of man, but the achievement of an organized society." It is not enough, in other words, merely to affirm the theoretical importance of a politics of participation: one has to ask, Through what institutions will that politics be conducted, protected, and nurtured? The whole panoply of "mediating structures" is important here. Are theologians of liberation willing to defend the prerogatives of free trade unions, an independent business sector, a free press, free peasant cooperatives and credit associations, a free church, or free political parties who may campaign for public support without fear of *turbas divinas* (the "divine mobs" of Nicaragua)? Will schools independent of state control be encouraged? Will neighborhood associations be truly independent, or will they be instruments of the state security apparatus? Trotsky's dictum, "Who says A, must say B," surely applies here: who says "participatory politics" must also say "the independent institutions that make genuine participation possible."

A commitment to "participatory politics" would also require a rethinking, in liberation theologies, of the idea of violence. To the Greeks, violence was "extramural," outside the walls of a true *polis,* a true political community. To some theologians of liberation, the very concept of violence has been traduced (by references to "first" or "structural" violence) to the point where violence in its classic sense is considered a redemptive reality. Commitments to participatory politics mean a rejection of that fascination with revolutionary violence that seems such a distinguishing psychological (and, occasionally, political) dimension in theologies of liberation. To take up politics means to lay down guns: "Who says A, must say B."

Perhaps because of their commitments to Marxist analysis, perhaps because of the distinctive experience of Latin America, the various theologies of liberation have not, to date, given much attention to the essential distinction between "society" and "state" that lies at the heart of both classic Catholic social theory (in the principle of subsidiarity) and the North Atlantic experience of liberal institutions. Yet this is an area that must be explored in depth if there is to be a "reformed" liberation theology that takes participatory politics and non-Marxist social analysis seriously.

There is surely room for dialogue here between "liberation south" and "liberation north." But the dialogue, to be intellectually fruitful, must begin with honest expressions of dissatisfaction and concern. Those theologians of liberation who wish to bring participatory politics and non-Marxist social analysis into their intellectual kit bag might signal more than an abstract interest in these questions by prophetically criticizing two societies in which the mediating structures essential to a genuinely participatory politics are now absent, or under intense pressure: Cuba and Nicaragua. Such a critique would carry immense weight throughout the Americas. It would indicate a genuinely new moment in the debate between theologians of liberation and theologians in the liberal tradition. It would persuasively demonstrate the commitment of liberation theologians to a *praxis*-oriented reflection.

Will we hear it? I am not holding my breath, but I hope so.

# Underdevelopment Revisited

*Peter L. Berger*

The poverty in which large numbers of human beings live has been a stubborn and morally troubling reality for a long time. The terminology describing this reality has often changed, however. During the hopeful years of decolonization in the aftermath of World War II, "backwardness" (a term suggesting mental retardation) gave way to "underdevelopment" (implying a merely physical lag). This "underdevelopment" was to be cured by "development," in turn identified with "growth" (as a child catches up with an adult). The manifesto of this period was Walt W. Rostow's *The Stages of Economic Growth,* first published in 1960, and reminiscent of Jean Piaget's child psychology in its self-confident prescription of how a country develops from "take-off" to "maturity."

Then came the late 1960s and early 1970s, when this entire way of looking at the poorer portions of the globe was radically debunked, both in the "underdeveloped" countries themselves and in influential academic sectors of the West. Not only did the "children" throw the book at their "teachers," but many teachers recanted their earlier pedagogic doctrine. The quasi-mythological phrase "third world" came into vogue, while the bureaucratic agencies concerned with the poorer regions fell back either on the relatively optimistic term "developing countries" or on the seemingly neutral term, "less developed countries" (with its official acronym, LDCs).

In the last few years, as the revolutionary redemptions of the "third

EDITOR'S NOTE: Because of intensive commitments abroad, Peter Berger was unable to prepare a formal lecture, but agreed in advance to speak from notes. Alas, despite a careful check before and after his delivery, a technical error wiped away the record of his talk. Only a portion of the discussion was spared. Therefore, we have substituted a related paper by Professor Berger (through the courtesy of *Commentary Magazine,* which first published it in 1984). The editor appends a summary of Professor Berger's oral presentation, based on notes taken as he spoke and approved by Professor Berger.

world" have proved ever more disappointing, the favored term has become "South," as in "North/South dialogue." "South" suggests sunshine, perhaps even natural abundance, but also languid siestas in the heat of the day. The ambiguity is telling.

Changes in terminology sometimes reflect advances in knowledge; sometimes they are covers for ignorance. Which is the case here? How much have we really learned about the world's poverty and the remedies for it?

If one is in the habit of writing books, these books can sometimes serve as convenient landmarks to measure both advances in learning and perduring ignorance. It is now almost exactly ten years since the publication of my *Pyramids of Sacrifice,* which was a tentative summing-up of what I had learned about "development" since becoming involved in the topic a few years earlier. As it happens, this book (somewhat to my surprise) is still being read; more importantly, it reflects a particular phase in the intellectual and political debate over the issue of poverty and development. For this reason a look at what I said in 1974 may be a useful exercise.

I wrote *Pyramids of Sacrifice* in response to two powerful experiences. One was my first contact with third world poverty, which shocked me morally as well as emotionally. The other was the eruption in American academia of a neo-Marxist rhetoric, which purported to understand the causes of third world poverty and which also claimed to know the remedies. I was never convinced by this rhetoric, but I wanted to be fair to it. More than anything else, I wanted to explore, with moral engagement and skeptical rationality, an area which at that time was suffused with violent emotions and blatantly irrational opinions.

The book argued that both capitalism and socialism had generated myths that had to be debunked—the capitalist myth of growth, which mistook an increase in GNP for improvement in the condition of the poor, and the socialist myth of revolution, which provided an alibi for tyranny. In the service of demythologizing these ideas, the book advocated an open, non-doctrinaire approach; neither capitalism nor socialism, it argued, offered a panacea. Each country would have to think through, in pragmatic terms, what its most promising development strategy should be. As far as moral criteria were concerned, such a pragmatic assessment should be guided, I thought, by two calculi—a "calculus of pain," by which I meant the avoidance of human suffering, and a "calculus of meaning," which I defined as respect for the values of the putative beneficiaries of development policies.

A centerpiece of the book was a comparison of Brazil and China, important respectively as the largest capitalist and the largest socialist case. I had traveled extensively in Brazil just before writing *Pyramids;* although I had not been to China, I had read voraciously about it. I

74

concluded that both "models" should be rejected—curiously, for the same reason. Both were willing to sacrifice a generation for an allegedly certain goal of development, Brazil through the adoption of economic policies that condoned widespread and bitter misery as the short-run price for long-run prosperity, China through terror and totalitarianism. Neither the Brazilian technocrats nor the Chinese ideologists, I wrote, could be certain about the eventual outcome of their policies. This being so, they lost any moral warrant for the sacrifices they were imposing on their peoples.

Yet neither case, the book suggested, exhausted the possibilities of the capitalist or socialist development models. Capitalism need not be practiced as brutally as in Brazil, and there could be a more humane socialism than that of Maoist China. In this connection, I said some nice things about Peru (then under Velasco's left-leaning regime) and Tanzania; I had been briefly in both places and had been favorably impressed.

A number of readers of *Pyramids of Sacrifice* were misled by my wish to be fair to the left (which, practically, meant that I desired to go on talking with most of my colleagues). They read the book as advocating democratic socialism. That had not been my intention at all. What did come through, however, was some vague notion of a "third way," perhaps some sort of a so-called mixed model. I had no clear conception of what this might look like; I was unsure of much, and I admitted it. I did feel sure of two things, however: that people should not be allowed to starve if the means to feed them were at hand, and that people should not be subjected to totalitarian terror under any circumstances.

Obviously, *Pyramids of Sacrifice* is today obsolete because of the changes that have taken place in the world (more of this below). But looking back on it now, I am struck as well by the changes that have occurred in my own perspective. Not to put too fine a point on it, I am much less evenhanded today in my assessment of capitalist and socialist development models: I have become much more emphatically pro-capitalist. Some part of the shift I have undergone is undoubtedly due to personal experience. In 1974, except for one foray into Africa, my acquaintance with the third world was limited to Latin America; inevitably, this made for a very specific bias. In 1977, however, I had my first experience of East Asia and since then my attention has turned very strongly to that region. East Asia is inconvenient territory for those who want to be evenhanded as between capitalist and socialist development models. Specifically, the capitalist "success stories" of East Asia and the lessons they hold must be confronted by any reflective person with a concern for world poverty.

To speak of success stories implies a definition of success. And

75

here I would today insist that, minimally, there are three criteria to be applied.

First, successful development presupposes sustained and self-generating economic growth. To that extent, at least, Rostow and the other enthusiasts of the 1950s were perfectly right, while the late fantasists of zero growth were perfectly wrong. We have a pretty clear idea of what a zero-growth world would look like. It would either freeze the existing inequities between rich and poor, or it would see a violent struggle to divide up a pie that is no longer growing. Neither scenario holds out the slightest promise for such values as human rights or democracy. The existing inequities would have to be brutally defended or brutally altered. I daresay that this root insight of political economy is by now widely recognized, even on the left (except, perhaps, among the remaining holdouts of romantic environmentalism).

Secondly, successful development means the large-scale and sustained movement of people from a condition of degrading poverty to a minimally decent standard of living. In insisting on this point, I continue to give credence to the critique (mostly from the left) of the earlier development theories, which tended to see economic growth as a synonym for development rather than as its precondition. On that point, the critics were right: the most impressive growth rates can cover up massively inequitable distribution of the benefits of growth; there can be growth without development, and there can even be what André Gunder Frank has called "the development of underdevelopment." Brazil in the early 1970s was a striking example of this—staggering economic growth, so maldistributed that abject misery (measured by hunger, infant mortality, low life expectancy, and the like) not only continued unabated but, in parts of Brazil, worsened.

I would even go a step farther in conceding a point to the left. The advocates of liberation theology have contributed a phrase, "the preferential option for the poor," which sounds like a bad English translation of a bad Spanish translation of neo-Marxist German, but means simply that one is morally obligated to look at things from the viewpoint of the poor. Fair enough. After all, it was Dr. Johnson, not exactly a premature Marxist, who said that "a decent provision for the poor is the true test of civilization."

In focusing on this particular criterion for defining successful development I am invoking, of course, the ideal of equity; but I am *not* invoking "equality," a utopian category that can only obfuscate the moral issues. It is inequitable and immoral that, next door to each other, some human beings are starving while others gorge themselves. To make this situation more equitable and thus morally tolerable, the starvation must stop and the poor must become richer. This goal can be attained without the rich becoming poorer. In other words, I do not assume the need for a leveling of income distribution. Western societies (including the United States) have demonstrated that dramatic improvements are possible in the condition of the poor without great changes in income distribution; the poor can get richer even while the rich get richer too. And there are good economic grounds for thinking that income-leveling policies in the third world inhibit growth, with the poor paying the biggest price for this inhibition. "Equality" is an abstract and empirically murky ideal; it should be avoided in assessing the success or failure of development strategies.

Third criterion: development cannot be called successful if the achievements of economic growth and equitable distribution come at the price of massive violations of human rights. This criterion applies to both of the calculi formulated in *Pyramids of Sacrifice*. In 1974 it seemed to me and to many others that China offered an illustration of the "calculus of pain." We now know that the economic and egalitarian achievements of Maoism were themselves largely fictitious. Still, I believe that I was correct to insist that, *even if* it were true that Maoism had vanquished hunger among China's poor, this achievement could not morally justify the horrors inflicted by the regime—horrors that entailed the killing of millions of human beings and the imposition of a merciless totalitarian rule on the survivors.

As for the "calculus of meaning," Iran now offers a good instance. The shah's regime undoubtedly achieved economic growth, it ameliorated the condition of many of the poor (even if a corrupt elite greatly enriched itself in the process), and its violations of human rights, ugly though they were, did not come even close to the horrors of Maoism (not to mention the nightmare of terror of the Khomeini regime). However, as Grace Goodell has persuasively argued, the reform program of the shah systematically trampled on the mores and values by which the largest number of Iranians gave meaning to their lives. It was a program of rapid and coercive modernization, contemptuous of tradition and indigenous institutions. Logically enough, this alliance of technocrats, profiteers, and secret police evoked a neotraditionalist reaction. The tragic consequences following the triumph of these reactionaries, and the fact that the new regime has worsened the condition of the Iranian people, cannot provide an *ex post facto* justification of the shah's policies. (By analogy, the Bolshevik Revolution was a catastrophe for the Russian people; but it does not follow from this that czarism, though in many ways morally superior to its successor regime, was a wise and humane system.)

It should be clear what I mean by "massive violations of human rights": mass killings, concentration camps, forced deportations, torture, separation of families, pervasive intimidation—in other words, the standard practices of 20th-century totalitarianism. But I should stress at the same time that I do *not* include democracy as a necessary element in this criterion for successful development. Democracy is the best available form of government in the modern world; moreover, I consider it the only reliable protection of human rights under modern conditions. (I have explained why at some length in "Democracy for Everyone?" *Commentary,* September 1983.) In the long run, I also believe that democracy and development are necessarily linked realities. All the same, the case regrettably cannot be made that democracy is indispensable to successful development.

Armed with these criteria for development we may now turn to the evidence that has accumulated over the last ten years. Perhaps the most important piece of evidence is negative: the absence of even a single successful case of socialist development in the third world.

Even in the early 1970s it should not have been news that socialism is not good for economic growth, and also that it shows a disturbing propensity toward totalitarianism (with its customary accompaniment of terror). What has become clearer is that socialism even fails to deliver on its own egalitarian promises (the second criterion of success). In country after country, socialist equality has meant a leveling down of most of the population, which is then lorded over by a highly privileged and by no means leveled elite.

Put simply, socialist equality is shared poverty by serfs, coupled with the monopolization of both privilege and power by a small (increasingly hereditary) aristocracy. That this was so of the Soviet Union had already been accepted by most Western and third world leftists by the late 1960s and 1970s. What is evident now is that a Soviet-style *nomenklatura* seems to spring up predictably wherever socialism extends. It has done so in China, in Vietnam, in Cuba, and in such lesser socialist experiments as Angola and Mozambique. None of these countries, not even Cuba, is directly or entirely under Soviet rule. It seems to be the intrinsic genius of socialism to produce these modern facsimiles of feudalism.

The fact that there is not a single case of economically successful and nontotalitarian socialism has begun to sink in. (The social democracies of the West, of course, should not be subsumed under the category of socialism.) The monumental failures of Maoism, failures proclaimed to the world not by its old enemies but directly from Peking, have made a deep impression in Asia; so have the horrors of the triumphant socialist revolution in Indochina. In Asia more than elsewhere in the third world, there now seems a new openness to the possibility of capitalist models, even if the word itself is avoided in favor of circumlocutions like "market mechanisms" or euphemisms like "pluralism." The radical shift from a socialist to a capitalist model in Sri Lanka illustrates this tendency, especially because it came about as the result of open debate and democratic politics.

Two cases touched upon in *Pyramids of Sacrifice,* Peru and Tanzania, are interesting in this connection. The socialist experiments of the Velasco regime ended in economic disaster, after which, prudently, the military handed the mess back to a civilian government that stopped the experiments. It is not clear, however, to what extent the brief and limited socialist policies of the Velasco regime can be blamed for economic problems that antedated it.

The case of Tanzania—an economic fiasco—is much more instructive. Here was a country that in the early 1970s had much going for it— reasonably good resources (especially in agriculture); a dubiously democratic but relatively humane government led by Julius Nyerere, an intelligent and attractive leader by most standards; and freedom from foreign domination. What is more, Tanzania had long been the darling of devlopment-aid institutions, which poured vast amounts of money into the country. Whatever else one may say about the economic and political failures of Tanzania, these cannot be blamed on corrupt leadership, on bad Soviet influence, or on the hostility or destabilizing policies of Western capitalism. The fiasco was self-made.

Tanzania's much-vaunted Ujamaa program of socialist agriculture has come close to destroying the agricultural productivity of the country. As the program has failed economically, it has become more coercive. The government had at first tried to persuade peasants to move to Ujamaa villages by means of incentives; by the later 1970s, pressure had to be applied. As for the non-agricultural sector of the economy, small enough to begin with, the "para-statal organizations" that operate it have succeeded in running that little into the ground. This particular failure has been augmented by systematic pressures on the Indian minority, who (in Tanzania as in other East African countries) comprise much of the small entrepreneurial class. Not surprisingly, the economic failures have gone hand in hand with increasing political repressiveness; Tanzania today is even less democratic and certainly less humane than it was in 1974.

Events in China and Brazil, the two countries discussed at greatest length in *Pyramids of Sacrifice,* have been momentous. In the book I rejected the Maoist model because of its human costs; now the model must also be rejected because of the costs brought about by economic and social mismanagement. To put it differently, where I rejected Maoism on non-Maoist grounds, now the Maoist experiment can be shown to have failed even by its own criteria of success.

79

Brazil is a more complicated .case. Before the oil shock and the ensuing indebtedness crisis, there were some modest signs of a more equitable distribution of the benefits of growth. There has also been an impressive move from harsh military dictatorship toward democracy. It is noteworthy that Fernando Henrique Cardoso, the father of Latin American "dependency theory," is today a federal senator of the largest opposition party and speaks more in the moderate tones of Swedish social democracy than in the fiery neo-Marxist rhetoric of the early 1970s. All the same, by the criteria set forth above, Brazil cannot be cited as a case of successful development, and cannot (yet) be used as an argument for capitalism.

One other case in the Americas, that of Jamaica, is interesting because it (like Sri Lanka) abruptly veered from a socialist to a capitalist course, and did so as a result of democratic politics. Jamaica, however, is beset with manifold troubles; the capitalist experiment of the Seaga regime is still very new; and the place of the experiment remains uncertain.

A number of other cases (such as the Ivory Coast) are sometimes cited in favor of capitalism. But these aside, the most dramatic and convincing success stories today, and the one offering the strongest brief for capitalism, are in East Asia.

There is, first of all, the astounding instance of Japan. To be sure, Japan is no longer regarded as anything but a highly advanced industrial society—in some ways a more successful one than the societies of North America and Western Europe. This very achievement, however, is what makes Japan crucial for any responsible theory of development. Here is the only non-Western society that has moved from underdevelopment to full-blown modernity within the span of a century. Moreover, whatever variables may have been in play (political, cultural, geographical, and so on), Japan is a successful *capitalist* society. How did the Japanse pull this off? And can others learn from their success? Not surprisingly, third world politicians and intellectuals, even in countries that have reason to fear Japanese power, such as those of Southeast Asia, talk of the "Japanese model" as something to be admired and emulated.

But Japan no longer stands alone as a success story. There are the four countries of what may be called the Asian prosperity crescent—South Korea, Taiwan, Hong Kong, and Singapore. Despite important differences among them, each has employed an exuberantly capitalist strategy to move out of underdevelopment to the newly designated status of "new industrialized country" (or NIC). And this has happened with breathtaking speed and thoroughness, within the span of two decades. In no meaningful sense can these countries any longer be regarded as parts of the third world (though Hong Kong, depending on China's policy toward it, may fall back into underdevelopment in the near future). There are even grounds for thinking that their prosperity is pushing into other countries, especially in Southeast Asia (Malaysia, Thailand, and possibly Indonesia).

South Korea, Taiwan, Hong Kong, and Singapore are successful by all three of the criteria listed above. Their rates of economic growth continue to be remarkable. They have completely wiped out third-world-type misery within their borders. What is more, they (especially Taiwan and South Korea) have forcefully challenged the so-called Kuznets curve by combining high growth with a highly egalitarian income distribution. Their regimes, while not democratic, are authoritarian in a generally benign way (especially when compared with others in the region).

These four countries, only one of which, the Republic of Singapore, operates within the United Nations system, are increasingly attracting the attention of analysts of development and are more and more frequently cited as examples to be emulated. They constitute the most important evidence in favor of a capitalist path of development.

What, then, do we know today about development? We know, or should know, that socialism is a mirage that leads nowhere, except to economic stagnation, collective poverty, and various degrees of tryanny. We also know that capitalism has been dramatically successful, if in a limited number of underdeveloped countries. Needless to say, we also know that capitalism has failed in a much larger number of cases. What we do *not* know is why this is so.

It seems to me that the issue of socialism should be put aside for good in any serious discussion of development; it belongs, if anywhere, to the field of political pathology or *Ideologiekritik*. The question that should be of burning urgency (theoretical as well as practical) is why capitalism has succeeded in some places and failed in others. What are the variables of success and failure? That is the crucial question.

The success stories of East Asia have, very understandably, led some analysts to think that an important causal factor may be the culture of the region. A "post-Confucianist hypothesis" proposes that all the successful societies and ethnic groups (notably the overseas Chinese) share a common economic ethic derived from Confucianism, deemed to be a functional equivalent of Max Weber's famous "Protestant ethic." But Confucianism is by no means the only cultural element that may be relevant. Others may include the political traditions of East Asia, patterns of family and household, and different components of the area's religious heritage (such as Mahayana Buddhism).

One does not have to be a disciple of Weber to want these hypoth-

81

eses addressed. Indeed, if one is concerned with third world development in general, one would dearly love to see them falsified—not out of antagonism toward East Asia, but because the East Asian success stories can only become models for other parts of the world if they do not hinge on a non-exportable cultural factor. One might advise an African country to adopt the economic policies of South Korea; one can hardly advise the Africans to adopt Korean culture.

In *Pyramids of Sacrifice* I put forward a "postulate of ignorance": we are compelled to act politically even when we do not know many of the factors determining the situation in which we find ourselves. I formulated this postulate in the context of recommending a non-doctrinaire approach to development policy. I would reiterate it today. We are less ignorant than we were ten years ago, but there is still much that we do not know. Those charged with political responsibility in the matter of development, however, do not have the luxury of the social scientist who can always say that more research is needed. Science is, in principle, infinitely patient; politicians must act out of the urgencies of the moment. In such a situation the morally sensitive politician should be fully conscious of the fact that, whatever he chooses to do—and often the range of choices is narrow—he will be gambling. The evidence today strongly suggests that it is much safer to bet on capitalism.

# A Summary of
# Peter Berger's Oral Presentation

In measuring development, three criteria of success must be met: (1) sustained, self-generating economic growth; (2) notable improvement in the condition of the poor and the least privileged; and (3) no massive violations of human rights.

Behind liberation theology, in particular, and dependency theory, in general, there stand several empirical assumptions. These conceptions stand or fall by their empirical validity. My own studies in development persuade me, for reasons I do not here go into in detail, that several cases of successful development in East Asia constitute the major empirical falsification of these conceptions.

Rather than concentrating on liberation theology and Latin America, however, I want to concentrate on the cases of successful development in Japan and the "four little dragons": South Korea, Taiwan, Hong Kong, and Singapore. It seems crucially important to draw attention to stories of success.

What happened in these cases of successful development? Within one generation, these five non-Western societies fulfilled the three criteria mentioned above: self-generating economic growth; the lifting up from misery to a decent material standard of life of significant numbers of the poor; and no massive violations of human rights. These are not cases of perfection, but they are stories of very rapid and very successful development—certainly as compared with many other nations that began even better off than they, such as many in Latin America, and with a higher measure of natural resources.

The case of Japan is instructive. Consider the first period of development from 1868 to 1912 under the Meiji Dynasty. First came, virtually overnight, the abolition of feudalism, a civil rights revolution for Japanese males. The feudal gentry were forced to take cash or government bonds in compensation and were obliged to invest these in industry. Thus indigenous capital formation was induced, and a class of investors in the future was formed: a capitalist class. Basic rights of movement and property ownership were guaranteed. The national industries built by the Meiji were subjected to massive privatization (except for naval shipyards) and sold to the new capitalist class at below market prices. No welfare state was introduced, except for one crucially important innovation: enormous state investment in education. There followed a rapid development of a literate working class. (This was parallel to Abraham Lincoln's insistence on the land-grant colleges in 1862 and followed from Adam Smith's insight that the cause of the wealth of nations is intellect.)

Did the condition of the poor in Japan improve? On this, there are mixed reviews, and no consensus. Educationally for certain, materially maybe. As the Kuznets curve would lead us to expect, during periods of economic growth, inequality at first increases and then levels off or declines. During the first stage of Meiji development, the picture was mixed.

What do the "four little dragons" have in common? They are all capitalist societies, committed to growth and invention, and to multiplying the numbers of economic activists and decision makers at the bottom of society.

They are different in culture from the West, but rather like Japan both internally and in their links through trade and export to overseas markets. Like Japan, they have launched programs to spur domestic investment.

## On the Positive Side

In the 1950s, all four of these nations were marked by extreme poverty, even by third world standards. Today, third world misery no longer exists, and the poorest are much better off than they were thirty years ago, not only in life expectancy and infant mortality, but also in income, education, and other measures.

Interestingly, as well, development in these countries has created problems for the Kuznets theory. Taiwan, for example, had one of the most egalitarian distributions in the world during its period of highest growth.

These societies are committed to universal upward mobility and have concentrated their efforts on education. Otherwise, they have only very weak forms of the welfare state, with virtually no redistributive policies.

## On the Negative Side

One must note the following deficiencies. First is mild authoritarianism. Politically, none of the four is a democracy, although each experiences pressures toward democracy. Their regimes might accurately be described as "mildly authoritarian"—tyrannical if you will, but with no massive violations of human rights. A number of civil and political liberties are abridged.

Second is human costs. The educational system is a ruthless meritocracy, almost merciless in its sense of its own justice. Education is universal and wide-open, but every youngster is so thoroughly tested that by the age of twelve his or her fate for life is decided. Thus, society vigorously seeks out and promotes its most talented members. It is a frighteningly just society, in which it is held that failure is deserved and that life exerts a brutal justice.

By the three criteria established at the beginning, Japan and the "four little dragons" have achieved a level of development still sought by the vast majority of the other third world nations. In fact, it is hard to think of these five as "third world." If nations are looking for a path that can take them in one generation out of poverty and beyond massive and brutal violations of human rights, in these five East Asian nations they have a model.

But the sixty-four billion yen question is, Is the East Asian model exportable? It has achieved what most third world leaders say they want to achieve. Can they achieve it in the East Asian way?

Parenthetically, let me say that I have just returned from a trip to South Africa. It is clear that one day soon, perhaps sooner than many think, the blacks will inherit South Africa. The question is, When they do inherit it, will they inherit Uganda or Taiwan? This brings us back to our question, How exportable is the model of Taiwan?

I see two problems here. How many Taiwans can the world economy accommodate—that is, how many economies based so heavily on trade and export? But, of course, some nations are much wealthier in natural resources than Taiwan and in this respect would not have to follow the Taiwanese marketing strategy.

A question more serious and more interesting than the economic one concerns the cultural factor. Is the success of Japan and the "four little dragons" due to the culture of East Asia, to the particular commitment to family and to learning, to loyalty and to cooperation, to honesty and to hard work taught by Confucian and other moral elements in East Asia? As a way of organizing passion and energy, is East Asian Confucianism a better cultural base for economic development than Latin American Catholicism? Do Jamaicans act, think, and organize themselves like Chinese?

One way of thinking about this is to try to imagine the interchangeability of 18 million Taiwanese with 18 million Brazilians or 18 million Africans. Imagine them changing places. If they did so, would

85

one predict significant consequences for change, as each group inherited its new environment?

We know surprisingly little about the cultural causes of wealth and development. My hunch is that the cultural factor is enormously important and that it provides a significant comparative advantage to some, disadvantage to others. To test this as a hypothesis, we would need to gather together a much more thorough comparative picture of the relation of the world's cultures to development than we now possess. Acquiring that picture is a major task of the future of developmental research.

# Discussion

MR. NOVAK: Would another piece of evidence in this argument be that the two most significant measures in American history are the Homestead Act and the Loan Grant College Act, which achieved both these purposes in the Civil War period? I think the arguments that American development depended more on those measures than on anything else are very plausible.

DAVID BECKMAN, World Bank: I would like to respond to the question about how many Taiwans the world can tolerate. Economically we would all be much better off if we had a lot of Taiwans. It is a question of political decision, whether we want to proceed with the kinds of changes that would be necessary to accommodate many more prosperous countries.

This is a point of practical convergence between Hugo Assmann and Nick Eberstadt and Michael Novak and Arturo Fontaine and you. We all agree that it is important for poor people in developing countries to resist protectionism. It is important for the heavily indebted countries; it is important for the economies that you are talking about; it is important for poor people because it encourages labor-intensive manufacture, labor-intensive production so that a continual redistribution of income goes on. It is not a small matter that virtually all of us agree on that.

MR. BERGER: I agree with you. But it is very difficult to oppose protectionism without some imaginative domestic social policies.

A couple of months after I had been in South Korea, when people were talking about the Korean steel industry, I was invited to Bethlehem, Pennsylvania, to speak to a seminar of Bethlehem Steel people about Asia. I know nothing about the steel industry, but I talked about the kind of thing I am talking about tonight. Everyone agrees that the American steel industry has no future, except maybe in some very specialized things; and then you go to a place like Bethlehem, Pennsylvania. What do you do with large numbers of people in their fifties, some without even a high school education? They own their own homes, they are not mobile, they are not retrainable; and you say you are against protectionism.

I am against protectionism, but I think an antiprotectionist philosophy has to be coupled with some imagination about what to do in domestic social policy. I asked an economist, What does it cost the United States to have trade barriers for steel, as against what it would cost to have some imaginative modification of the social security system, allowing people in certain designated industries to retire earlier?

COMMENT: You are advocating a redistributionist policy.

MR. BERGER: No, that is not redistribution.

COMMENT: It certainly is, if you take the money from somebody and give it to somebody else.

MR. BERGER: But it is not an incomes policy. It would be no different logic from the social security system today.

COMMENT: Which is a redistributionist policy. The social security system is highly redistributionist.

MR. BERGER: I don't want to get into the semantics of what redistribution is at the moment. Let me just finish my point, that all we would have to do is to have a differential notion of when people are allowed to benefit from the social security system. It would be very important to think of those issues in conjunction with antiprotectionism.

EDWARD LYNCH, National Forum Foundation: I agree that the most important question you could address is the exportability of the East Asian model even though it may or may not be the major empirical falsification of dependency. Proving one theory false without replacing it with something else seems to me less than useful.

I would like you to comment a little more on something you mentioned in the Japanese experience: indigenous capital formation. I ask that, first, because it is very important to development and, second, because it is part of the dependency theory that such indigenous capital formation is rendered difficult by the actions of other states. Would you comment specifically on the exportability of that part of the Japanese Meiji experience?

MR. BERGER: All I can say is that I think it has been successfully repeated in the four little dragons. Those societies have rather powerful indigenous capital formation. I am not enough of an economist to tell you just what the mechanics have been. We see the results: certainly very successful multinationals have come out of indigenous capitalism in Korea and Taiwan.

MR. LYNCH: Do you think it is applicable to non–East Asian societies, such as Latin America and Africa?

MR. BERGER: The honest answer is, I don't know. I am thinking of a recent conversation in Capetown, where every single person was talking of some sort of future socialist society in South Africa. I don't think it will work.

We do not really know how to bring about successful development. Nobody fully understands the dynamics. I am very impressed by the fact that the only successful cases are capitalist cases. In talking to Africans or Indians or Latin Americans, I find that in forming national policy, those who are honest know they are betting. Nobody knows— not the right, not the left. Nobody knows. I would bet on some form of the East Asian model, but I would be a totally immoral liar if I said that I knew what the outcome would be in any country.

MR. NOVAK: I want to act as a friendly critic here and say that you have left out the capacity for invention—whether it is the invention of new processes or new methods or new products. I think that is crucial. It was brought home to me by a man in Korea. You said nobody knows the answer. Well, this fellow did.

"The secret to development is very simple. To develop a country, you must play baseball and use chopsticks or calligraphy." He explained: "Baseball taught us Confucians, who are collectivist, to respect individuals because they come to the plate one at a time and the ball singles them out one at a time and yet they work in association; baseball also taught us the relation between law and liberty: nothing happens in baseball without an umpire, but it is a game of great spontaneity and liberty and checks and balances." I won't go into the whole argument, but it is a beautiful argument.

Then he said, "The problem with the Chinese is that they use chopsticks but they don't play baseball, and the problem with the Cubans is that they play baseball but they don't use chopsticks. The chopsticks thing is very important because chopsticks and calligraphy relate the brain to the hand and in manufacturing cultures, which work with the hand and invention, this is crucial. The emphasis on education and the emphasis on high achievement are very much a part of the culture, and they are there in the calligraphy and the chopsticks."

89

I just want to tell you that somebody has the answer even if you don't.

MR. BERGER: Let me expound. This gentleman looks frustrated by my answer, and rightly so. Let me go one step further.

What do we know, and what don't we know? By "we" I don't mean some mythical we. I mean, what is social science in a fairly good position to tell us?

I think we know now (we should know—I realize that many people claim the contrary) that socialism is not a development model. We also know why. Socialism is no longer a utopia. There are real existing socialist societies in the world. I think we can understand the mechanisms by which failure is produced under a socialist project. That is, to me, not terribly interesting anymore because I think I understand it.

We also know that there are fabulously successful capitalist cases and many cases of capitalist models of development that have not been successful. The intellectual edge lies in beginning to understand not why socialism does not work but why capitalism works under certain circumstances and not under others and what the variables are— economic, social, political, and cultural. That, to me, is the agenda.

JOAN ANDERSON, School of Business Administration, University of San Diego: Let me start with a couple of technical points. The Kuznets curve is a cross-section curve, examining where countries are at a certain time in level of development. You really cannot take that sort of analysis and talk about it in terms of a time series—that is, looking at one country's rate of change of growth and calling that anti-Kuznets. What you were saying was not anti-Kuznets, technically, because it confuses cross-sectional with time series data.

To go to a more important point—Why did South Korea succeed? That is one of the key questions.

South Korea started by doing some redistribution in the initial stages—a really important precondition for any kind of capitalist market system. It also started with a strategy for export promotion of developing a vertically integrated textile industry. It was integrated completely from the agricultural level all the way up. It was a highly labor-intensive industry, so that at the same time it was developing human capital in a needs-based development model. That is one of the real keys to South Korea's successful development.

Taiwan has a similar history. Instead of copying U.S. models as many Latin American countries have tried to do, it developed its own land-intensive agriculture. The yields per acre are about twice the U.S. yields; the Taiwanese work their land much more intensively because it is scarce. Now they are developing new models to fit their factor allocations, which were extremely important in the beginning of their development.

One more side issue: a whole body of literature in economics addresses the costs of the various trade barriers, which have been measured econometrically.

MR. BERGER: Has anyone figured out what it would cost to have people retire at fifty-five under social security? That would be the calculus that would interest me—in specific industries.

MS. ANDERSON: I don't know. I thought you were talking about the cost of trade barriers. There is a body of literature on that.

MR. BERGER: About your point on the Kuznets curve: I am the first person in the world to be intimidated by economists. But most other developing countries going through a rapid growth cycle had increasing inequality. Why did Taiwan have decreasing inequality?

On redistribution: If you want to call land reform and an educational push redistributionist, fine, but I don't think that is what most people have in mind by redistribution. In other words, Taiwan did not have the kind of populist income policies found in countries such as India or Sri Lanka before the present government, which were deliberate interventions in the wage system. I agree that land reform and education seem to be very important ingredients of the model.

MS. ANDERSON: And ones that are directly applicable to Latin America.

MR. BERGER: I would think so.

MS. ANDERSON: I would, too.

NICK EBERSTADT, Harvard University: First, a couple of points of information about the Koreas. Both North and South Korea are extraordinarily difficult to find research on. Even for South Korea it is difficult to find accurate and comprehensive evaluations of the social and economic changes that have taken place.

On Father McGovern's point, the CIA did, indeed, assess agriculture during the 1970s in North Korea as having been extraordinarily rapid. That was based on a false reading of North Korean information.

North Korea's industry, by its own calculations, has had one of the more rapid rates of growth in the socialist world. That is, of course, because it started from a lower base than some of the more advanced societies. The growth was also, even by its own highly optimistic calculations, somewhat less rapid than South Korea's.

Professor Berger, there is much that I agree with you on, but there are two questions in particular I wonder if you could address. The first is the question of the first non-Western nation to industrialize. How would you assess the Russian Empire under Nicholas II? Of course, the Russian Empire was mainly populated by Caucasian people. But these people had principally been beyond the experience of the Renaissance and the Reformation. I wonder whether you take the Reformation and the Renaissance as integral to the experience of being a Western nation

The second question has to do with the nature of capitalism in the four little dragons or, putting Hong Kong aside, in the other three dragons. Singapore, of course, has always insisted that it is not a capitalist nation but a Socialist nation. The People's Action party was a member of the Socialist International until it was forced to withdraw from it. In South Korea until the death of President Park virtually all the finance capital was controlled by the government, and the economy was managed through five-year plans. In Taiwan a governing party, the KMT, was set up by Borodin, Stalin's agent, and organized very explicitly along Marxist-Leninist lines. Where does capitalism end and something else begin?

MR. BERGER: You may know the book by Gilbert Rozman comparing Russian and Japanese development. It is an interesting question. Where do you draw the lines? What about Germany after the unification of 1870? Is Germany a Western country?

Russia, whatever its specific characteristics, was shaped by Christian civilization. I would regard Russia as a part of the West, without trying to say that what happened in Russia was the same as what happened in England earlier. What happened in Germany in the second half of the nineteenth century was also quite different from what happened in England in the preceding century. We are still talking about a Western world, and the Japanese case is so glaringly outside, that I would stick to my point that it is the first successful non-Western case.

On the other question—certainly East Asian capitalism is characterized by very high degrees of state intervention, as many people have pointed out. Chalmers Johnson, for example, uses specific categories to describe this statist orientation to capitalism. Whether state intervention is any greater in Japan than, for instance, in France I am not absolutely certain. The French bureaucrats—not just under the Mitterrand government but always—have intervened in this way. I think we can say that capitalism in East Asia is more state guided than it has been in the Anglo-Saxon countries.

92

The defining characteristics of capitalism are two: one is the predominance of market forces in making production decisions; the second is private ownership of the means of production. Certainly all these cases fit under that definition and are emphatically capitalist societies. The relation between state and economy is different, on the whole, from those in the Anglo-Saxon countries, but so are there differences within the Western world.

MR. NOVAK: Those two criteria—market forces and private property—will not quite work, because they would include the most traditional societies, which we might want to say are precapitalist in other ways. You have to add what Mr. Levine said earlier—a sustained and systemic commitment to economic progress, or economic growth, and a capacity for invention, an emphasis on the head, the source of creativity.

Those are the two points that Nick Eberstadt made when he talked about the spirit of capitalism as something new, as distinct from the ancient traditions of property and markets. They apply to East Asian models very well, because those societies understood from the beginning that after World War II machines equalized the work forces of the world and therefore those nations that used machines with the maximum intelligence would succeed in markets.

MR. BERGER: With enormous reluctance I disagree with you. You are introducing cultural variables into the definition of capitalism. If you do that, you forgo the possibility of assessing those variables empirically.

In other words, I would stick to an economic definition, and what I do not agree with is your point on markets. Yes, there have always been markets—in the Stone Age there were markets—but what characterizes capitalism is that industrial production and the entire society are geared to markets. Brodell has a very nice picture of the market economy: at first it was like islands, then the islands became joined, then they became a continent, and then the entire economy became a market economy. So it is not the existence of markets but that under modern conditions an entire economy is primarily oriented toward the market.

I would prefer to define capitalism that way rather than introduce cultural variables into the definition. If we have a lean definition, we can ask, How does this kind of economic mechanism relate to the kind of thing you were talking about—inventiveness, innovative spirit?

QUESTION: I would like to ask Professor Berger about something that I hear said—that in all four of these countries development is linked with authoritarianism. Does that mean that political democratization in such a society will be a dangerous threat to economic development? Or just the opposite? Does it mean that democratization of the political sphere will lead to more successful capitalistic development because all capitalist countries in history except in eastern Asia have been linked with political democracy? If democratization of the political sphere can be dangerous to economic development, that is very important not only for eastern Asia but also for Latin America. Do we have any example of a country with democratization not only in the economic field but also in the political field?

MR. BERGER: My very tentative answer is that, much to my regret, I cannot honestly argue that democracy is a precondition for development. It does not seem to work that way.

You can make the argument that as development is successful under capitalist conditions, it contributes to the buildup of democracy. Thus I would not accept the notion that the democratization of Taiwan will be hostile to development—on the contrary. But it is evidently possible to have an enormous development spurt under authoritarian conditions.

I think that is the case, whether one likes it or not, under capitalist development. It does not seem to work under socialism, but under capitalism it does. Once that is successful, for reasons that are not at all difficult to understand, people want more than the material benefits of development; they want political rights—at least in the modern world. It is extremely unlikely that as these democratic processes succeed, development will be hurt.

MIHAJLO MIHAJLOV, Radio Free Europe/Radio Liberty: When you talk about capitalism, at the same time you say that it is economically free. So in part of society there is freedom, political democracy, economic democracy.

MR. BERGER: I know it is a favorite argument of the right that capitalism is democracy, but I think that is confusing terms. Democracy has a very specific meaning, and it applies to the governmental sphere; to be sure, capitalism involves free choices of individuals in the economic sphere, but I would hesitate to speak of democracy here. There is a very important empirical link between capitalism and democracy, but they are two different things.

MR. NOVAK: What is the link?

MR. BERGER: The link is that as successful capitalist development proceeds, a democratization dynamic is released. To put it more sharply—and I would put it as a hypothesis—capitalism is a precondition for democracy; even more logically, capitalism is a necessary but not a sufficient condition of democratic government.

QUESTION: But did not the U.S. Constitution marry democracy and capitalism?

MR. BERGER: That would not falsify the hypothesis. What would falsify the hypothesis would be the first successful case—the first case—of socialist democracy.

JAMES WEAVER, Department of Economics, American University: Three questions. What role would you ascribe to foreign aid in Korea and Taiwan, both of which were recipients of enormous quantities of such aid? Second, do you have any hypotheses about why almost no country in Latin America would meet your three criteria of success? why none of those countries that attempted capitalist development would measure up? Third, in light of your statement that socialism is not a successful development model, would you comment on the case of Yugoslavia?

MR. BERGER: The first question was foreign aid. The facts are very clear. Taiwan and South Korea received enormous amounts of foreign aid in the early years. That aid virtually came to an end by the mid-1960s, so that during the period of the real economic miracle it was a negligible factor. How important it was to development I am not in a position to say. In Hong Kong and Singapore, as far as I know, foreign aid was not a factor at all, at any point.

Your third question was on Yugoslavia. What was the second?

MR. WEAVER: Do you have any hypotheses about why virtually none of the Latin American capitalist countries, with the possible exception of Costa Rica, would meet your criteria of success?

MR. BERGER: That is part of the 64 billion yen question. If I knew that, I would be rich and powerful. I can spout hypotheses, none of them original; all of them you know. Some have to do with the position of Latin America in the world economy. Some have to do with Latin American statism, which I suspect is very important—the particular character of the state and the political culture of Latin America. Some, of course, have to do with culture, with religion, with moral values.

Yugoslavia is a place that I know a little bit about. If I were a socialist, Yugoslavia would be the most important place to look at. It is a very mixed picture. It has experienced some economic growth, but on

95

the whole it has had a very precarious economic history. I have recently read that if it were not for Yugoslavia's relationship to the EEC and especially if it did not have the safety valve of massive export of labor to the EEC countries, the mess would be even greater than it is. The self-management, worker-management model, which has many attractive features, does not seem to work well at all, even according to Yugoslav analysts.

Economically, then, it is not very successful, and much of the reason why it is not has to do with its socialist system. As for the other two criteria, if something is not economically successful, it is not very good for the poor. One of the main features of Yugoslavia is the terrible discrepancy between north and south; southern Yugoslavia has something pretty close to third world conditions, especially among the poorer people in Montenegro and places like it.

On the third condition, I would grant that Yugoslavia is a mild authoritarian regime. I would not be terribly hard on human rights violations in Yugoslavia, although of course it is not a democracy.

MR. NOVAK: Our colleagues at Radio Free Europe, Radio Liberty, tell me that Yugoslavia and Hungary have produced more free market economists per capita than any other country on earth.

MR. BERGER: Yes, but very frustrated ones.

JAMES THORNBLADE, Bank of Boston: I want to go back to the second question that Mr. Weaver asked. One possible hypothesis about the 64 billion yen question is that a factor in the economic development may be some kind of shock effect, such as land reform or educational change—a severe disruption that challenges the established order.

The Korean War was a traumatic experience for the Korean culture, and Taiwan experienced a dramatic change in the arrival from the mainland of the remnants of the Nationalist regime. South America has not had that kind of disruptive experience. It has never been invaded, it has never suffered an extensive disruption of its culture or the arrival of a group of people such as the Chinese Nationalists.

PETER SKERRY, Brookings Institution: It has been said by a number of people—and it is a Toynbeean sort of hypothesis—that all five of these societies have been in extremity, in civil war, in international war, with many refugees. For Singapore, with its extremely precarious position on that little island surrounded by basically hostile cultures, and for Malaysia and Indonesia, that is possible. Perhaps extremity is an important stimulant.

PAUL SIGMUND, Woodrow Wilson Center: I feel that my role here is to recall the theme of the conference periodically, and the theme is liberation theology and liberalism. My sense of your attitude toward liberation theology is that it is not very interesting because it has been refuted, dependency has been debunked, and socialism does not work. Marxism you did not get into, but I assume you would hold a similar attitude toward it.

Earlier we were exploring some other aspects of liberation theology, looking at it a little more broadly, particularly this morning with Hugo Assmann's emphasis on grass-roots democracy as a very important thrust of liberation theology, and more broadly the question of dependency, which many liberation theologians today will admit was overemphasized at the beginning. There remains a kind of structural critique that Bill Glade got into last night. Do you feel there are important structural changes that must be made if we want successful development? You have already emphasized agrarian reform and education. But am I right that you would say that participation is something that should come later and that development must come first? That too much participation at the beginning, especially in the forms of trade unions and political democracy, can impede the early stages of development? That participation will come as a consequence of development, rather than being for moral reasons, as it is for liberation theologians, one of the primary objectives of your state?

MR. BERGER: No. I did not make myself clear. I would not take the position that authoritarianism must come first and democracy has to come later. My position is more careful: that we cannot argue that democracy is a precondition for development. I am not arguing that democracy is an impediment to development, because I don't think that can be shown.

MR. SIGMUND: A lot of Latin Americans do argue that way.

MR. BERGER: Then I disagree with those Latin Americans. It is a nuance, but I think it is an important nuance.

MR. SIGMUND: What do you think about the argument that what is needed for development is investment? With democracy comes a strong push for consumption. The populist policies you criticize are part of democracy, and part of participation is the presence of organized trade unions. Trade unions will press for better wages, and that will make it much more difficult to build up investment and infrastructure and capital and all the things needed for development. You have not really

97

faced that issue, which is absolutely central in Latin America and has been for about twenty years.

MR. BERGER: I am very empirical about this. I am not sure there is one answer for all countries. It depends on the kind of trade unions. It depends on what the ethos of consumerism is. In Japan it has not worked as you have just described. This may be because of Japanese culture, but it has not had the effect that people fear who argue this way.

As to what you said about participation, it is quite possible that what is really happening is very different from what the intellectuals think is happening. The intellectuals may think that what is being mobilized is some sort of revolutionary political force, and what may really be happening is much more mundane: that people begin to think of where their advantage lies, not so much politically as economically, which may have paradoxical results given the rather grandiose expectations of what these communities may do. Fernando Cardoso has said some things like this very recently. I am very open to that.

I do not claim great expertise in liberation theology, but I read a lot. Some of this literature is a socialist vision of the future, and I cannot help thinking that it is a case of people desperately trying to get on a bus that has already landed in a ditch. What I would say to such people is, Why do you want to do this? There are much more important questions to be settled, such as the ones you have just mentioned.

MR. SIGMUND: My response would be that it is not just socialism. There are other and very important aspects of participation and of structural critique, not necessarily with a socialist solution.

MR. BERGER: If to be a liberationist means that there must be structural changes for development to occur, we are all liberationists. Isn't that stretching the term a bit? I don't know.

MR. SIGMUND: The first point is the priority of participation.

MR. BERGER: What is the meaning of participation?

MR. SIGMUND: Going to the poor, finding out what their problems are, the base community as a central focus of the effort of theologians and democracy through direct, face-to-face dialogue and solving of problems. That has been there from the beginning. To say that this is just a kind of warmed-over seminary Marxism is to dismiss what is only one aspect of an important thrust in Latin American thinking and to ignore this other aspect.

MR. BERGER: Is it such a terribly difficult problem to find out what the poor want? In most places I have been the poor want to be less poor and are very anxious to find ways to accomplish this task. I speak very hesitantly because I do not know the Latin American situation in recent years. In the early 1970s, when I did, I found that most of the intellectuals who wanted to find out what the poor wanted were extremely disappointed when they found out because the poor wanted something very different from what the intellectuals had in mind. If this has changed in the meantime, glory be. I don't know what else to say.

MR. SIGMUND: The critique by many of the liberation theologians of what appeared to be a democratic system was that for various reasons it did not reach out to the people who were in need and relate to them in a significant way. We have examples in this country of that kind of critique, and we have a response to it.

In other words, is that not an important element of liberation theology—the concern that the political system be responsive to the poor and to ethnic minorities and to women, in ways that it has clearly not been in Latin America? There has been formal democracy and some expansion of participation, but there have been enormous blocks. How can people know their problems when they cannot express them at all, when they cannot read and do not have jobs? That kind of critique is important and should not simply be dismissed as one more example of a discredited social theory.

MR. BERGER: I am not here to polemicize against liberation theology. When I said it does not interest me, I meant not so much to dismiss it as to say that what I have seen of it does not address questions that I regard as crucial.

I am perfectly happy to regard the preferential option for the poor as a valid criterion. It was Samuel Johnson—hardly a liberation theologian—who wrote that a fair provision for the poor is a moral test of any human society. If someone looks at Latin American societies and says that the condition of the poor is a scandal, morally, I would fully agree. The important question is, What can one do to change that situation?

MR. SIGMUND: A liberation theologist's answer is grass-roots democracy, and your answer is, look to Asia.

MR. BERGER: The liberation theologians that I used to talk to said the answer was socialism. If they now say grass-roots democracy, that is a slight improvement but not a very good answer. As much as I am in favor of democracy, we cannot argue, on the basis of what we know empirically, that democracy is a precondition of development. It just ain't so.

I am passionately in favor of democracy, and I am not saying that it has to wait until later. But if the primary moral criterion is to improve the condition of the poor, grass-roots democracy is not a very good recipe.

MR. SIGMUND: For certain kinds of improvement.

MR. BERGER: I am talking about material improvement. I am talking about poverty.

HENRY NORMAN, Volunteers in Technical Assistance: I would like to address the question whether the East Asian model is adaptable and suggest that it has very limited application. I head an organization that seeks to create wealth through the transfer of technology at the micro-level.

The countries you have mentioned have approached development from the top down. They had special circumstances—the enormous presence of Americans in Korea, the foreign aid, the Vietnam War, which spread large sums of money in that area.

The minister of technology of Korea once said that the Korean miracle was based on the very simple practice of importing nonproprietary technology, improving it, and using the advantage of cheap labor. Cheap labor is rather a tenuous basis for development. The textile industry, for example, went from New England to the South, to Korea, to Taiwan, and will ultimately end up in the People's Republic of China and India. You cannot get labor much cheaper than there.

I do not think the East Asian model is applicable to places like Africa (I am not familiar with Latin America). The advantages that existed in Asia—the high rate of literacy, the tremendous input of capital from outside—simply do not exist. I see no alternative to working up from the bottom to build up skills and all the elements required for development.

MR. BERGER: I don't know what you mean by working up from the bottom. In Japan's first economic miracle, none of the conditions you mention were present. The land reform I mentioned is certainly from the bottom. The distribution of educational skills among the lower strata of the population is from the bottom. Of course there were economic policies from the top, but I don't see how it could be otherwise in a modern state.

MR. NORMAN: A hundred years ago the advantages I have cited would not be as important. But the very success of these countries is defeating the advantages of cheap labor, because labor gets more and more money; that is the whole purpose of development. In recent months I have talked to people from each of the countries that you cite, and I find a great deal of anxiety about the future. In Singapore you can no longer start a business that is labor intensive. They want high-technology businesses. In each of these countries except Japan, the research and development capacity will simply not sustain competition in high technology.

COMMENT: The advantage they enjoy is being weakened.

MR. BERGER: But isn't that true of every economy? A number of Western economies have lost some of the advantages they once enjoyed. There is no recipe that I know of—although I will bow to economists who claim to have one—that means an everlasting prosperity for any society.

In other words, we are talking about strategies that improve the conditions of people and seem to last for a while. If we are talking about anxiety, American businessmen have a lot of anxieties about the future. I don't know what that proves. Development is not the achievement of an eternal state of contentment, even economically.

MR. NORMAN: No, we are talking about whether we can use the East Asians as a model for development, and I am suggesting that it is probably not a valid model, at least for places like Africa.

MR. NOVAK: Before you desist, could you say a little bit about the practical methods you teach, because I understand your programs have not failed wherever they have been used. I would be interested in what you do in a practical way.

MR. NORMAN: Some time ago we made a survey in forty-five countries of development organizations, private industries, and government people to determine what elements they found essential to development. In the best of all worlds, what could be made available to them that they felt would enable them to bring about development?

We were amazed by the unanimity of the responses. Three elements were named. One was technical information—meaning technology. The second was technical assistance, available very rapidly so that people would be able to learn how to do something and see models

101

of it and so on. The third was capital—not huge sums of capital, but small sums.

We have designed our programs around those responses. We try not to put in large teams of people, not to put in very expensive expatriates, but to try to make available the best possible technical information, not appropriate technology but serious technology, at a level where the skills of the community can handle it. Where possible we take volunteers from as close by as possible to work with them so that they can have hands-on experience. We try to specialize in commercially viable technology and to make small sums of money available as capital for them to develop. Sometimes the start is only a one-man operation, and sometimes it develops into larger operations. It makes a genuine impact in the community.

MR. NOVAK: It is like water in the desert. Could you give one or two examples of a concrete project that you got started?

MR. NORMAN: We respond to 2,000 to 3,000 inquiries a year for technical information. In Cameroon a woman who was the head of a cooperative for tie-dyeing cloth asked for information about that. We sent the information to her from a volunteer who was an expert on the subject. She wrote back and asked for help with a silk-screen process to make high-quality cloth for sale to tourists and others in the capital. We sent that information, and then she asked for technical assistance. We located a volunteer who would go over for nothing but expenses. We asked people in the community in Cameroon whether they would pay local costs, whether they would put the person up, whether they would pay for the per diem and so on, and they agreed. Then we went to a foundation in California, and they sent us a check for $2,500 to pay the transportation over and back. The volunteer is now over there providing technical assistance to the cooperative; the members of the cooperative will all increase their income from this technology.

It is relatively simple technology, it does not require a lot of capital, and it will keep a lot of people busy; it will increase rural income. This is what we are all about, and that is what we think development is all about.

MR. NOVAK: Thank you very much.

ANTHONY DOWNS, Brookings Institution: I realize that East Germany does not meet your third criterion concerning human rights. But you appear to say there are no socialist countries with reasonably successful economic development even if the criterion of human rights is ignored. Would you say that East Germany had been successful at development?

MR. BERGER: It has certainly been more successful than other East European socialist countries, no question about that.

MR. DOWNS: How does it rank among the lesser developed countries of the world?

MR. BERGER: That is not a very fair question. How can you compare East Germany with a third world country? The logical comparison is with West Germany.

MR. DOWNS: Not necessarily. It does not work as well as West Germany, I agree. But my impression is that you are saying that socialism never creates significant development, and I question whether that is not untrue of East Germany.

MR. BERGER: I said that by my definition of success, there is not a single successful case. I was very careful to define what I meant by success.

We cannot argue that a socialist society cannot have high growth rates. It can, and East Germany is a case in point.

MR. DOWNS: It would therefore meet your first two criteria but not your third?

MR. BERGER: It would meet my first criterion.

MR. DOWNS: The second?

MR. BERGER: The second I am less sure about. Again, what are we comparing?

The East German welfare state is a wretched thing if we compare it with Western Europe, and we have to compare what is comparable. It makes sense to compare North and South Korea; it makes sense to compare Kenya and Tanzania; and it makes sense to compare Hungary and Austria. It does not make sense to compare East Germany with a third world country.

MR. DOWNS: It might make sense to compare East Germany today with East Germany at some period in the past.

103

MR. BERGER: If we compare its industrial potential and what it has done with it with what West Germany has done with its industrial potential, it is not a very encouraging comparison.

MR. DOWNS: I agree with that. But have the East Germans engaged in a process that, if it happened in Africa, you would consider successful development by your first two criteria?

MR. BERGER: Of course, but I don't know what you want to do with this. Many Africans would love to have the standard of living of the East Germans, but what follows from that?

MR. DOWNS: It follows that it is not always true that socialism cannot work in the sense of raising the standard of living of the people in the country. Maybe it cannot work and also secure human rights. That is a very important distinction that I am not trying to argue with. But at least socialism has raised the standard of living considerably, although not as much as it would have been raised in the absence of socialism.

MR. BERGER: From a very high base. It was already a very highly industrialized country when the socialists took over.

MR. DOWNS: Nevertheless, it raised the standard of living?

MR. BERGER: I don't have those data at my fingertips, but the way that I would describe it is this. If a socialist system is imposed on a modern industrial society, it is not going to become an undeveloped society overnight; of course not. Not even socialism can accomplish that miracle. Being industrially productive is not the be-all and end-all of human existence. Otherwise I would be very happy about East Asia, which I am not. Of course East Germany and Czechoslovakia, in the socialist world, are relatively successful economically. But think of what they would be capable of if they did not have this crippling system.

LESLIE LENKOWSKY, Institute for Educational Affairs: I want to try to clarify the point about democracy and participation. You would not dispute, would you, that at some point in the East Asian countries political decisions are made that set those nations on a course for either more successful or less successful development?

The question about democracy and participation would resolve itself into a testable one. On balance, are political decisions that favor successful development more likely in a more or a less participatory regime?

104

MR. BERGER: Two points before I try to answer you. One, the purpose of democracy is not to foster development. I believe in democracy for its own sake; the argument that I am making is not antidemocratic. The other point is that I don't think anybody knows the answer to that question. It would be wrong to suggest that we know the answer.

Let me give you a hypothesis. I don't know whether a left-winger or a right-winger would be more upset by this hypothesis. It is that the degree of democratic participation is probably irrelevant to the question you raise.

What is more relevant is the nature of the elite that makes the decisions. There is a very good book by an American political scientist, John Higley, on elite theory. What I find interesting is the nature of the elite in those countries, whether they have a democratic regime or not. My hypothesis is that it is very important to have a clearly defined elite that overlaps economic and political spheres and is capable of engaging in a continuing communication process that makes such decisions possible. Whether that elite has to sell itself to the electorate as it does in Japan or can do things in a more authoritarian manner as it does in the four little dragons may be an important question for other reasons, but I doubt if it is the crucial variable.

# Latin America and "Dependency" Theory

### Arthur F. McGovern, S.J.

In 1984 Michael Novak wrote an essay for the *New York Times Magazine* entitled "The Case against Liberation Theology." His criticisms were focused on liberation theology's reliance on Marxist analysis and dependency theory, criticisms he noted also in his books *The Spirit of Democratic Capitalism* and *Freedom with Justice*.[1] His critique of dependency theory, which he judged "largely false," prompted my research for this paper and the questions that I brought to my study. So by way of introduction I summarize briefly, and I hope accurately, his arguments.

Novak sees dependency theory as placing the primary blame for Latin American underdevelopment on external causes, on the activities and decisions of foreign capitalist countries and corporations, with the United States as the chief offender now. He believes this charge is wrong on many counts. The United States certainly does not need Latin America for its own development; only 1 percent of the U.S. gross national product is related to Latin America. If being a major supplier of raw materials makes one dependent and underdeveloped, then the United States would certainly qualify. Multinational corporations, far from being exploitative, provide the capital, technology, skills, and jobs needed and requested by Latin American countries. The United States and foreign powers are not to blame. "Latin America is responsible for its own condition."[2] Its problems are internal. It had rich resources available but did not develop them. It could have developed technology but did not. In the mid-nineteenth century, the per capita incomes in Latin American countries were not that different from those in the United States.

The real problem, says Novak, is that Latin America lacked the system, ethos, virtues, and institutions needed to create the kind of wealth that could eradicate or minimize poverty. He blames, in part, the Catholic Latin culture for failing to inculcate the work ethic and creativity esteemed by the North, though he also recognizes, as an internal obstacle, extreme concentration of economic and political power in the hands of a few. He thus sees Latin America not as true democratic capitalism but as existing in a precapitalist stage of development. He counsels liberation theologians and other Latin Americans to "look North," not blaming the United States in anger, but learning from the United States and Western Europe about the system, ethos, virtues, and institutions that have made them successful. They should look also to the successes of newly industrialized countries of the Far East, such as Taiwan and South Korea. These, not Marxist models that promise much but lead to greater evils, should be their guide.

Some of Novak's points appear to me quite valid. Indeed, my most serious reservations about liberation theology have been regarding its overreliance on Marxist analysis and dependency theory. My major criticism of Novak is that he moves to the opposite extreme, seeing little or no truth in Marxist analysis or in dependency theory. This position leads him to pose options for Latin America in overly simple terms (democratic capitalism versus Marxist-Leninist socialism). I see the situation in Latin America as far more complex. I do not have the professional expertise in economics or in Latin American studies to make definitive judgments about dependency theory. But I have tried to draw from dependency theory what appear to me the most insightful and cogent arguments worthy of further study. The results of my study are presented here in three parts: a look at how dependency theory developed; an examination of what I see as major themes or insights in dependency theory; and some brief reflections about the labels (Marxism, capitalism) that cause discussion about Latin America to become polarized.

### Background: The Development of Dependency Theory

After World War II social scientists and political leaders directed special attention to problems of development in the southern half of the world, to countries designated by various labels: backward, underdeveloped, less developed, developing, or third world. The debate that developed in Latin America produced several contending, though sometimes overlapping, theories about development. To understand how dependency theory entered into this debate, one must consider each of the characters that played significant roles.[3]

**The Modernization Paradigm.** Conventional wisdom, labeled modernization by many dependency theorists, viewed the problem in terms quite similar to those articulated by Michael Novak. Latin America faced the same problems once encountered in Europe, such as scarcity

107

of capital, undeveloped technology, and traditional mores. To achieve development, underdeveloped nations must break out of traditional mores, adopt a profit incentive, and discover newer ways to become productive. All countries must pass through certain stages, though time spans may vary considerably. W.W. Rostow, in *The Stages of Economic Growth,* spelled out the steps.[4] Advanced industrial countries had all passed through a necessary "take-off" stage; underdeveloped nations would have to do the same. Development meant primarily economic growth, and to achieve growth constraints and obstacles (for example, traditional cultural modes) had to be overcome. Advanced countries could play an important role in supplying some of the missing components needed to "prime the pump" of development.[5] Most of the arguments in defense of multinationals are based on the modernization model of development. Multinationals bring the technology and managerial know-how needed to break through old patterns of production. They bring needed capital for investment; they create new jobs and train both workers and local managers with requisite skills. They help countries to specialize in what they can do best (comparative advantage); and, through multinationals, developing countries can penetrate new markets in advanced countries. Some theorists include in this modernization model the thesis that economic growth creates conditions for democracy; economic growth and democratic political stability are seen as mutually reinforcing.

If any one point unites all the dependency theorists, it is a rejection of this linear model of progressive modernization to explain all development. Some feel that the very use of this model implies a dependent relationship: the capitalist world of the North stands for modernity, development, rationality, and superiority; the world of the South, which manifests backwardness and inferiority, needs the help and example of the North to change. But, more important, dependency theorists argue that Latin America's present situation is quite different from that once faced by countries like England, Germany, and the United States. These now-advanced nations may once have been *un*developed, but they were never *under*developed: they did not have to contend with the power of nations ahead of them.[6] Latin America's condition, these theorists conclude, should be described not as feudal or precapitalist but as "peripherally" capitalistic, forced to confront and adapt to dominant "centers" of capitalism in the North.

**Raúl Prebisch and ECLA.** Before World War II, social sciences were themselves quite underdeveloped in Latin America.[7] But they developed quickly after the war and were used effectively by the United Nations Economic Commission on Latin America (ECLA). Dependency theory would come later, but Raúl Prebisch, as director of ECLA, laid the groundwork by challenging an important modernization thesis. ECLA studies done after the war seemed clearly to show that the conventional wisdom about international trade was contradicted by the effects on Latin America. Conventional theorists saw trade as mutually benefiting both trading partners and believed contact with advanced productive centers would spur productivity in underdeveloped countries. In contrast, ECLA studies (later disputed) showed a long-term deterioration in terms of trade; and Prebisch sought to explain why. Latin America's thrust had been outward for many decades, relying on export of primary goods (for example, bananas, coffee, minerals) to provide income to finance the buying of imported industrial goods. But Latin American countries were running a deficit balance of payments, caused by the rising costs of imported manufactured goods and the decreasing, unstable prices of exported primary goods. (To use a later example: in 1960 three tons of bananas could buy a tractor; in 1970 the same tractor cost the equivalent of ten tons.)[8] One reason for this discrepancy, ECLA argued, was that the advanced, center countries had nearly full employment and a highly organized labor force; the peripheral nations of Latin America had masses of unemployed and underemployed workers. As a consequence, productivity gains stayed in the center in the form of higher wages; productivity gains in the periphery led only to cheaper commodities and a net loss. The oligopolistic nature of center corporations also gave them greater power.[9]

Prebisch and ECLA sought to counter this situation by an inward, industrializing thrust. They urged import substitution and state protection and subsidy of national industries. To build up domestic industrialization, however, they still encouraged controlled foreign investment. They also noted that social issues (for example, land and income distribution) created power struggles that impeded economic growth. ECLA policy recommendations had a concrete effect, influencing the strategy of import substitution and encouraging the reforms undertaken in Chile in the 1960s, in Brazil until 1964, and in Argentina until 1966.[10]

Economists would later challenge the statistical basis of ECLA's studies about terms of trade, and in fact the terms improved in contradiction to ECLA forecasts. The strong role of the state and reformist strategies stirred even stronger reactions on the Right, while the Left criticized continued adherence to capitalist principles and the worsening of conditions brought on by ECLA policies. Thus, for example, A. G. Frank showed that the deteriorating effects of trade continued into the 1960s. The growth rate in per capita income had declined from

4.8 percent in 1945–1949 to 1.9 percent in 1950–1955 and then to 1.2 percent in 1960–1966.[11] But Prebisch had set in motion a new way of thinking about Latin America's problems and established a core idea that would become part of all dependency theory—the peripheral position of Latin America in the world capitalist system.

**Marxist Analysis.** More explicit and forceful statements about dependency emerged in the late 1960s. Modernization assumptions about development continued to be a primary target for criticism, but the developmentalism proposed by Prebisch and ECLA was attacked by the Left as being too reformist and too attached to capitalist principles. Such language suggests Marxism, and indeed Marxist analysis did figure prominently in dependency theory. Marxism would provide useful insights and concepts for dependency theory (for example, about exploitation and the appropriation of surplus value, about class formations and class conflicts, and about the dynamics of capitalist expansion). But orthodox Marxism also became an additional target of dependency theorists, so the relationship needs to be examined.[12]

Ironically, Karl Marx's own writings on colonialism supported the linear modernization paradigm. Marx believed that colonialism was a brutal but historically necessary step if backward countries were to develop. Since they lacked the inner dynamism to develop spontaneously, backward countries would have to be jarred out of their stagnation. Advanced countries would have to provide them with the economic and technological components they needed. Moreover, Marx believed that capitalist modes of production were highly successful at creating wealth and had to run their course before socialism could emerge.[13]

Lenin's writings proved more helpful. He had analyzed the backward nature of Russia's development (and its dependence on foreign capital for industrialization) and had written a major work on capitalist "imperialism." But Lenin's theories on imperialism focused almost entirely on the center, on the needs of advanced countries to find new sources for investment, cheap labor, and control over raw materials. One could perhaps deduce from Lenin's writings the effects of imperialism on underdeveloped countries (for example, keeping wages low and products cheap), but they contributed little to understanding the specific conditions of peripheral countries like those in Latin America.

Communist party strategies in Latin America also influenced the dependency debate. In 1928, the Comintern had determined that the advanced capitalist countries were working to hinder the industrial development of backward nations and would ally with traditional land-owning oligarchies in those countries to impede change. So the strategy adopted by Latin American Communist parties—convinced also that socialism could only follow upon capitalism—was to favor the kinds of progressive reforms promoted by ECLA and to encourage the national bourgeoisie in its efforts to develop autonomous industrialization. This strategy, especially after the Cuban revolution, was attacked by Marxist dependency theorists. Dependency theory, then, found itself drawing upon some aspects of Marxist analysis at the same time it attacked others.

**Dependency Theory: Cardoso and Frank.** Two figures stand out prominently in the late 1960s debate: Fernando Henrique Cardoso and André Gunder Frank. Although I am now convinced that Cardoso is the more important of the two in understanding Latin American dependency theory, and especially its use by liberation theology, Frank's work has most influenced perceptions of dependency theory in the United States. His thinking is also more clearly related to the Marxism just discussed.[14]

André Gunder Frank was raised in middle-class America and trained in economics at the University of Chicago; his ground-breaking work, *Capitalism and Underdevelopment in Latin America* (1967), was published in English. His work, observes one commentator, was "very much a North American product."[15] Frank acknowledges his debt to North American Marxist Paul Baran who, in his *The Political Economy of Growth,* had argued that no third world country could hope to break out of a state of economic dependence and become a competitor equal to advanced countries. Frank's work became part of the *Monthly Review* development debates carried on by Baran, Paul Sweezy, Harry Magdoff, and others. His work had a significant impact in Latin America and on Latin American dependency theorists, however. (Frank taught and did research in Latin America in the early 1960s, an experience that led him to reject the conventional views on development that he learned at the University of Chicago.)

Drawing upon Baran's ideas, Frank asserted the thesis most often associated with dependency theory: underdeveloped nations were made and kept underdeveloped to support the development of advanced capitalist countries; "the development of underdevelopment" represented two sides of the same coin. Spurred by the success of the Cuban revolution, which declared itself socialist without waiting for progressive capitalism to prepare the way, Frank called for a revolutionary breakaway from the whole capitalist system. Latin America would remain stagnant and could not develop if it remained in the world system of capitalism. Frank further argued that Latin America had been capitalist from colonial times on; it was not feudal or precapitalist

111

now or even then, as both modernization and orthodox Marxism suggested. Latin America was capitalist because it used exploited labor to accumulate surplus value (capital). It manifested no progressive development and remained stagnant because the accumulated capital was not reinvested for growth in Latin America but appropriated by foreign monopolies or consumed by domestic elites. Only through socialist revolution could it hope to develop.

Critics have attacked Frank from all sides and on many counts.[16] Marxists have criticized him for attempting to define capitalism simply as any exploitation and appropriation of surplus value, ignoring all differences in modes of production. Other critics say that his stagnationist thesis has been empirically contradicted by growth figures in the 1960s and 1970s. Others say that, while insisting on the specific nature of Latin American development, Frank ends with a generalized, mechanistic explanation of underdevelopment. Even his defenders find significant inconsistencies in his theory.

Some Latin American dependency theorists have developed neo-Marxist views similar in many ways to Frank's, most notably Ruy Mauro Marini (revolutionary like Frank), and Theotonio Dos Santos (more reformist). Dos Santos's oft-quoted definition of dependency uses the same "two-sides-of-one-coin" metaphor. "By dependency we mean a situation in which the economy of certain countries is conditioned by the development and expansion of another country to which the former is subjected."[17] But Dos Santos criticizes Frank for oversimplified explanations, and the words "conditioned by" are important modifiers of the "development of underdevelopment" thesis. External factors are not the whole cause of the problem, but they do determine the limits and possibilities of action available.[18]

Fernando Henrique Cardoso represents a dependency approach more distinctively Latin American in origin, and far more modest and nuanced in its claims, than Frank's. With Enzo Faletto, Cardoso published his *Dependencia y Desarollo en America Latina* in 1969 from manuscripts written before the publication of Frank's work. Many view this work as the *locus classicus* of dependency literature.[19] In a more recent essay, Cardoso insists that when he wrote *Dependencia* he never claimed or intended to present a new paradigm or a *theory* of dependency. He sought rather to criticize weaknesses in prevailing methods and to explain what Latin Americans had for years experienced and discussed, the *fact* of dependency.[20]

In common with all dependency theorists, Cardoso believes that external factors are important, that one cannot understand Latin American development without considering its dependent position in relation to advanced capitalist nations. But his primary focus is internal, on the social process through which, under the impact of external forces, different classes, alliances, and conflicts are formed. Indeed, so much of his original work focused on internal dynamics that he felt obliged, in response to Marxist critics, to *add* to the English edition of his work (1979) a section on U.S. interventions, which were not treated in his original book.[21] Cardoso's work is distinctive in that he avoids general theorizing and insists on studying "situations of dependency" in their specifics. Even within a given country, he finds very different dynamics at work in "enclave economies" (formed with foreign capital and producing goods for external markets), nationally-owned economies, and multinational economies.[22] He also stresses that new factors must be studied; thus, for example, he believes that manufacturing for domestic Latin American needs is now a goal of multinationals.

As the dependency debates continued, Cardoso clearly and sharply distinguished his views from those of Frank, stating with Faletto that "we do *not* see dependency and imperialism as external and internal sides of a single coin."[23] He finds several of Frank's theses to be erroneous: for example, that capitalist development of Latin America is impossible (Cardoso believes that Latin America *has* developed, albeit in the form of "dependent development"), that the domestic bourgeoisie are no longer a signficant force, and that the only options available to Latin America are socialism or facism. Though socialist in vision, Cardoso is generally classified as a moderate nationalist, concerned with developing greater autonomy for Latin America. Critics focus on the vagueness of his socialist vision and the weakness of empirical data.

A fuller study of dependency theory would have to include many other figures, such as Osvaldo Sunkel and Celso Furtado, both of whom are considered moderate reformists following, but revising, the work done by Prebisch and ECLA. Many of the studies done on dependency theory classify theorists on the basis of their political stances. The evaluator's own political bias usually shows itself in the process.

**Liberation Theology.** I do not know of any study devoted to the use of dependency theory in liberation theology. At this stage of my own investigations, I can only offer a few impressions focused chiefly on Gustavo Gutiérrez and Leonardo Boff. At one level, reliance on dependency theory, or at least on the "fact" of dependency, appears integral to the development and message of liberation theology. The word "liberation," in addition to its theological meaning (God/Jesus as liberator), stems from an analysis of Latin American dependence. Thus Gutiérrez wrote: "Dependence and liberation are correlative terms. An analysis of the situation of dependence leads one to attempt to escape

113

from it."[24] Hugo Assmann develops this same point in his *Theology for a Nomad Church*.[25] Without the conviction that the poor of Latin America are in a situation not just of poverty but of a poverty linked to oppressive structures, the whole enterprise of liberation theology would make little sense. Poverty might evoke compassion and a call for charity but not a call to "opt with and for the poor" that they might liberate themselves. At another level, however, the centrality of dependency theory can be exaggerated. Many works of liberation theologians (for example, Jon Sobrino, Juan Luis Segundo, and Segundo Galilea) make little or no reference to dependency. Nevertheless, it will be useful to examine some works that do deal in some detail with dependency to determine where they fit in the spectrum of theories outlined above.

In his first major work, *A Theology of Liberation*, Gutiérrez deals at length with the issue of dependence, taking up first the criticisms of the development model followed by ECLA in the 1950s and 1960s. This model failed, says Gutiérrez (echoing Cardoso), because it did not recognize development as a "total social process," one that demands consideration of all the external and internal factors (economic, social, political, and cultural) that affect the economic evolution of a nation. Development became synonymous with reformism and modernization, its proponents never recognizing the need to break dependence on rich nations and to create a new socialist society.[26] Gutiérrez's longer treatment of dependency derives primarily from Cardoso: Latin American countries are constitutively dependent on rich nations, "but we are not dealing with a purely external factor."[27] Leninist theories of imperialism do not take into account the experiences of peripheral countries. Much needs to be done, says Gutiérrez, to work out an adequate theory of dependency, to eliminate ideological factors that impede a true scientific understanding. He cites Carsodo's warning that "one can have recourse to the idea of dependence as a way of 'explaining' internal processes of the dependent societies by a purely 'external' variable . . . which is regarded as the real cause."[28] In his first work, then, Gutiérrez writes extensively about dependency theory, relying most on Cardoso and espousing radical change.

In a more recent work, *The Power of the Poor in History*, Gutiérrez returns to the issue of dependency. "External dependency and internal domination are the marks of the social structures of Latin America."[29] Looking back on the early theories of dependency, Gutiérrez feels that their analysis has been, by and large, a boon.[30] But they sometimes failed by focusing too much on the conflict between nations (center versus periphery) and not enough on class analysis.[31] In the meantime, Gutiérrez observes, a "new form of domination" has developed, one that requires new instruments of anticapitalist analysis. This new form of domination includes great expansion of foreign investment in manufacturing; an even greater draining off of capital; fiscal stability achieved by "brutally devaluing the contribution of the world labor force"; and greater control of technological, political, military, commercial, financial, and now "food" power by a few countries headed by the United States.[32] The gap between the rich and the poor has only widened, and political repression and persecution of the Catholic church have intensified. The book also includes a brief history of Latin American dependence as Gutiérrez sees it.

Most probably in response to Vatican criticism, in 1984 Gutiérrez wrote an essay, "Teologia y ciencias sociales." In respect to dependency theory, Gutiérrez refers to Cardoso as the "most important figure" and notes that Cardoso considers his own attitude situated at the opposite end *(antipodas)* from Marx.[33] Gutiérrez sees dependency itself as a fact but affirms that liberation theology should be more attentive to variations of the theory and to criticisms of it and that it should avoid generalizations and be "enriched by other types of analysis."[34] Much of the rest of the article deals with "critical use" of Marxism and class struggle. On this last point Gutiérrez cites various Catholic social teachings, including John Paul II's *Laborem exercens*, in affirmation of the fact of class struggle.

Leonardo Boff also views Latin America as dependent. Paradoxically, while Gutiérrez draws from the more nuanced Cardoso but rejects the reformism Cardoso would accept, Boff uses the language of Frank and Dos Santos when describing Latin America but rejects Frank's call for a revolutionary breakaway. Boff writes: "Latin America stands on the periphery of the big-power centers and is dominated by them."[35] "Development and underdevelopment are two sides of the same coin."[36] Boff, too, has his brief history of Latin American dependency: the plunder of its resources by Spain and Portugal, production determined by Europe in the colonial period, the newest dependency shaped by multinationals that determine Latin America's productive system and priorities. But Boff has serious reservations about dependency theory, quite different from those noted by Gutiérrez. Boff writes: "It is only a theory, not an established truth. It is one stage in an ongoing investigation and has its own intrinsic limitations. It offers a good diagnosis of the structure of underdevelopment, but it does not do much to offer any viable way out."[37] Expanding on this last point, Boff expresses skepticism regarding revolutionary change: "More moderate advocates of the theory of dependency showed greater historical sense" and recognized the need to work for change within the system.[38] Citing Joseph Comblin, Boff says that one cannot choose both complete

115

autonomy and development. Compromise is necessary. If development is the goal, one has to work within the international system. Remarkably, Boff even mentions, as a "more pragmatic and immediately viable" option for Brazil, the acceptance of a Canadian form of dependency with its promise of economic growth.[39] His strategy, then, appears sharply at odds with Frank's call for a revolutionary breakaway from capitalism.

Most studies classify dependency theorists by their stated or implied political strategies. The same could well be true for liberation theologians. Gutiérrez's work certainly contains a continued hositility to all that the word "capitalism" represents and a continued faith that the "popular movement" (represented in Peru by the United Left?) will eventually create a new form of socialism serving the great popular majorities but avoiding the deficiencies of existing socialist countries.[40] Boff, however, if he has maintained the position noted above, appears quite open—or perhaps resigned—to reformist efforts with the system.

### Major Themes in Dependency Analysis

Two connected goals governed this study, and they affect this section especially. One goal was to understand and to begin to assess dependency theory. The second and more important goal was to understand better the sources of development problems faced by Latin American countries. Certain a priori convictions, arising from studies in epistemology, influence my judgment about attaining these goals. I am skeptical of theories that claim to offer *the* explanation of complex social situations, but I also believe that most theories that rise to prominence have *some* important insights to contribute to our understanding. These convictions apply to dependency theory.

Dependency theory can take the form of reducing Latin American problems to one cause (or at least one primary cause)—foreign imperialism. Frank's "development of underdevelopment" suggests this form, and two North Americans who support dependency theory assert as its principal thesis that "Latin America is underdeveloped because it has supported the development of Western Europe and the United States."[41] This simplistic form I would reject. But dependency analysis can take the more nuanced form used by Cardoso, as a study that recognizes external factors as significantly affecting and conditioning Latin American development but acknowledges and studies also the internal factors involved. (I use the expression dependency "analysis" rather than "theory" since Cardoso disclaims calling his studies a theory and theory implies a set of theses that can be empirically tested and proved.) This form I do find insightful and fruitful in attempting to gain a more comprehensive understanding of Latin America. Using dependency analysis in this second sense, I will in this section examine three themes: (1) the distinctive social factors that have influenced Latin American development; (2) the issue of dependency; and (3) issues about the social effects of Latin American development. The first theme offers a general historical overview; the second and third themes deal with specific contemporary issues.

**Distinctive Social Factors in Latin American Development.** Dependency theorists criticize traditional economics, and the modernization model in particular, for focusing narrowly on economic factors (for example, scarcity of capital, marginal costs, technology) while ignoring distinctive sociopolitical factors. They argue that Latin America cannot and should not be fitted into any a priori models of development—modernization, Marxist, or otherwise—and that the whole social context of Latin America must be analyzed. "Development is itself a social process," Cardoso insists, and social factors in Latin America have caused it to "deviate" from the pattern of development in advanced countries.[42] What are the important and distinctive factors that have made Latin America a deviant case? (My attempted answer goes beyond points stressed by dependency analysis.)

Spanish-Portuguese colonization unquestionably shaped Latin America in ways that made it far different from the United States. Culture affected its economic development. Michael Novak and others stress this link as highly significant, arguing that Catholic Spanish culture failed to inculcate a work ethic, a spirit of entrepreneurship, a sense of individual responsibility, and a willingness to risk, all of which are characteristic of the North American ethos. The culture also reinforced strong class divisions—Spaniards, Creoles, Mestizos, Indians—with Indians remaining the most impoverished class in Latin America.

Politics in Latin America has been closely linked to economic development in various ways. Property was seen not as a human right open to all individuals but as a patrimony bestowed by the crown on a few.[43] In many Latin American states, even when forms of democracy were observed, oligarchies, representing dominant or contending economic classes, ruled in fact. The state has played a much more dominant role in economic policy decisions than in the United States. The military, likewise, not only has exerted far more political influence but, in recent decades especially, has assumed direct political rule and set economic policies.[44]

The link between economic development and foreign powers has been stressed most by dependency theorists. They see foreign influence as changing through various stages and forms: the plunder of natural riches by Spain and Portugal, the production of crops primarily for foreign export by local plantation owners, industrialization developed or taken over by foreign investors, the penetration by multinationals, and finally dependency on international banks.[45] Some dependency theorists unquestionably assign the blame for this distorted development to foreign powers. Cardoso and Faletto are more concerned with describing how Latin America became dependent. Thus their study of how British and North American capital investment in the mining industries of Chile and Peru rose from 13 percent in 1878 to 55 percent by 1901 is related without an assessment of blame.[46]

Setting aside the who-is-to-blame issue, I am struck by one aspect concerning the external factors as the most significant: how much of the economy has been, and is now, geared toward agricultural production to meet domestic needs? John Willoughby argues that Latin America has not followed the "natural path of growth" that Adam Smith claimed societies should follow: first, to develop its agriculture (through relatively egalitarian free enterprise in rural areas): second, to produce for the urban market; and, third, to produce for international trade. He sees production for export as having truncated Latin American development.[47]

W. Arthur Lewis makes a similar point about the need for a strong agricultural development for domestic markets as a basis of industrial growth. Moreover, he believes that underdeveloped nations cannot escape from unfavorable terms of trade without greater and more efficient agricultural productivity.[48]

From my own study of Latin American history and present conditions, the most significant obstacle to Latin American development has been concentration of ownership, particularly land ownership. In the United States, before 1850, four out of five white Americans owned their own land or had their own trade. Such has never been the case in Latin America. Restricted ownership may have begun with the patrimony idea of property. But so-called government land reforms in the late nineteenth century also led to transfer of lands from small individual farmers and Indian communal farms to large plantation owners for use in growing export crops. In Mexico, Cardoso notes, eight persons gained control over 22.5 million hectares from 1881 to 1889.[49] Michael Todaro asserts that 1.3 percent of the landowners in Latin America control 71.6 percent of all the land under cultivation.[50] Had the plantation owners been more efficient, reinvested in the domestic economy, developed more domestic markets, and paid fairer wages, size might not have been an obstacle. But they did not; and I perceive most of the cultural, social, political, and economic factors discussed in this section to be closely linked to the issue of concentrated ownership and power.

The validity of some of the points raised in this section may be challenged, and the relative importance of factors can certainly be disputed. But the importance, stressed by dependency theorists, of studying linkages and of acknowledging the distinctively different pattern of development that these linking factors created appears incontestable.

**The "Fact" of Dependency.** However different Latin American history may have been, for dependency theory to have merit it must be able to show that Latin American countries are in "fact" in a more vulnerable, disadvantaged, dependent position in respect to advanced industrial nations (whatever causes may be to blame). Historians writing on U.S.–Latin American relations have certainly perceived the relation as one of power versus dependence.[51] Even U.S. allies in Latin America have acknowledged it. (Luis Somoza, former president of Nicaragua, once confided to a reporter: "We are economically, politically, and militarily dependent on the United States.")[52] More than a battery of quotes is needed, however. First, what is meant by dependency? Cardoso and Faletto offer this definition: "From the economic point of view a system is dependent when the accumulation and expansion of capital cannot find its essential components inside the system." They add that mere interdependence becomes dependence when the partners are in vastly uneven positions of power, such that one partner has almost exclusive possession of the technological and financial sectors needed for expansion.[53] Raúl Prebisch, in "The Dynamics of Peripheral Capitalism," defined dependency in terms of decisions taken in the center to which peripheral countries are subjected.[54] Each of these authors believes that dependency exists when external and not internal factors most determine the development of a country.

The 1984 annual reports of the International Monetary Fund (IMF) and the World Bank make strikingly evident the dependency and disadvantaged position of Latin American countries as judged by the norms set down by Cardoso and Prebisch. The IMF report notes that Latin American countries experienced a growth rate averaging 5–7 percent annually from 1967 to 1980. Then their growth rate plummeted to $-2.3$ percent in 1983. The reasons given by the IMF are consistently external. A major factor in the problems faced by developing countries has been "the recession in industrial countries." Weakness of foreign exchange earnings and indebtedness made developing countries "particularly vulnerable" to interest rate increases in 1980. The weakness of economic activity in the industrial world had a "substantial adverse effect" on the terms of trade of the non-oil-developing countries.[55]

Does the decision-making power to reverse these conditions lie

119

primarily inside or outside the developing countries? The IMF report gives quite clear indications of the subordinate, reacting position of developing countries (though the dialogue form is my own addition). Decision (center): High interest rates have greatly increased Latin American debts, but these rates are "a result of industrial countries' 'new-found determination' to confront inflation." Reaction (periphery): "Faced with an abrupt change of external finance, many developing countries had no option but to cut back sharply their current account deficits."[56]

The World Bank report reflects this same causal relation: restrictive monetary policies (center) "pursued on their part to control inflation" had a "profoundly adverse effect" on the rates of growth of many developing countries (periphery). "Enormous pressures" have been exerted on the positions of countries in Latin America.[57]

Throughout these reports the language of cause and effect consistently mirrors causes in the advanced industrial world (center) and effects in developing countries (periphery). Certainly in more prosperous times the effects may be positive, but they would still reflect dependency. To counter this conclusion, one would have to show instances in which the cause-effect relation is reversed, so that decisions or changes in Latin America became the primary factor in determining the growth or decline in the U.S. economy.

Michael J. Francis, in a paper on dependency for an AEI/Notre Dame seminar last summer, divided his assessment into "easily defensible" propositions about dependency and "controversial" propositions. He asserts as an easily defensible proposition that "the peripheral countries are experiencing a growing loss of national control over their economic, political, social, and cultural life due to their dependent situation." It is this proposition, in even narrower terms, that I have been addressing. Francis does not say that developing countries have no options; but he does argue, in defense of dependency theory, that economic growth in developing countries is now closely tied to the prices of certain primary products, the availability of credit, and the viability of foreign investment, and that policy decisions in the center greatly affect the periphery. He demonstrates his proposition with several examples: (1) the power of the IMF to impose austerity programs, which set externally a number of internal policies, for example, on taxes and government spending; (2) the devastating effects of the international economy on Chile, which sought to pursue a free market model; (3) the use of foreign aid to influence governmental decision making, for example, in Brazil in 1964; (4) military assistance to Latin America to counter leftist groups.[58]

Many dependency theorists focus their criticisms of external factors on the power that multinationals exert on Latin America (such as draining off capital through excess profits and transfer pricing or undermining domestic industries). But to treat each of the indictments brought against multinationals and to assess counterarguments would require a book-length study. Some criticisms, however, do concern the social effects issue, which I now wish to discuss.

**The Social Effects of Latin American Development.** The dependency arguments just considered deal chiefly with relations between nations; center versus periphery; rich, developed nations versus poor, underdeveloped ones. Equally important to dependency analysis are socioeconomic problems centered on conflicts within nations. What are the social effects of the particular forms that development has taken in Latin America? Have all sectors of the society benefited (or failed to benefit) or only certain sectors? The modernization model stresses growth in the GNP as the key to development. Growth can come only through increased productivity, which multinationals can help to achieve through the benefits of their capital, technology, and organizational skills. With growth will come benefits for all, a higher standard of living, and increased levels of political participation and democracy. Dependency theorists see things quite differently. They do not have faith in the trickle-down effects of increased growth; they did not see such effects occurring during the recent years of economic growth nor throughout Latin American history. They believe that only policies that from the outset involve economic and political participation of the lower 40–50 percent of the population and address their basic needs can hope to achieve any equitable growth.

Raúl Prebisch states this dimension of dependency analysis quite forcefully: "Peripheral capitalism, particularly in Latin America, is characterized by a dynamic which excludes the great masses of the people. It is a dynamic process oriented towards the privileged consumer society. . . . It is also incompatible with the process of democratization."[59] Prebisch discusses three areas in which elitism is manifested: the markets for goods produced, employment and income distribution, and the political process. Each of these merits some brief discussion.

Dependency analysts believe that production of goods in Latin America has been oriented to satisfy foreign needs or the desires of the upper classes and not to meet basic domestic needs. Certainly automobiles, if geared for a mass consumer market in advanced countries, remain a luxury item for the vast majority of Latin Americans. The same is true for refrigerators (an example that Novak puts forward). Most of the rural families I visited in Latin America were without

121

electricity, and a nun working in an urban barrio (population 100,000) outside Lima told me that milk itself was a luxury that few families could afford. One cannot generalize on the basis of a few examples (though more could certainly be cited).[60] Some goods, including some produced by foreign companies, do meet basic domestic needs. But the issue is serious enough to have generated wide discussion of an alternative basic needs strategy of development.[61]

Latin American countries rank among the worst in the world in respect to income distribution. Several empirical studies have focused on the problem of income distribution in developing countries, on the negative effects of multinationals regarding income inequity, on the limited benefits of growth for the bottom half of the population, and particularly on Latin America's highly uneven distribution.[62] André Gunder Frank focuses on Brazil since its growth rate had been lauded as an "economic miracle." He claims that in relative and absolute terms the poorest sectors of society suffered. From 1960 to 1970 the top 5 percent of income recipients saw their annual income increase from $1,645 to $2,940 and their share of national income rise from 27 percent to 36 percent; the poorest 40 percent of the population endured a reduction in share of national income from 22 percent to 9 percent, or to $90 per capita. The change was reflected in absolute terms as well. By 1975 minimum wages had been cut to 29 percent of the 1958 level and 45 percent of the 1964 level. The number of hours of work necessary to buy a subsistence diet for a worker and his family at the minimum wage was 5.7 hours in 1960, 7 hours in 1965, and 8.5 hours in 1970.[63]

The relation between concentration of ownership and poverty is not difficult to judge. In El Salvador, during the 1970s, landless peasants worked on coffee and other plantations for $1 to $2 a day; the owners of these plantations, the twenty wealthiest families in El Salvador, had wealth estimated at $70 million to $300 million per family.[64] Distribution of income is also linked to the consumer-market problem discussed earlier. The more inequitable the income distribution, the more the market will reflect goods produced for higher-income groups. But mere distribution of wealth would only equalize poverty, so the main argument of dependency analysts focuses on job creation. Multinationals are criticized for using capital-intensive technology and for creating "regressive competition" by pitting skilled workers against a waiting pool of unskilled and unemployed workers.[65] (The effect on jobs by multinationals is exaggerated by the opponents and defenders alike; multinationals account for only one-half of 1 percent of the jobs needed in developing countries).[66]

Political rule has also been affected by the elitist factor in Latin American development. Free enterprise and democracy may have developed together in Europe and the United States. Economic liberalism and political liberalism had the same philosophical sources in Europe. But in Latin America, Prebisch contends, economic liberalism has been achieved by force to the destruction of democratic liberalism. José Nun confirms this observation: "The exclusion and marginalization of the popular sectors have been the preconditions of Latin American liberalism," and when even a partial integration has taken place "it has occurred under the auspices of populist, not liberal, movements."[67] To these internal factors, dependency analysts would add the intervention of the United States and its military aid to right-wing regimes as important factors impeding democratization.[68]

As a distinct theory of development, dependency may have little future. But the aspects I have tried to underline, far from fading away, have been incorporated into the structuralist method now used by many in the field of development economics. Michael Todaro's widely-used textbook, *Economic Development in the Third World,* includes almost every point I have noted in this section—criticism of neo-classical, modernization approaches; the link between sociopolitical systems and economics; the phenomenon of dependence as a common linking factor; and the importance of strategies that deal with equity and meeting basic human needs.[69] The continuing influence of dependency analysis is clear.

### Polarization of Options: Marxism and Capitalism

Disagreements can arise on many levels, about facts and their interpretation, about values and the institutions best suited to achieve these values, and finally about concrete realistic options. Most of the discussion of the last section on themes will focus on the factual accuracy of statements made or the comprehensiveness of the data presented. (The number and complexity of the variables involved make any judgments about causes of problems extremely difficult.) But value concerns also greatly affect one's analysis and proposed solutions. (I assume here a discussion of what kinds of options one can encourage and support in Latin America; even with the power to do so, imposing solutions would run counter to the tenor of my paper.)

All of us share many of the same values and would like to see Latin American countries able to experience growth and equity, development and autonomy, freedom and justice. But the weight given certain values may differ considerably. Many may feel that growth is the most essential value, that without it other values cannot be realized and with it they are most apt to follow. I believe that liberation theologians and dependency theorists assert a different priority set of values: autonomy (a sense of worth and self-respect as nations and individuals), liberation (from servitudes of every kind, economic and political; the ability to gain greater control over one's life), and life-sustenance (the ability to provide as many as possible with the basic needs required for a decent life).[70]

Values must be translated into specific structures, institutions, and policies to be realized, however. Many would argue that the institutions that succeeded in the United States are the institutions still best suited to bring development to Latin America—free-enterprise, free-market, political democracy. In contrast, liberation theologians and dependency theorists, while quite articulate about what they oppose, can appear vague and utopian about what they favor ("a system that truly represents the vast majority of the people"; "a socialism without the deficiencies of existing socialist countries"). I believe, however, that there is a way of articulating this option more clearly and that its merits might be discussed more objectively if no label were attached to it.

Imagine for a moment contemporary Nicaragua without Marxism but with Sandinista "professed" goals and some of its attempted changes. Nicaragua would be a country in which land reform was carried out, giving landless peasants new opportunities. It would be more autonomous by expanding its export markets to more countries and by adopting a nonaligned foreign policy. It would be more self-determining by diversifying its production while maintaining income from some exports. It would be a mixed economy with state banks and with some collective and state enterprises, but it would retain and encourage private ownership and free enterprise for 60 percent to 70 percent of the economy. Socioeconomic rights and basic needs would receive a high priority: production to meet basic food needs would be stressed; free or low-cost medical care for the poorest sectors and efforts to eliminate illiteracy would be greatly expanded. At the same time political rights would be safeguarded: open and fair elections, pluralism of political parties, no government repression, independent unions, true freedom of the press, and guaranteed freedom of religion.

Even with this idealized form some might quarrel (for example, against nationalization of banks and any significant degree of state ownership). Some of the goals may be unrealistic or inadvisable (for example, how can a poor country afford significant expenditures on medicine and education before it has ensured sufficient economic growth?). But this idealized picture of Nicaragua does represent, I believe, the kind of society most liberation theologians envision, and one I could support with enthusiasm. No doubt an equally attractive model might be imagined closer to the ideals of democratic capitalism.

But polarization sets in the moment one moves from this idealized form to judgments about the real situation. If one excludes from consideration those who would explicitly favor a Soviet-style, Marxist-Leninist rule, the polarization comes from differing views about the nature of Marxism. The same polarization often occurs, especially in Latin America, regarding the nature of capitalism. Both words carry connotations heavy with emotion.

For most North Americans and many Latin Americans, the word Marxism has almost entirely negative connotations. For them, Marxism means simply "Marxist-Leninist" totalitarian regimes. They judge as naive anyone who cannot recognize what Marxism, despite its alluring appeal of liberation, has in fact brought—repressive rule without even its vaunted promises of growth and equal distribution. The proof can be seen in the Soviet Union, Eastern Europe, Vietnam, Cambodia, and Cuba. The fruit of its actions lie in the seeds of its doctrines, in Lenin's espousal of a single vanguard party and dictatorship of the proletariat, in strategies of violence and class struggle, in its atheism and materialism, in its misguided conviction that human nature can be changed by changing structures and systems, and in its claim to represent *the* scientific truth about society and history.

Liberation theologians and many of their supporters view Marxism differently. They do not see it as one inseparable piece. They perceive Marxist analysis as separable from its atheism (which they believe is based on an inadequate understanding of religion) and from any one set of tactics. They believe that one can learn from Marxist analysis about the fact of class struggle and the causes of exploitation and domination without espousing hatred or violence. They see Marxist analysis as distinctive in Latin America, shaped not by Lenin but by Gramsci in Italy and indigenous Marxists like Mariátegui in Peru. They believe that Latin American Marxist movements and groups, like the Sandinistas, should be judged on their own policies and actions not by what Marxists elsewhere have done. They know, moreover, that right-wing governments have used the label "Marxist" or "Communist subversive" to block reforms. In Central America, land reform has long been equated with Marxism. In El Salvador, in 1976, even given the more euphemistic expression "agrarian transformation," the model of land reform used in Taiwan was sharply rejected.[71] Workers and peasant unions, attempts to form peasant cooperatives, even protests against government repression, have been suppressed as Marxist measures.

The word "capitalist" can also be charged with emotion and connote different meanings to different people. While critical of some specific features, most U.S. Americans would certainly give positive marks to the overall political and economic systems of our country. They might resonate more with the expression "free enterprise," but most would acknowledge the opportunities and the actual achievements that U.S. capitalism has bestowed.[72]

In most of Latin America, however, the word "capitalism" carries very different connotations. Even conservative U.S. Americans would not use "democratic capitalism," "free enterprise," or "true capitalism" to describe the systems that have prevailed in Latin America. Capitalism, as Latin Americans have experienced it, has not brought a high standard of living or even significant progress toward such a standard to the vast majority. It has not opened up widespread opportunities for individual free enterprise; instead, concentration of ownership and wealth prevails. State power has been used more often to protect this system and its privileged elites than to safeguard human rights and include the majority. Foreign ownership in industries, whatever benefits it may confer, diminishes autonomy and national pride; hence many do not see capitalism as their system at all.[73] In the Latin American church, even the staunchest critics of liberation theology do not attempt to defend Latin American capitalism. Bishop Alfonso Lopez Trujillo affirms: "We are convinced that capitalism is a human failure."[74] Roger Vekemans, S.J., calls for a "Christian socialism" to avoid the evils of capitalism and Marxist socialism.[75]

To all this some will reply that trusting Marxism or the untested and vague options proposed by dependency theorists will lead to worse, not better, conditions. They may be right. But Latin Americans know from experience what trusting U.S. interventions has brought. The CIA planned and succeeded in overthrowing the Arbenz regime in Guatemala in 1954 (a democratically elected reformist government, accused of letting Communist labor leaders become too influential). Then Vice President Nixon proudly proclaimed: "This is the first instance in history where a Communist government has been replaced by a free one. The whole world is watching to see which does the better job."[76] The "better job" included rescinding almost all of the land reforms, disenfranchising all illiterates (then 70 percent of the population), executing an estimated 30,000 civilians over the next thirty years, causing hundreds of thousands of Indians to become refugees, and establishing a human rights record judged to be the worst in all of Latin America. Nor is Guatemala an isolated example. The United States sought to block the Marxist but democratically elected Allende regime in Chile and left that country with a repressive military dictatorship; it supported the overthrow of Goulart in Brazil in 1964, leaving that country with twenty years of military rule. Some Latin Americans may exaggerate the U.S. role (it was one of many factors in Chile and not a primary factor in Brazil), but their skepticism about U.S. promotion of democracy is hardly unfounded.

The countries of Latin America have no easy options. Most are likely to continue along established paths, by methods that have not been beneficial economically or democratic politically for the majority of their people. Some may move in nationalist-populist directions but will face enormous problems dealing with the passions that far-reaching social change awakens. The polarizing labels of Marxism and capitalism will only add intensity to the problems. Hence, for most Latin American countries, I consider the real options available to be, not democratic capitalism as experienced in the United States versus Marxist-totalitarian socialism (Novak) or the extremes of fascism versus true socialism (Frank), but restrictive capitalism versus more leftist-populist alternatives.

Throughout this paper, I have tried to show Latin America from the perspective of liberation theologians, modified by my own reformist political values. In the first section, I explained what dependency theory is and how it developed. In the second section, avoiding the extreme statements of some dependency theorists, I presented what I found most fruitful in the insights and arguments of dependency analysis. In the last section, at the risk of polarizing the discussion, I felt it important to underline strongly conflicting perceptions of Marxism and capitalism. Such efforts are needed to attain a broader and deeper understanding of the complex problems confronting Latin America.

# Notes

1. Michael Novak, "The Case against Liberation Theology," *The New York Times Magazine* (Sunday, October 21, 1984); Novak, *The Spirit of Democratic Capitalism* (New York: Simon & Schuster, 1982), chaps. 16–18; Novak, *Freedom with Justice* (San Francisco, Calif.: Harper & Row, 1984), chap. 10.

2. Novak, *The Spirit of Democratic Capitalism,* p. 301.

3. My presentation of the development of dependency theory is a summary of several studies and commentaries. A brief word about each may be helpful.

a. Gabriel Palma, "Dependency: A Formal Theory of Underdevelopment or a Methodology for the Analysis of Concrete Situations of Underdevelopment?" *World Development* (July–August, 1978), pp. 881–924. This prize-winning essay is the best and most comprehensive study of dependency theory. It includes an extensive study of Marxism; it comments on most of the dependency theorists; and it judges Fernando Henrique Cardoso's method of analysis to be the most fruitful.

b. Philip J. O'Brien, "A Critique of Latin American Theories of Dependency," in Ivar Oxaal, Tony Barnet, and David Booth, eds., *Beyond the Sociology of Development* (London: Routledge and Kegan Paul, 1975). This also is a very useful study, particularly of the United Nations Economic Commission on Latin America (ECLA), Fernando Henrique Cardoso, and André Gunder Frank (with a good critique and defense of Frank).

c. Ronald H. Chilcote has edited or coedited several helpful studies dealing especially with the debate between Marxism and dependency: *Dependency and Marxism* (Boulder, Colo.: Westview Press, 1982)—this book contains essays originally published in *Latin American Perspectives: Issues of Theory in Dependency and Marxism* (Summer–Fall, 1981); Ronald H. Chilcote and Dale L. Johnson, eds., *Theories of Development* (Beverly Hills, Calif.: Sage, 1983)— an introductory essay by Chilcote covers modernization, imperialism, dependency, and a neo-Marxist "modes of production" model; Ronald H. Chilcote and Joel C. Edelstein, eds., *Latin America: The Struggle with Dependency and Beyond* (New York: John Wiley & Sons, 1974).

d. Richard C. Bath and Dilmus D. James, "Dependency Analysis of Latin America," *Latin American Research Review,* vol. 11, no. 3 (1976). This study summarizes common elements in different forms of dependency theory but focuses most on North American theorists. Other studies on more specific points will also be noted.

4. Walt W. Rostow, *The Stages of Economic Growth: A Non-Communist Manifesto* (New York: Cambridge University Press, 1960).

5. Kenneth Prewitt, "The Impact of the Developing World on U.S. Social-Science Theory and Methodology," pp. 3–19, and Paul Streeten, "The Limits of Development Research," in Lawrence D. Stifel, Ralph K. Davidson, and James S. Coleman, eds., *Social Sciences and Public Policy in the Developing World,* pp. 21–56 (Lexington, Mass.: Lexington Books, 1983). Both essays include critiques of modernization, pp. 3 ff., 21 ff. See also Michael P. Todaro, *Economic Development in the Third World,* 2d ed. (New York: Longman, 1981), pp. 8 ff., 57 ff.

6. Paul Streeten, "The Limits of Development Research," p. 24.

7. Eduardo Venezian, "The Economic Sciences in Latin America," *Social Sciences and Public Policy in the Developing World,* pp. 189–210, notes that, apart from one university in Mexico, no schools or faculties of economics existed in Latin America before the 1950s. He credits U.S. aid for spurring their rapid development. Jorge Balán, in the same volume, studies the development of "Social Sciences in the Periphery: Perspectives on the Latin American Case," pp. 211–47.

8. Frances Moore Lappé and Joseph Collins, *Food First: Beyond the Myth of Scarcity* (Boston: Houghton Mifflin, 1977), pp. 182–83.

9. These ECLA arguments are noted by David Booth, "André Gunder Frank: An Introduction and Appreciation," *Beyond the Sociology of Development,* p. 55. His whole treatment of ECLA-Prebisch (pp. 52–61) was helpful.

10. On the practical effects of ECLA policies, see Balán, "Social Sciences in the Periphery," p. 215.

11. Cited by Booth, "André Gunder Frank," p. 62, from A. G. Frank, *Lumpenbourgeoisie: Lumpenproletariat—Dependence, Class and Politics in Latin America* (New York: Monthly Review Press, 1972), p. 93.

12. Most of my summary on Marxism is drawn from Palma's article in *World*

*Development*. Most Marxists find dependency theory inadequate; many reject it as largely incompatible with Marxism. On this issue, see *Dependency and Marxism,* especially essays by Colin Henfrey, John Weeks, and Ronaldo Munck. Munck's essay includes reasons the Communist party of Mexico gives for their perception of dependency theory as "an obstacle to the advancement of Marxism" (p. 163).

13. See the Introduction by Shlomo Avineri (ed.) to *Karl Marx on Colonialism & Modernization* (Garden City, N.Y.: Anchor Books, Doubleday & Co., 1969), p. 13.

14. For more on Frank, see Booth, "André Gunder Frank"; and Tulio Halpérin-Donghi, "Dependency Theory and Latin American Historiography," *Latin American Research Review,* vol. 17, no. 1 (1982), pp. 115–30.

15. Halpérin-Donghi, p. 115.

16. See Palma, Booth, O'Brien, and Halpérin-Donghi for critiques of Frank.

17. Dos Santos cited by Bath and James in "Dependency Analysis," p. 5.

18. O'Brien, "A Critique of Latin American Theories of Dependency," p. 15.

19. Robert Packenham, "Plus ça change . . . the English edition of Cardoso and Faletto's Dependentia y Desarollo en America Latina," *Latin American Research Review,* vol. 17, no. 1 (1982), p. 131, cites several authors who view the Cardoso-Faletto book as the *locus classicus.*

20. Fernando Henrique Cardoso, "The Consumption of Dependency Theory in the United States," *Latin American Research Review,* vol. 12, no. 3 (1977), p. 8.

21. See Packenham, "Plus ça change."

22. See Fernando Henrique Cardoso and Enzo Faletto, *Dependency and Development in Latin America* (Berkeley: University of California, 1979), p. xix and passim.

23. Ibid., p. xv.

24. Gustavo Gutiérrez, *A Theology of Liberation,* trans. and ed. Sister Caridad Inda and John Eagleson (Maryknoll, N.Y.: Orbis, 1973), p. 81.

25. Hugo Assmann, *Theology for a Nomad Church,* trans. Paul Burns (Maryknoll, N.Y.: Orbis, 1976), pp. 45–56.

26. Gutiérrez, *A Theology of Liberation,* pp. 26–27.

27. Ibid., p. 85.

28. Ibid., p. 87. See also Gustavo Gutiérrez and Richard Shaull, *Liberation and Change* (Atlanta, Ga.: John Knox, 1977), pp. 77 ff.

29. Gustavo Gutiérrez, *The Power of the Poor in History,* trans. Robert R. Barr (Maryknoll, N.Y.: Orbis, 1983), p. 45.

30. Ibid., p. 78.

31. Ibid., pp. 45, 192.

32. Ibid., pp. 83–88.

33. Gustavo Gutiérrez, "Teologia y ciencias sociales," *Christus* (October–November, 1984), p. 12.

34. Ibid.

35. Leonardo Boff, *Liberating Grace,* trans. John Drury (Maryknoll, N.Y.: Orbis, 1979; original 1976), p. 65.

36. Ibid., p. 66. See also Leonardo Boff, *Jesus Christ Liberator* (Maryknoll, N.Y.: Orbis, 1978), pp. 276–77.

37. Boff, *Liberating Grace,* p. 66.

38. Ibid., p. 77.

39. Ibid., p. 78.

40. Gutiérrez, *The Power of the Poor,* pp. 46, 188–91.

41. Chilcote and Edelstein, *Latin America,* p. 27.

42. Cardoso and Faletto, *Dependency and Development,* pp. 8, 11.

43. See Paul E. Sigmund, *Multinationals in Latin America* (Madison: University of Wisconsin, 1980), p. 24.

44. See Margaret E. Crahan, ed., *Human Rights and Basic Needs in the Americas* (Washington, D.C.: Georgetown University, 1982). Crahan's own chapters are excellent studies of the state in Latin America.

45. Eduardo Galeano, *Open Veins of Latin America: Five Centuries of the Pillage of a Continent,* trans. Cedric Belfrage (New York: Monthly Review Press, 1973), pp. 30–68, develops the thesis that transfer of wealth from Latin America to the "center" served to finance the Industrial Revolution.

46. Cardoso and Faletto, *Dependency and Development,* p. 121.

47. John A. Willoughby, "International Capital Flows, Economic Growth, and Basic Needs," *Human Rights,* p. 200.

48. W. Arthur Lewis, *The Evolution of the International Economic Order* (Princeton, N.J.: Princeton University Press, 1978), pp. 9–10, 16–18.

49. Cardoso and Faletto, *Dependency and Development,* p. 106.

50. Michael P. Todaro, *Economic Development in the Third World,* 2d ed. (New York: Longman, 1981), p. 260.

51. Gordon Connell-Smith, *The United States and Latin America* (London: Heinemann, 1974), observes: "What above all distinguishes Latin America from the United States is the disparity of power between them" (p. 2). He adds, "Latin America is heavily dependent upon the United States as a market and as a source of investment capital" (p. 8). Similarly Cole Blasier, *The Hovering Giant* (Pittsburg, Pa.: University of Pittsburgh, 1976), writes that Latin American countries have been dependent on the United States and that "in great measure dependency has been the inevitable result of disparities in economic and political power" (p. 6).

52. Cited in "Trading with Multinationals," *Multinational Monitor,* vol. 6, no. 4 (April 1985), p. 6.

53. Cardoso and Faletto, *Dependency and Development,* pp. xx–xxi.

54. Raúl Prebisch, "The Dynamics of Peripheral Capitalism," in *Democracy and Development in Latin America,* ed. Louis Lefeber and Liisa L. North (Toronto: CERLAC-LARU, 1980), p. 25.

55. *International Monetary Fund Annual Report, 1984* (Washington, D.C.: IMF, 1984), pp. 9–11.

56. Ibid., p. 31.

57. *The World Bank Annual Report, 1984* (Washington, D.C.: World Bank, 1984), p. 32.

58. Michael J. Francis, "Dependency: Ideology, Fad *and* Fact," in *Latin*

*America: Dependency or Interdependence?* Michael Novak and Michael Jackson, eds., (Washington, D.C.: The American Enterprise Institute, 1985), pp. 92–94.

59. Prebisch, "The Dynamics of Peripheral Capitalism," p. 21.

60. Lappé and Collins, *Food First,* includes numerous examples: Mexico's growing strawberries and cantaloupes for export, a Colombian grower's shifting from grain production to flowers for export, Peruvian fish sold as pet food in the United States (pp. 255–56).

61. See essays by John F. Weeks, Elizabeth W. Dore, John A. Willoughby, and Richard E. Feinberg in *Human Rights.*

62. Francis, "Dependency," states as an "easily defensible proposition" that economic growth in less-developed countries is unevenly distributed in a way that results in the poorest half of most societies being relatively untouched by economic growth. He cites studies by Volker Bornschier in *American Sociological Review* (June 1979); Patrick Nolan in *American Journal of Sociology* (September 1983); Peter Evans in *American Sociological Review* (August 1980); Keith Griffin in *World Development* (March 1978); David Felix in *Latin American Research Review* (1983), and others.

63. André Gunder Frank, *Crisis: In the Third World* (New York: Holmes and Meier, 1981), pp. 7, 12. Frank's inference about the buying power of minimum wages assumes the same proportion of workers receiving only minimum wages. I have no data on this.

64. Paul Heath Hoeffel, "The Eclipse of the Oligarchy," *New York Times Magazine* (September 6, 1981), p. 23.

65. Prebisch, "The Dynamics of Peripheral Capitalism," p. 23.

66. C. Fred Bergsten, Thomas Horst, and Theodore H. Moran, *American Multinationals and American Interests* (Washington, D.C.: Brookings Institution, 1978), pp. 356, 367.

67. Prebisch, "The Dynamics of Peripheral Capitalism," pp. 22–23; and José Nun's *Democracy and Development,* comments on Prebisch's essay, p. 31.

68. See Crahan, ch. 3, "National Security Ideology and Human Rights," in *Human Rights,* and Brian H. Smith, ch. 9, "U.S.-Latin Military Relationships," in the same volume.

69. Todaro, *Economic Development,* pp. 12–18, 117–19, and passim.

70. Ibid., pp. 68–73, expresses the same values in slightly different terms.

71. See Phillip Berryman, *The Religious Roots of Rebellion* (Maryknoll, N.Y.: Orbis, 1984), p. 115.

72. The expressions "free enterprise" and "capitalism" connote, for me at least, different things. Free enterprise suggests opportunities for individuals to begin their own businesses. Capitalism suggests ownership of factories or other large businesses with physical work done by hired laborers. Thus I view the United States as a free enterprise system from the outset—four out of five white Americans owned their own farm or trade before 1850—but as capitalist (with continuation of free enterprise) only from the mid-to-late nineteenth century on.

73. I cannot imagine that U.S. pride in its system would be the same if, from

the outset, the major auto, steel, and oil companies were foreign owned.

74. Alfonso Lopez Trujillo, *Liberation or Revolution?* (Huntington, Ind.: Our Sunday Visitor, 1977), p. 101.

75. See Padre J. Guadalupe Carney, *To Be a Revolutionary* (San Francisco, Ca.: Harper & Row, 1985), pp. 199–200.

76. Cited in Stephen C. Schlesinger and Stephen Kinzer, *Bitter Fruit: The Untold Story of the American Coup in Guatemala* (Garden City, N.Y.: Doubleday, 1982), p. 234.

# Discussion

PAUL SIGMUND, Woodrow Wilson Center: I lived in Chile at the time of the adoption of the Agrarian Reform Act, and there were some problems with the confrontational approach taken. There was a problem of concentration of landholding and especially of inefficient production. Chile was not producing enough food to feed itself and had to import increasing amounts. Part of the problem was related to price structures and state intervention and import substitution, but part also was the inefficiency and primitive organization of large landholdings in certain areas—not the whole country; there were different patterns of distribution. But some kind of reform in some areas was necessary.

In retrospect, using the tax system would probably have made more sense than the kind of much debated thing that took place. It did not cause the coup and was not a major factor in the triumph of the left; it was one of many factors that contributed to the polarization of politics. But there was a consensus that some kind of change in the land tenure system was needed in parts of Chile.

If Peter Berger is calling for another paradigm, we have it alive and well from the previous speaker. The fact that liberation theology is generally leftist is better known in this country because the liberation theologists write books and the books get translated; often they have time to write books because they are in exile or persecuted, not in power. One almost has the impression that all Latin Americans are leftists. In fact, there is a strong populist element, and there is an extremely vigorous libertarian, free-market-oriented group of people—economists and political scientists and publicists—who are increasingly important in Latin America.

If Mr. Berger is looking for a new paradigm, then, it is there, and it is a paradigm that is much influenced by American economics. Milton Friedman is available in every bookstore in Latin America, and "Free to Choose" is on television, but we are not going to find a single new paradigm. I think that is why liberation theology is important, because what is happening there is a revival on the left, just as the right has discarded the old hierarchal, organic, traditionalist, patrimonial paradigm and replaced it with a modern paradigm of free markets and a

133

development oriented toward production. There has been a paradigm shift on the right.

A paradigm shift on the left is also taking place. The old Marxist categories are being rethought and some of them abandoned, and there is a sense that the whole basis of the reformist or radical thrust of the left can come from somewhere else. It can come from the cultural tradition of Latin America, which is Catholic.

Marxism made lots of progress among the intellectuals, but how many Communist parties are or ever were important in Latin America? The Chilean one was and is and will be, despite all efforts to reverse the process. The Cuban one was, but Castro was an opponent until he co-opted it, until he took it over and used it. So liberation theology is important because it is seen as part of a left paradigm that is populist and either reformist or radical and has a base in popular culture and in the history of Latin America in a way that the Marxist parties never had. The Marxist parties in Argentina, for example, were always looked at as following a bunch of Italians; they are not Argentine. Most of the guerrillas in Argentina were not Marxists but Peronists. The Montenegros were Peronist left.

What I am saying is that liberation theology, and the Marxist leftists as well, is part of a search for a new paradigm there. The right has found its new paradigm in the free market, but the left is not as sure. That is why there is an interest in liberation theology as part of the search and a way to formulate the populist tendencies that have always been important in Latin American politics.

For that reason we cannot and should not dismiss liberation theology. We should try to find out what is positive about it.

In response to Father McGovern, let me say you appear to make Prebisch into a dependency theorist when historically he was not. The dependency theory grew out of the Prebisch group in Chile; someone associated with Prebisch wrote an article in the first issue of *Estudios Internacionales* in 1967, in which he talked about dependency theory, and the term began to be used. The criticism that Gunder Frank and others on the left have made about the development of underdeveloped countries was made earlier, but the label emerged in 1967 from people associated with Prebisch in the Economic Commission for Latin America, not from Prebisch himself. Prebisch, as you say, was pushing import substitution and the decline of the terms of trade. Although that is related, I don't think you should label Prebisch a dependency theorist.

Second, there should be some discussion of income distribution in Brazil, on which there is a huge literature. The minimum wage, for instance, is sometimes set low, to save employers money. That is an administrative decision and does not necessarily measure the decline of purchasing power. The real purchasing power of the minimum wage may be one-third what is was ten years earlier because of high inflation.

You have to think some more about those measures. I would urge you to think more about the decline of the absolute standard of living, or absolute per capita income. So much of the literature is on deciles—the top 10 percent or the bottom 40 percent. The problem with that is that the gap may widen but the rising tide may have lifted all boats. It is important to focus, as you did, on the absolute decline in living standards at the bottom, and that is very hard to measure.

Finally, I am sorry that you did not talk more about the last part of the paper, because I am very sympathetic to your critique of the polarized view—either Marxism or capitalism, either Adam Smith or Karl Marx. That is not what Latin American politics, if it is going to be democratic, is going to be about. It is going to be what you correctly identified, a kind of left populism. I don't know what restrictive capitalism is, but I know what you mean; that is, an emphasis on growth and an emphasis on distribution. But if one is sacrificed to the other, even an authoritarian regime will be in big trouble.

ASHLEY TELLIS, Woodstock Theological Center: In the paper you distinguish between various trends in dependency theory in an attempt to isolate those ideas that might be more serviceable than the rest. Toward that end you distinguish between two sets of ideas, what we might call the simplistic thesis of Frank and the nuanced thesis of Cardoso.

The nuanced thesis does allow the possibility for dependency theory to be judged as furthering the aims of liberation theology. But creating this kind of dichotomy does not get out of the bind that dependency theory is in.

I will try to demonstrate this by showing the strengths and weaknesses of the positions. The crucial strength of the simplistic position is that it is an explanatory model with a very clear line of causation—the poverty of the underdeveloped countries is a function of development in the first world. If this is empirically true, it is a novel claim that is worthy of consideration. The weakness of the theory is that it can be shown to be empirically false. Therefore, one may adopt the nuanced thesis. The strength of the nuanced thesis is that it does not make external relations the crucial factor but allows room for many interplaying variables, such as domestic considerations. That is its strong point.

It is also its weakness, because it destroys the causal clarity of the simplistic thesis. In the simplistic thesis we have an explanatory model that is very clear in the interrelations that it isolates—the first world versus the third world—whereas the nuanced thesis brings in a lot of quality variables.

What, finally, are you suggesting? What is dependency after all? Cannot the interdependence model of liberal economic theory also be used to explain this kind of case? If you are saying that dependency is one factor among many, surely neoclassical economics can accommodate this kind of problem without any difficulty. The weakness of the simplistic strategy thus flows from its very strength. Its strength is that it is nuanced, and its crucial weakness is that it says nothing, in terms of clean lines of causation. Dependency derives its success simply from the fact that it can show that one is responsible for the other. In the nuanced strategy this kind of line of causation gets blurred. I am only saying that there are two ways out of this. One way is to drop dependency analysis altogether, on the grounds that the claims of the nuanced analysis can be served by the neoclassical theory of international trade, in some variant or another.

The second is to create a scale of dependency whereby one demonstrates that all countries are in some sense dependent. It is problematic simply because the moment that one creates a scale of dependency, the attractiveness of the dependency theory is lost; the absurd conclusion is that everyone is dependent, in some degree, on everybody else. So what is new?

The literature today offers two ways out. The first is the resurgence of the modernization paradigm. The so-called new right has rediscovered Rostow, particularly the crucial fact, which had somehow been lost, that what was as important as his celebrated takeoff was his claim that the third world needs a cultural framework to sustain expansion. In the height of the modernization debate, everybody stuck to the takeoff and forgot that Rostow was the first to talk of the creation of a cultural framework to sustain expansion. That is one option.

The second option is to revert to an orthodox Marxism. Some have argued that dependency analysis has lost its explanatory powers and one must therefore switch to the orthodox Marxist model, which talks of global modes of production. The limiting case of this kind of analysis is the world order systems of Immanuel Wallerstein, which is Marxism in a new dress. We are left with a very peculiar choice of alternatives. It comes back to the old ideological choices: a resurgent modernization paradigm, of which Arturo Fontaine has been labeled as one embodiment, and the alternative of a reversion to orthodox Marxism. I found it interesting that in a 1982 book André Gunder Frank acknowledged that dependency theory is an unserviceable proposition and that one must now talk in terms of global accumulation. It is no surprise that the antagonists of the dependency theory in the 1960s and 1970s, such as Frank in South America and Samir Amin in Africa, have today been talking of global accumulation and world order models.

What does this mean for liberation theology? To my mind the aims of liberation theology are furthered more by dropping dependency analysis altogether.

FATHER MCGOVERN: I would respond to your question by asking another question of you. Either you are saying that we need a new simple causality theory that is not nuanced, and that is the modernization theory, or you are saying that the modernization theory is now nuanced and includes bargaining power, scales of dependency, and so forth. Basically you are saying that a lot of dependency theory can be absorbed in a modernization theory. I agree with Paul Sigmund that the other way around is also valid, that much of modernization theory can be absorbed and nuanced in dependency theory.

I do not see, I do not agree with, I am distrustful of a single causality thesis. If you are arguing for a nuanced modernization theory, I am arguing for a nuanced dependency theory, which includes some of the elements of the modernization theory. I think that you are talking about competing paradigms. Cardozo never said that he was inventing a new paradigm with a single causality; he was criticizing what was left out of the modernization paradigm. So we can talk about competing paradigms, and both have to be nuanced to be significant.

MR. SIGMUND: I don't deny that ultimately it comes to a choice of competing paradigms. What I am saying is that the crucial attractiveness of dependency theory lies precisely in the fact that causality can be demonstrated across a very clear nexus—

FATHER MCGOVERN: I agree that it had a lot of ideological power as a starting point, but I think that—

MR. SIGMUND: No, I am saying something else too. I am saying that if one talks of a nuanced dependency theory, this kind of a situation can be well accommodated within the neoclassical theories of international relations. Therefore, one does not require a nuanced dependency theory. Maybe you are saying that it comes to the same thing, but then why keep the label?

FATHER MCGOVERN: I am arguing simply for leaving open—not classifying or labeling—a dependency theory and saying the only kind that makes any sense is a single-causality version. Some people have oper-

137

ated on very simplistic modernization theses that have not included the social factors.

One of the things my paper is appealing to is an openness to many different variables. That is probably why we have disagreement on the importance of land reform. There is no way of creating a chemistry laboratory where we can eliminate some variables and put in some others and come up with the solution. I am simply making the case for what needs to be included in whatever paradigm we are talking about.

MR. NOVAK: One reason for being skeptical about the dependency theory is that one of its effects is that people begin thinking of themselves as victims. It is hard to become responsible and autonomous and creative if you think of yourself as a victim who can do nothing.

Therefore, it seems to me very important to make dependency theorists argue for every inch they claim. Whatever can be shown needs to be shown, but other people are in this until proved guilty. It is not healthy to think of oneself as a victim, particularly if the aim is to produce creative growth. In addition, many people who are discriminated against and are actually victims turn out to be the most economically successful.

The second point that I would like to make is that I believe that Father McGovern and many people interpret the concept of democratic capitalism too much in an Adam Smithian mode as free enterprise, free markets. That is not what democratic capitalism means. It means a political economy; it means many things that states must do. The Homestead Act in the United States was an act of the U.S. Congress. The land grant colleges were acts of the U.S. Congress. States need to do many things to empower people, and it is important to remember the political side of political economy.

The choice is not between Adam Smith and Marx. Democratic capitalism is something rather stronger on the side of the state than the invocation of Adam Smith tends to suggest in people's minds. Adam Smith himself allowed sixteen functions to the state.

Democratic capitalism is something different from the mixed economy, but the concept does imply political economy, a clear role for the state, also in economic matters. The Constitution of the United States talks about promoting the general welfare, and so on.

The last point that I would like to make is that when I speak about institutions, the institutions I have in mind are those precisely at the bottom of the ladder. I do believe that wealth begins from below. That is the democratic capitalist idea—send me your tired, your poor, your huddled masses yearning to breathe free—on the great symbol of liberation theology, the Statue of Liberty.

What strikes me on my visits to Latin America is how difficult it seems to be for people at the bottom of the ladder to have any institution equivalent to the American savings and loan institutions or the farmers' credit bureau, which specialize in small loans to previously unknown people—loans up to $5,000 or $10,000, say, so that a fellow in a village can have credit to buy a truck to bring the produce of his village to market and through those earnings pay off the loan. It is very hard—and Archbishop McGrath made this point very clear last year from Panama—for poor people in Latin America to get credit, but credit is the lifeblood of autonomy and independence. Unless you have institutions that specialize in empowering people at the bottom to become economic activists, you don't get capitalism at the grass roots, and you don't empower independent citizens who become the basis for democracy. Citizens who have a certain independence vis-à-vis the state become the best bastions against the state and the real resource of democracy.

When I talk about institutions, I don't mean only free markets, I mean credit institutions. In Germany, for example, it is extremely difficult to start a corporation. It takes a long time, and the state loads on so many obligations toward employees that an entrepreneur must think twice about doing it. We don't see small business formation in Europe, and we do not see it in Latin America, but we ought to.

Finally, several people have said that in the next few years multinationals will probably be employing fewer people in Latin America rather than more. It is quite clear that even with land reform, Latin Americans will never be able to live on the land. There are not enough jobs in agriculture, especially under modern means of production, even on small farms. Yet people already born, who are below the age of fifteen, will be coming into the labor market every year from now until the end of the century, and they number between 60 and 70 million. Apart from unemployment and underemployment in Latin America, 60 million new people are coming into the job market. If multinationals are not going to hire them, if the state cannot hire any more than it has, if agriculture cannot absorb any more, there is only one solution: millions of small businesses—10 or 20 million small businesses. And in Latin America the formation of small business is very, very difficult. I wish that the base communities in Latin America would become sources of economic enterprise and empower people. That is the kind of institution that I had in mind.

JAMES THORNBLADE, Bank of Boston: I find myself in the curious position of being by training a macroeconomist, doing arms-length macrocountry risk analysis in a bank that is stingy about staff resources, so that I am forced to range very widely and very superficially over Latin America and Asia, but there may be a certain advantage in having a broad comparative perspective. That is why I find the introduction of the Asian experience into what has essentially been a discussion in a Latin American context very useful.

I find myself increasingly drawn toward a microsolution: the building up of grass-roots credit associations and microenterprises in the context of base communities in spiritual growth. That is my ending point.

I second the observation of others that Father McGovern's paper is an excellent and a balanced summary of an area that I know relatively little about. But he said that we can find confirmation for the dependency, the sensitivity, the vulnerability of the periphery to the policies and the business cycles in the center in the language in the IMF and World Bank annual reports. I would take issue with that. This leads very nicely into some wild theories and hypotheses about governmental legitimacy in Latin America, which leads me to my point about building from the base communities.

I often quote from speeches by de Larosière. In a speech in February 1984, he argues that the debt crisis, which was prompted by external shocks like higher oil prices and high U.S. interest rates, had very uneven effects on third world countries. Some countries suffered a more severe debt crisis than others because their internal policies had made them more vulnerable.

What I find strikingly missing from the discussion in the past three days is that Latin America has had—even in Chile, although the Pinochet government reacted strongly against it—a history of inflation in orders of magnitude more severe and persistent than other parts of the world. My thesis is that this inflation is symptomatic of a fundamental problem of internal mismanagement. It follows along the classic IMF lines—inability to make tough decisions between guns and butter, between more guns and butter and higher taxes, which leaves the Ministry of Finance to turn to the Central Bank to print more money.

Chile broke that nonvirtuous circle under the current regime, but that has been the history in Latin America. The symptom of it is a long period of much greater inflation than in most other countries in the world.

Some Asian countries had similar experiences. The Chinese had a traumatic experience of inflation on the mainland that determined them, when they arrived in Taiwan, never to let that happen again. The Koreans were slipping in that direction by 1980, as inflation began to move up into double digits, and they reacted strongly and vigorously.

The United States was moving in the same direction in the late 1970s. Many people will tell me not to preach monetary and fiscal morality when we have this severe fiscal problem in the United States.

The important difference is that we have the Federal Reserve system, which is independent of the fiscal authorities. It has pursued a tight money policy since 1979, which has been a fundamental factor in reducing the rate of inflation. Latin America, however, has consistently been unable to develop a monetary authority independent of the Ministry of Finance. That is a very important factor that has been left out.

What is missing from the paper, then, is that domestic monetary and fiscal management lays the groundwork for how vulnerable a country is to the shocks that come from the center, through higher interest rates, for example.

Why did Latin American governments—with the notable exception of Chile—find it difficult to make tough monetary and fiscal decisions? (Chile, by the way, is a fascinating and tragic country. When I have taught economic development, we have constantly gravitated toward Chile because it has been, to the misfortune of the populace, the laboratory for many economic experiments.) Why this inability to come to grips with monetary and fiscal orthodoxy, which has made certain countries much more vulnerable to external shocks than others? I think it is the lack of legitimacy of government, the lack of national identity, the lack of a sense of belonging to a nation-family. That is a problem in Latin America and less of a problem in Asia. Korea and Taiwan are ethnically much more homogeneous and have a sense of being one large family. Government therefore has greater leeway to make tough monetary and fiscal decisions.

The striking counterexample of that in Latin America is in Argentina during the period of Roberto Aleman. He was going in very much the right direction, but he was blown out of the water by the bankrupt policy of the military government, its inability even to fight a war, much less run an economy.

Aleman had some very good ideas about selling off the state sector to the private sector, breaking the monetary and fiscal spiral. His efforts were destroyed by the blatant illegitimacy of the government that emerged from the inability to prosecute the Malvinas war.

Finally, we do not have a national consensus on the legitimacy of the governments in Latin America. Carlos Fuentes said, "Leave us alone to work out our problems." He was critical of U.S. intervention in Central America, but he went further than many Latin American philosophers in admitting that they have a problem in working out their identity. That lack of national identity has been a fundamental reason for the difficulty of implementing trade-offs in government monetary and fiscal policy and hence for the high inflation.

Perhaps the way to go is to build from the bottom up. I am intrigued to learn more about base communities, to learn more about what Rabbi Klenicki talks so eloquently about: how we can, through wandering in the desert for a generation, renew ourselves, develop our own internal disciplines, and then use this greater sense of discipline and charity to develop collective, cooperative grass-roots economic associations.

This is getting back to the point that Michel Novak made so articulately. I was on the board of Oxfam America, which tends to take an angry, confrontational stance toward goverment authority, both in the United States and in the countries in which it works, but does have a strong element of grass-roots self-reliant development.

What I find so appealing about the Oxfam mode and that of my new extracurricular activity, IIDI, a little organization in Vienna, Virginia, is that they try to break bottlenecks at the local level: the credit bottleneck, the reluctance of the local banking system to extend credit to the small entrepreneur. The big question to keep in mind is, To what extent should money and support and technical assistance from the United States come into these organizations to encourage them to grow and to break bottlenecks? Is there a danger that we will corrupt and distort the goals of these excellent grass-roots organizations?

The Institute for International Development Incorporated (HDI) is an organization of evangelical Christian businessmen. The vision came from Alfred Whittaker, president of Bristol Meyers International. The idea was to supply capital or loans to a local board in a developing country that makes loans to small entrepreneurs, loans of $400 to $2,000 or somewhat more. The recipients of the loans are identified through local parishes, or some kind of association—in most cases, the evangelical Protestant church community.

The progress in developing this kind of credit reference through the Catholic churches has been slower, but it is developing in the Philippines through the charismatic Catholic churches. One of the most successful programs has been in Indonesia, in Java—I assume in an entirely non-Christian context—so it is possible to transfer this into a non-Christian community.

The idea, again, is to identify responsible potential entrepreneurs who will take $400 and not squander it on drink or easy living or a bank account in Miami but will create jobs. The donors have generally been individual American businessmen giving $500 to $1,000. That money is lent to a family in the Dominican Republic, for example, and that loan will create two or three jobs.

Some 35 percent of this revolving loan fund comes from AID money. I would like to see IIDI get away from AID money, but it is an important factor still. Fairly quickly the income from the interest on these loans is plowed back into the local fund, which is spun off. It becomes independent. Six to eight independent local associations now no longer need capital infusions from the United States.

The IIDI program also provides technical assistance: how to arrange books, how to do simple bookkeeping, how to arrange finances, how to prepare to become a borrower from the established banking system. The IIDI needs to begin to pull in the local banking system. Once skeptical local bankers understand that the loan repayment record of the organization has been very good, they may begin to support the program.

I am very intrigued by the potential for this kind of activity to grow out of base communities, and in which there is an important spiritual context. Again, the Dunn and Bradstreet effect here is to identify responsible entrepreneurs who are committed to creating jobs for persons in their local community. These people will often be identified in the context of a religious community. I find this very exciting. I have gone essentially from a macrocountry risk analysis perspective to what may be part of the paradigm we are seeking for Latin America.

The question for us to ponder is, What kind of support should we offer to these organizations without steamrolling over them and destroying their unique grass-roots nature?

DAVID BECKMAN, World Bank: I would like to start by recommending a book and also recommend a program of work that is along the lines of this discussion. The book is the *World Development Report* of the World Bank. This year's *World Development Report* is entirely about developing country debt, capital flows, and the development crisis. It is extremely comprehensive and includes a wealth of data, so that whatever you set out to prove, you can find some data to help you along the way. Most of the report is about reforms that developing countries, especially heavily indebted countries, need to adopt to encourage and reaccelerate growth and regain credit worthiness. By and large, those are market-oriented, efficiency-oriented reforms.

I was struck by the fact that the report also gives great prominence to the policies of the industrial countries, which have made an extremely difficult situation for virtually all developing countries, even the best-managed. It argues, as Hugo Assmann argued yesterday, that a continuation of the past few years in the management of the debt crisis will not work. Even if there is not another recession, simply going along as we have been going the past few years will not work. Perhaps the crucial change that is needed is better economic management in the industrial countries: policies to foster more rapid growth than we have seen in all except this past year, policies to lower interest rates, policies to reduce the fiscal and trade deficits of the United States, and policies to encourage capital flows to developing countries, including increased official flows, both nonconcessional—that is, lending—and concessional.

The report argues strongly that dependency is still a factor in the life of the developing countries. It argues the need for negotiations, although the kinds of policies it advocates are not debt forgiveness or a debt moratorium but rather policies that someone like Michael Novak would find congenial.

The program of work that I would like to suggest, especially for those of us who are U.S. conservatives, is a program of fresh thinking along conservative lines about the problems of third world development and poverty. Around this table is assembled a very extraordinary gathering. Many of us are U.S. conservatives, but probably a disproportioinate number are conservatives who agree, as Peter Berger does, that God is on the side of the poor, and we somehow want to be there too. Part of the program of work, then, is to do the kind of thinking that Michael Novak was talking about or the kind of experimentation that the IIDI represents, that is, thinking and demonstration that show how capitalists or democratic capitalist policies can assist in the reduction of misery and poverty in the developing countries.

Perhaps more important for the credibility of U.S. conservatives who are concerned about third world poverty is the need for fresh thinking and higher priority political action on U.S. and other industrial country policies—the policy changes that are almost certainly necessary for a successful resolution of the debt crisis and to create an international environment in which the developing countries can make progress against poverty.

JAMES WEAVER, Department of Economics, American University: I want to echo those people who appreciate what Arthur McGovern has done today. Although I was an early adherent of dependency theory, I have come to reject it, but it is important to take it seriously, because it grew out of a concrete reality. Dependency theory did not just emerge out of someone's head. It grew out of the experience of the Great Depression and the fact that laissez-faire and free market solutions had failed. Import-substituting industrialization was an attempt to deal with the reality that Latin America had been depressed for over a decade and was in serious trouble with its free-trade, free-market orientation.

Before people rush too enthusiastically into free-market solutions, they ought to look at Chile under Pinochet. No one who advocates free market ever finds a test case that falsifies his model, because the country always did something wrong: it was not really a free-market test, because, say, they pegged the peso to the dollar. There has never been a falsification that any free-market economist would accept. Nevertheless, there is a great deal to be learned from dependency theory and its critique of free-market solutions.

My third point concerns the question of a new paradigm. I agree with Peter Berger that a new paradigm will be capitalist, but it certainly will not be laissez-faire or free-trade capitalist. It will be much more along the East Asian line, requiring an enormous role for the state. It will also require redistribution, certainly in some of the Latin American countries where the income distribution and the wealth distribution are so skewed.

I agree with Mr. Fontaine, however, that it will probably not require land reform. Cries for land reform keep everybody nervous but never get implemented. If they are implemented, they fail, as in Vietnam, where the United States sponsored land reform, or the Dominican Republic.

We do need redistribution, but land reform is not the answer. We need to be creative in thinking of alternatives to land reform that would redistribute wealth and power.

My fourth point is that liberation theology has a great deal to offer in the search for a new paradigm. No development economics book that I know of, including my own, deals with religion at all. Some of the early ones used to talk about Weber and Tawney and capitalism and development and Protestantism, but now none of them deal with religion. Religion has been excluded from development economics for the past twenty years, despite the enormous impact of Islam and liberation theologians and people allied with the Catholic church in Latin America in much of the world.

Liberation theology can contribute a great deal to our thinking about structuring a society and a world economy, in which, as David Beckman said, we agree that God is on the side of the poor and that we need to be there too. I appreciate your efforts, and I hope that we will take many of your points very seriously.

JOHN LANGAN, Woodstock Theological Center: The tone of these remarks will reflect the fact that I am a philosopher and not an economist or a practitioner. Partly because I am a philosopher, I have experienced some frustration at certain phases of the conversation so far. I would begin by putting a few questions on the table—questions that come partly from the conference title and partly out of the last part of Father McGovern's paper.

To what extent can liberation theology accept liberal institutions? Hugo Assmann's response yesterday was rather encouraging, although he speaks more about democracy than about strictly liberal institutions.

But liberal institutions are a particular concern to American citizens as we look at Latin America, and there are certain ambiguities in the notion of democracy that I will get to in a minute.

Second, to what extent can a liberal society respond effectively to liberationists' concerns—to the concern of the poor, to national feeling, to the national-identity-building aspects of the liberationist movement? This gets us back to the problem of those societies that had an impressive façade of liberal institutions that did not seem to work very effectively to improve the lot of the poor or to generate a sense of widespread participation and satisfaction.

Related to that is a third question: To what extent can a program of liberal institutions draw on genuine popular support in Latin America? That is a question of persuasion and an articulation of some of these things in a way that makes sense for a Latin American public.

Fourth, what kind of population are we looking for in successful development? I detect a number of divergent emphases here. One is that we should have a relatively patient population that will understand that quick results are not to be expected. Perhaps the willingness of the populations of East Asia to provide cheap labor and so on is helpful here or is being recommended.

Or do we need an independent and productive peasantry to provide a solid agricultural base for development? Or do we need primarily an educated working force, as seems to be implied by some of Peter Berger's remarks? We need more clarity about what kind of answer we are prepared to give to that question.

Participation and democracy are important values and terms that are used in many senses. In addition to the two senses that Tony Downs mentioned, another lurks in the background, partly because of its use in antidemocratic movements. That is the notion of mobilized population, in which people participate, but in a spirit that is fundamentally inimical to the development of liberal institutions.

This is one of those shadows that bother North Americans looking at Latin American appeals for greater democratization and participation. Does this really mean something like active local groups, or does it mean something approaching a totalitarian party? That has to be recognized as a continuing source of anxiety in North American perceptions.

As we look at liberation theology from the north, one of the things we must appreciate is that we are dealing with something that has mythic power, that articulates the situation of large numbers of people in a way they find convincing. We may find it unsatisfactory, because it does not respond to our consciousness, and we may find it unsatisfactory also because it seems to lead in a policy direction we think will be counterproductive in the long run, but we have to recognize the great

146

power of the scheme and the fact that it has both a grass-roots aspect and a very sophisticated interface with traditional Catholic theology or, more broadly, Christian theology. While the conversation is moving very much in a pragmatist, piecemeal direction, what I call the mythic and popular dimension of liberation theology is both an important resource and a potential stumbling block for this kind of micro-approach.

When we talk about solutions, there is a tension between people who are recommending, as Jim Weaver just did, something like a national economic strategy with an active role for the state and those recommending something that is much more populist and locally based. The discussion over the past couple of days has taken us beyond broad ideological categories, although the conference was originally conceived in those categories. Part of what strikes me as a noneconomist is the sense that whether proposed solutions call for active state involvement or much more of a laissez-faire approach, it helps to be smart. The programs that work do so regardless of their ideological labeling. Of course, once one says that, one has not said anything very helpful.

We are moving away from the grand ideological schemes to the more pragmatic. For me as a philosopher that is something of a source of pain, but as a participant in public policy discussions, I think that it is a gain.

The summary of the conversation so far that comes to me is that the North American line now is to plead with people coming at the problem from a liberationist perspective not to foreclose certain capitalist and decentralized options in the name of a big, socialist centralized solution. That gets a response from certain experiential elements in Latin America: the grass-roots orientation and the increasing skepticism about the actual record of socialism and the possibilities of implementing any broad socialist program in the current context.

If we as North Americans urge a more pragmatic view on Latin Americans, we must correspondingly take a more pragmatic view ourselves, both of a range of social experimentation and of things that may not look attractive or plausible from our perspective. We ought to avoid a kind of reflex support for movements or positions that simply present themselves as anti-Marxist or for proponents of capitalism whose interests may be damaged by particular policy shifts within these countries.

NICK EBERSTADT, Harvard University: I would like to elaborate on a couple of points made by Michael Novak, Ashley Tellis, Arturo Fontaine, and Jim Thornblade. These remarks concern three concepts: dependence, development, and poverty.

It is quite clear to all of us that we live in a world interconnected by flows of finance, by flows of money, by flows of trade, and by political

147

relations. Whether one calls that a dependent world or not depends very much on one's attitude. Indeed, I would argue that the notion of dependence is very much a state of mind—perhaps also a self-fulfilling state of mind.

Look at perhaps the principal demon in the demonology of dependence, the United States. A fairly good argument can be made that the United States is quite dependent on the rest of the world. The U.S. dollar, for example, is used as the principal denominator of international trade. What this means, of course, is that the United States cannot control its own money supply. A growth in world trade or a boom in the world economy will create an additional demand for dollars. This will have consequences for inflation at home and consequences for the U.S. balance-of-payments deficits. Similarly, European countries, especially those that seem to be having the most difficulty managing their own affairs, frequently talk about their dependence on the rest of the world, even though by objective measures they are clearly in a more powerful position than many of the weaker countries.

The world economy presents opportunities and potential risks for all that choose to participate in it. Nothing more than potential opportunities is guaranteed, nothing more than potential risks is threatened, and learning to make use of the world economy in such a way as to minimize the dangers for national populations is one of the principal things that a government can learn.

It seems to me to be instructive to look at the difference in the ways that East Asian small economies and the Latin American economies reacted to the oil shock of 1974. Of course, this political extraction was caused by forces to some extent beyond the control of actors outside OPEC. Nonetheless, it was a serious economic extraction from both the East Asian and the Latin American nations.

In the East Asian nations, the adjustment experiences were slightly different from one country to the next. Nonetheless, it was generally resolved that there would be a deflationary policy. The exchange rates were devalued, and there was an attempt to resolve the balance-of-trade deficit. There was a temporary contraction in some of those economies, but then the fundamental path for sound economic growth and competitiveness in the world economy was restored.

In Latin America, by contrast, there was an extreme reluctance to make the devaluations that would have been necessary to make exports more competitive. Borrowings were used largely to finance continued consumption at unsustainable levels, and the beginnings of what we have come to see as the debt crisis were in some significant sense already set.

If we wish to talk about dependence, the primary case we should look at in Latin America is Argentina. Here we have an example in which the fault does not seem to lie in the stars.

Until 1914 Argentina was a nation whose per capita income rivaled that of the United States. It was a magnet for migrants, much as the United States and Canada were—migrants from developed nations. The fact that Argentina was a developed nation in 1914 and is now considered a third world nation should give us pause and make us think about what precisely is encompassed in this dependence we are talking about.

A second set of points concerns development.

MR. NOVAK: May I interrupt? I saw figures recently; as late as 1939 Argentina was ranked seventh in the world and is now seventy-seventh.

MR. EBERSTADT: In 1914 Australia, Argentina, and the United States were the three highest countries in per capita income. Per capita income, of course, is often a misleading figure.

Let's talk about development for a second. What does development mean?

I do not presume to give a comprehensive definition, but I would like to give a very biased one. I think that development means the extension of human choice. And the extension of human choice means not only the alleviation of material poverty but also the extension of social and political liberties.

Father McGovern was talking a while ago about the richest national resource in Chile, by which he was referring to copper. I would argue instead that the richest national resource not only in Chile but in other countries is its human beings. It is necessary to concentrate on what can be done to maximize the ability of human beings to extend their choices. In this regard, much of the discussion of democracy we have had has troubled me.

Democracy seems to me to be a somewhat Orwellian word. I don't mean by that *1984:* I mean Orwell's politics of the English language. It is a word used by those who like it to mean whatever they wish it to mean.

If we were to talk about something that may be more fundamentally related to development and extending human choice, we would talk about two things. We would talk first about property rights and second about something we have not mentioned at all—the rule of law.

The rule of law seems to me to be extraordinarily important for the poor. The rule of law does not matter for the *caudillos,* who have the power of the state. *Caudillos*—strong people, rich people—can often do as they please. Soldiers in Africa can do as they please. The rule of law gives poor and unprotected people an equality in society that they are otherwise not guaranteed. The rule of law seems to me to be very important in any concept of development.

One of the things that generally seems lacking to me, in my admittedly very limited knowledge of Latin America, is the concept of the rule of law as it pertains to individual rights. We hear so much about corporate rights, about the rights of interest groups, and so very little about the rights of individuals. I wonder whether this has something to do with the manifestations of development we see in Latin America.

Finally, a few words about poverty. I have spent more time than I would care to bore you with delving into statistics of poverty in various areas of the low-income world. A number of the measures we seem to be very comfortable in using are virtually useless.

Principal among these is the notion of income distribution as it is currently used. Income distribution in contemporary economic literature refers to a dispersion usually taken at a point in time from a survey and usually measured by a gini-coefficient, a technical measure of dispersion. This is a very flawed measure, for a number of reasons.

The first is simply the problem of measuring incomes, especially for poor people. National surveys or limited sample surveys do not do a good job of it in rich countries and do an even less adequate job in poor ones.

The second is the question of the change in mortality rates. Clearly, every family likes to see its children survive, and the families that have the most difficulty in guaranteeing the gift of life to their children are the poorest ones. In any successful health revolution, the poor will benefit most. More will survive in poor families. This will make it seem as if inequality has increased, even though by any human measure, the well-being of the society has improved.

Third is the question of prices. To get some accurate measurement of income distribution, we must examine the prices facing different economic strata in any given location.

Finally, there is the question of lifetime incomes. Ideally one would wish to measure not transitory blips and dips but the sort of earning power one can command over the course of a lifetime. The problem is that a doctor who is still in graduate school can appear to be making very much less money than a busboy even though, over the course of their lives, their earnings streams are entirely opposite from that initial impression.

The whole problem of using income distribution is profound. I am much more comfortable with using differences in measures of mortality simply because, first of all, the meaning is intuitively clear and, second, it is very easy to tell whether someone is alive or dead.

If one were to look for meaningful differences in life chances between poor people in poor societies or poor nations and more affluent ones, one should look first toward life expectancy and mortality, not income distribution.

MR. NOVAK: P. T. Bauer makes the comment that it is an absurdity of statistics that per capita income goes up when a new cow is born and goes down when a new child is born. It is ridiculous, but that is the way the figures come out.

PETER SKERRY, Brookings Institution: I want to make a few comments that echo what Father Langan raised a few moments ago, although I might put a bit more of an edge on mine and express a bit more frustration and confusion. My comments have to do with the notions of participation and democracy that have been floated about the table in the past couple of days and what seems to me a somewhat overeager attempt to find something worthy of salvage in liberation theology.

Professor Sigmund, for example, suggested that Catholicism was an indigenous source of strength for liberation theology. That leaves me a bit confused because I understood Father Assmann as rejecting the institutional church and the cultural heritage of Catholicism as the source of liberation theology.

Perhaps you could speak to that a bit later. That is just one of the kinds of confusion I have been suffering from the past few days.

My problem with the notion of democratization or redemocratization is the assumption that seems to be made more often than not that this is the one new direction being reemphasized in liberation theology these days. I am not a specialist in this area, but I have no concrete sense of what the institutional forms are that give it any grounding in reality. I am simply not convinced that because a group of intellectuals declare an interest in democratic or grass-roots participation, it happens. Indeed, we have many examples where precisely the opposite occurs.

I am reminded of my college days in the heady 1960s when, at every demonstration around Boston, there seemed to be something called the Worker-Student Alliance. The Worker-Student Alliance generally consisted of about a dozen students and one worker, who turned out to be a student who had dropped out of school and was a janitor in the gymnasium.

I am very uneasy when intellectuals start talking about grass-roots participation in that way. Even if those forms do exist—and I could be instructed about where they exist—I would be tempted to say, so what?

There is a problem here of the kinds of manipulation that can go on when intellectuals and politically oriented elites go to poor people and try to find out what they are about and try to speak to their needs.

The possibilities for manipulation are endless. In our own society and in our own politics in the past ten years, it seems quite clear to me that the notion of participation—look what has happened in the Democratic party—is really an ideology for certain activist-oriented articulate individuals who have been able to maneuver themselves into positions of power and prominence and have excluded other elements. That may be good or bad, but I think something significant has happened there. Again, I am made uneasy by what is meant by these terms "democratization" and "participation."

Finally, I would make what to me is an obvious point. There is a certain hubris about the table about social institutions.

Suppose that social formations, grass-roots organizations, of this kind do exist and that there is an organic tie between liberation theologians and their political organs in these organizations. The problem with social institutions is that their functions are frequently ambiguous and conflicting. I am reminded of the situation of the Black slave family in the antebellum south. Frequently, the formation of strong family units was fostered by slave owners, because it was a means of social control—a means of keeping Black male slaves in line. It is also true that where strong families existed among Black slaves, they were a source of social and cultural support. That is just one example where the ambiguity of social functions of institutions is overwhelming.

The same could be said of political parties. Political parties can vent and can channel and articulate the needs of grass-roots elements, but they can also be used to manipulate those elements. It is just this sense of the ambiguity of social institutions—particularly in the context of Latin America, with its extremes of wealth and power—that I feel has been lacking in the effort to identify the new and, to some people here, reassuring trends in liberation theology.

BARRY LEVINE, Florida International University: What I want to do, in a very delicate way, is to put Father McGovern on the spot and challenge some things. I want to challenge his dependence on dependency theory.

In your response to Ashley Tellis, you said that each of these theories is to some extent accommodating the other. I think we have to choose; if ultimately they both say the same thing, we have to choose by the consequences of how they are presented.

As a sociologist, I spend a lot of time studying stratification, both within a society and among societies. I have come to the strange conclusion that stratification just means inequality. I have also come to the conclusion that having an unequal status is not the same as being victimized. Often the "victims" exploit the supposed victimizers.

In fact, I wrote a book—*A Picaresque Tale of Emigration and Return*—about a Puerto Rican, Benjy Lopez, who went to New York and never once thought of himself as a victim. He always thought that he was getting away with something. I think that can also apply to nations.

My problem with dependency theory is that it is victimology. It is a kind of ¡*ay bendito*!, to use the Puerto Rican phrase. "Oh, my God. Things are the way they are." It seems to imply resignation and determinism. It takes history as if it not only happened but had to happen as it did. That creates the same problem the ethicist has when he says he is a Marxian ethicist—he believes in determinism, but he is somehow going to come up with a set of ethics.

The question we must come to terms with is, What is the implication of believing in dependency theory? It is not simply—and this is a challenge to Mr. Glade—that dependency theory is the result of certain conditions. The belief in dependency creates certain conditions in turn.

Liberal modernization theory incorporates many of the dependency concepts, and dependency theory incorporates many of the liberal modernization concepts, and I have to choose. My gut reaction is that I would choose one that would promote the belief in choice, only because I would hope that people would try to actualize that possibility.

FRED TURNER, Department of Political Science, University of Connecticut: The great synthesizers are sometimes in error because they believe their sources. They are great because they are broad-minded and synthetic. But other synthesizers fall prey to a typical sort of error. One of the few books that remains magisterial in comparative politics is Sam Huntington's *Study of Political Institutions*. Yet Huntington is wrong on Cuba and wrong on Bolivia because he believed the Yankee sources that he read in English on those countries. It is an all-encompassing book, worldwide; but he cannot be right on every country.

Similarly, Seymour Martin Lipset, before recent years one of our greatest synthesizers, was wrong in *Political Man* on Peron because he believed Gino Germani—his colleague then and later at Harvard—who was wrong because of his ideology and his party affiliations. Germani convinced Lipset of one interpretation, and that chapter of *Political Man*—in both the revised and the original versions—is simply wrong.

What is the cure for this potential malady of great synthesizers? To the extent that a cure exists, it is prepublication distribution of the manuscript—get as many specialists who will disagree on Cuba or

Bolivia or Argentina or whatever to read the manuscript and comment on it before it is published.

I would like to comment very briefly on the Brazilian distribution material that Professor Sigmund has already commented on. The Gunder Frank material cited there is certainly controversial and, many scholars of Brazil would say, wrong. Father McGovern referred to World Bank data, which are generally far more reputable and accepted. There is also an excellent recent study in the *Journal of Economic Development and Cultural Change*. We need to compare the Frank material with what, as Sigmund says, is a very large literature; and it comes out as very one-sided.

There is a side of the situation in Brazil not in the other Latin American countries that we might look at for just a minute. Not only may Frank's numbers simply be wrong—and they are certainly very different from other people's numbers—but there is also the intellectually intriguing fact that the people in categories in different years are not the same people. That is, in survey research terms, we do not have a longitudinal panel study.

Alfred Stepan, when he was a graduate student at Columbia, wrote one of his best articles pointing out that in Brazil the people in the urban lower class were different people at different times, so that if rural migrants came in they might be better off; the people once in the lower class moving up might be better off. Even if the situation for the urban lower class is not greatly better—not as greatly worse as Frank suggests, but not greatly better—the situation of individual citizens in Brazil might be far better.

I would like to make a plea that the World Bank make the income distribution issue one of its focuses for the future. I have found the *World Development Report* very helpful. I assign it every year in class. Last year's issue was on population, and now we have another.

If the World Bank data are the best comparative data that we have, it could be very important for their economists and their statisticians to focus on the meanings of distribution, whether by mortality data or income distribution or a series of other measures. I would love to read an issue that had their expertise on this crucial issue.

Let me comment briefly on a couple of other matters. On land reform I come out quite differently from those around the table. I think it depends on what kind of land reform in what context. Some kinds of land reform, such as the family farm adequately supported by technology and by fertilizers, can be a crucial empowering mechanism, a vital means, along with education, to give more autonomy to the lower socioeconomic groups. They can, after all, have multiple crops. They do not have to have one crop on three acres, five acres, seven acres.

If this is true, as I think it is, what we may need to focus on for Latin America is the process by which effective land reform—not a formula assumed right for every country, but appropriate strategies for reform—can be engendered in each nation. After all, the United States is not and has not been antagonistic to land reform. Land reform was crucial in the Alliance for Progress. It has perhaps worked fairly in Vietnam. Perhaps we have not encouraged it in the right way, but there is a good deal of agreement that some reform is useful.

The Berger comments last night were especially apt because agrarian reform and education can empower people. They can give people increasing self-reliant control of their own economic situations and ultimately form the basis for a more informed and a more politically empowered population.

Therefore, I would like to conclude on the indigenous situation in South Korea that may have allowed early land reform. There were special circumstances in South Korea very different from those we find in most Latin American countries.

One was the class origin of the officer corps. Park Chung-Hee came from an impecunious rural family, essentially from the peasantry, as did a series of other senior officers in his age bracket. Saemaul Undong, the rural development program, might very well never have got started except for the concern among senior officers for the rural poor, which came, in no small part, from their private and familial experience.

Second, the South Korean experience is also different not only because of the historical civil war context, which was discussed last night, but because of the continuing threat from North Korea. The North Koreans have continued to tunnel under the demilitarized zone (DMZ); they continue to send commandos in rubber rafts on both sides of the South Korean peninsula. Several years ago their soldiers hacked to death two U.S. army officers at the DMZ. It is a threat that South Koreans naturally feel in a poignant way, not simply South Korean paranoia or government propaganda. At the bridges of Seoul, you would think you were in World War II. There are sandbags and machine gun emplacements on the bridges because Seoul is so close to the DMZ.

The threat is very evident, and that may be another reason for the emphasis on rural development strategies. Technically—but perhaps not so substantively—Professor Berger was right last night when he said that these were not government redistribution policies—they did not hand money over to the poor. But they were strategies that have built considerable support for the government by empowering the rural poor.

If we need to look at the indigenous causes for this sort of reform in

South Korea, perhaps we need to do exactly the same thing for each of the Latin American republics. It is in that context that I think the McGovern synthesis is especially important.

FATHER MCGOVERN: I have a few short comments. I have been happy to let the conversation flow; I think that worked well. I might start with the first two questions that John Langan proposed because they reflect the dual concern that I have. First, to what extent can liberation theology accept liberal institutions? That has been reflected in a number of comments.

If I were talking to liberation theologians or advocates of liberation theology, those are the concerns that I would raise. There is a risk, and I am not sure that they have taken sufficient account of the importance of political structures and not just economic structures.

I don't know how much to take on what Hugo Assmann said the other day about different currents and their emphasis on participation, but even someone like Leonardo Boff—who cites Jose Comblin, one of the most influential analysts used by liberation theologians—talks, in Brazil, not about revolution, not about socialism, but about Canada as a model of dependent development. I suspect that Cardoso is moving in that direction.

The other concern that I have is the second question: To what extent can a liberal society respond to the concerns of liberation theology? I agree with much that has been said about the danger of dependency theory as a victimology, as making people blame someone entirely outside. I responded, first of all, to the article in the *New York Times*. As a strategy for delegitimizing liberation theology and saying, "Don't take it seriously," the subheadlines were "Critics find it fundamentally naive" and, later in the article, "largely false." If we want to change liberation theologians in a church in Latin America, we cannot write them off that way. We have to say, "here is what we find is good and legitimate, but would you also consider this?" That was part of the emotional reaction that I had.

I think your concern goes both ways. There is a danger that participation and the lack of clear political identification can be used for manipulation; but I think if I were a Latin American I would say, "You guys do the same thing. You promise; you talk about democratic institutions; and you give us Guatemala and Chile. Then you walk away. Once you stop Communism, that's the end of your concern. You don't give us democracy. You don't encourage or support democracy."

I do a lot of counseling of married couples, and I try to get both sides to see that they are the problem instead of starting off by saying, "You are the problem." If I am talking to a Latin American liberation theologian, that is a perfectly legitimate approach. We want to get people to say, "Hey, it is our problem. Don't just blame someone else."

I would like to see people in the United States take the same attitude and say, "We are the problem, to some extent; and what can we do to make sure that we don't become a greater problem?" But the tendency is for us to say, "You are the problem."

I don't see that dependency is a phenomenon, and it is not just interdependency. The language that I would use now if I were redoing it, influenced by Moran, is "bargaining power."

The bargaining power is not equal. To use an analogy, I don't think the situation of ordinary workers was the same before they became members of a labor union. The bargaining power was entirely different, and the bargaining power is still not equal. Host countries have an increasing ability to get more bargaining power, but I don't think the bargaining power is equal.

Peter Berger said, "Socialism hasn't been able to lead to un-development or to worse development." The example you gave is one of capitalism in Argentina doing that. That was capitalism. They were not ruined by socialism. Granted, it may not be a very good form of capitalism. We agree on that.

On mortality, I don't think that is a sufficient norm. It struck me in Latin America that one simple change dramatically affects mortality. Simply having sewage disposal and potable water makes a dramatic change in mortality. Having simple drugs makes a dramatic change in mortality. Those are gains, but the people remain in every other way as poor as they were even though there is a dramatic decrease in mortality.

Finally, on choice, it is not just that we all agree on the same options. Some of the group have discarded the leftist, populist, tending-toward-socialism model and don't see it as a viable option.

Some of us who are with the dependency model see the possibility not of a Marxist totalitarian nation but of another model, though not necessarily the best model. I applaud Taiwan; I applaud Korea; but I don't rule out as bankrupt and impossible the other model. I appreciate the response to my paper; it is very helpful.

# Commentary

## Dean C. Curry

A major theme, perhaps the major theme, to emerge from our discussions on liberation theology and the liberal society has been the transformation of liberation theology from a more or less monolithic theological and socioeconomic paradigm into a pluralistic one encompassing a wide variety of assumptions as well as strategies.

From our vantage point as North Americans, committed to the validity—indeed the sanctity—of political and economic liberalism, the most encouraging note to be heard from the AEI Summer Institute was the assertion that Latin American theologies of liberation have now been denuded of their reliance upon Marxism and have become more concerned with democracy. Moreover, there is good reason to believe that dependency theory, as it has been articulated in recent years, has forsaken its sole focus on the dependency relationship itself (that is, the conscious exploitation of the periphery by the core or "the development of underdevelopment") and has been reformulated to take into account other variables—internal as well as external—to explain Latin American underdevelopment. In this sense, it has been asserted that dependency theory must now be seen as nuanced, a theory embracing a pluralism of understandings relative to poverty in Latin America.

It is within this context that the important question arises concerning the continued relevance of the dependency concept itself. It would seem that dependency theory, as it is now defined, sounds very much like the more traditional development theories of the North, at least in their acknowledgment of the variety of factors affecting development.

If a convergence of sorts has in fact occurred between dependency and more traditional North American interpretations of the causes of underdevelopment and the prerequisites of development, what is the continued utility of the dependency paradigm as a separate, distinct way of understanding the underdevelopment dynamic?

There is certainly no reason why the theologies of liberation must give up the dependency concept itself. In fact, one might want to argue that the concept has important symbolic status given the uniqueness of

158

the Latin American experience. Moreover, the evolution of the concept might be further cited as evidence of the growing maturity of liberation theology.

I find two dimensions of this "new" understanding of dependency, and by extension liberation theology, to be problematic, however. First, I would identify what might be called the Nicaraguan problem. The Sandinista regime is by any definition Marxist (leaving aside the issue of whether the regime is also Leninist). Marxism is the proclaimed ideology of the regime, and Marxist institutions are the chosen instruments of government. These facts are well known. So also is the reality of the support of the so-called "people's church"—a "church" fully committed to liberation theology—for the Sandinista regime. The point is clear: if Nicaragua is the laboratory for testing the assumptions and prescriptions of liberation theology (and dependency theory)—as many have proclaimed with great hope and anticipation—then there is good reason to be skeptical of the claim that liberation theology and the dependency paradigm represent a third way apart from democratic capitalism and Marxism. In short, the experience of Nicaragua as the grand experiment of liberation theology falsifies the third way thesis and goes a long way in casting doubt on the notion of a nuanced, pluralistic theology of liberation.

Nonetheless, Hugo Assmann as well as Arthur McGovern has persuasively argued that during the past decade there has been a growing disenchantment with Marxism and a growing appreciation of the internal factors affecting Latin American underdevelopment. It is here that my second concern arises. While the case for a nuanced understanding of dependency among Latin elites seems to be strong, the same cannot be said of those who are engaged in the popular debate in the United States, particularly in the American religious community. This point relates directly to the whole question of the continued utility of the dependency paradigm. For at the level of the popular debate in the United States (a debate that is not irrelevant to the actual formation of public policy as evidenced by the influence of the Maryknolls on Speaker of the House O'Neill), the dependency paradigm has become a conceptual magnet subsuming a specific set of ideological commitments, among them the inherent violence and brutality of U.S. foreign policy and ultimately, for the most radical, the illegitimacy of the American Proposition itself.

My point is simply that dependency theory has ideological uses beyond the relevance or irrelevance of its socioeconomic constructs. This may go a long way in addressing the question of why Latin American proponents of dependency theory and their North American counterparts are unwilling to let go of the paradigm. If this is indeed the case—and I believe a strong argument can be made for it—then the

159

integrity of liberation theology as a proclaimed theology of liberation must rightfully be called into question.

## Ashley J. Tellis

Arthur McGovern's paper, "Latin America, Dependency, and Liberation," represents an attempt to justify the liberation theologian's use of dependency analysis to demonstrate that the "link between economic development and foreign powers" in Latin America is exploitative. As part of this exercise, he surveys some of the permutations of dependency analysis and narrows the perspective to two archetypal forms represented by the "simplistic" formulation of André Gunder Frank and the "nuanced" formulation of Fernando Cardoso.

The tension between these formulations represents the crux of McGovern's justification. Given the choice between these two alternatives, he can easily reject the simplistic in favor of the nuanced form, because of its ability to accommodate a more complex reality. Thus, the aim of his paper, implicitly, is to salvage dependency analysis by demonstrating that at least one formulation of it is serviceable and, hence, that its use by liberation theologians can be justified.

My comments here address simply McGovern's crucial distinctions between the two formulations at an empirico-methodological level. I do not aim to develop either an all-encompassing theoretical and paradigmatic critique of dependency analysis, or even a comprehensive criticism of McGovern's paper. My comments have the limited yet important objective of demonstrating that McGovern's heuristic device of pitting a simplistic against a nuanced version is insufficient either to demonstrate the legitimacy of dependency analysis or to justify its use by liberation theology.

Prior to analyzing the two formulations, we must recognize that dependency analysis is essentially part of a renewed Marxism that seeks to "reestablish the tradition of economic structures and the structures of domination."[1] As such, it sustains the notion of "dependence" on an interrelated trio of core beliefs:

- Dependency is part of a historical process of the maturation of capitalism, whose motive force is "capital seeking profits."
- The consequence of this maturation has been the forced integration of the economies of developing countries into an inherently exploitative world capitalist system, wherein growth in the economies of the developed countries takes place at the expense of growth in the developing countries through various dependency mechanisms. Simul-

taneously, internal transformations within those countries make locally initiated change impossible.

• Economic growth in the developing countries is then possible only when ties of exploitation and dependency between them and the global capitalist system are severed, so that self-centered autonomous growth can take place.

These three elements unify the different formulations proposed by various dependency theorists. It is vital to recognize them prior to understanding McGovern's heuristic device.

The key strength of the simplistic formulation, as enunciated by Frank, is that it functions at the methodological level as an explanatory model employing a very clear line of causation that justifies a simple explanation with minimal qualifiers: the underdevelopment of the developing countries is a simple function of the growth of the developed countries. If such a proposition is true at the empirical level, the claim is indeed dramatic and worthy of consideration. For it diagnoses the wretched consequences of underdevelopment as a function of the technical character of the growth processes of the developed countries; hence, it assigns moral culpability as well. Thus, it is a clear and concise formulation because of the clarity of its line of causation and the empirical testability that that implies.

The crucial weakness of that formulation, however, is that it is empirically false. Dependency theorists do not usually operationalize their beliefs or specify empirical referents. Still, if their intuitions are expressed in the proposition "the greater the economic dependence, the more underdeveloped a country will be", the empirical evidence available falsifies this proposition.[2] McGovern concedes this point.

In contrast, the strength of the nuanced version that McGovern supports is clearly that it disallows the dramatic claims of the simplistic version and seeks to extend to other factors a role as well. In avoiding univariate terms of causation, which are no doubt methodologically attractive but have the disadvantage of obscuring the complexity of the reality they seek to explain, the nuanced version preempts the criticism that too much is based on a single explanatory variable—dependency. Thus, the nuanced version coincides with McGovern's skepticism "of theories which claim to offer *the* explanation of complex social situations."[3]

The weakness of this nuanced version is, paradoxically, a consequence of its strength. In trying to accommodate multiple variables in the formulation, the line of causation, which is crucial to giving the core beliefs of dependency their attractiveness, is blurred. Hence, the nuanced version succeeds only in suggesting that external links, *among other things,* affect the growth of developing countries—a bland formulation that contains nothing either new or unique. If such a formulation is admitted, then the central claim of dependency analysis, which lies in discovering a predatory line of causation of underdevelopment, is submerged among a plethora of factors—which, lacking any relative internal weights within the formulation, destroy the uniqueness of dependency analysis.

Hence, McGovern's heuristic device cannot succeed because it is locked into a circular trap: in order to function as a unique explanation, dependency analysis must assume the simplistic formulation—which is empirically false. To avoid empirical falsity, dependency analysis must lapse into a nuanced multivariate formulation—in which case it says nothing new. The debilitating problem with this approach, therefore, which McGovern does not clarify and which at any rate he cannot remedy, is that although dependency analysis developed as a criticism of the neoclassical theory of international economic relations and remains to date very radical *in its intentions,* it still subsists within the problematic realm of neoclassical theory. Hence, *any* systematization of dependency analysis in its nuanced forms will only produce a revised version of neoclassicism and a nonradical one at that.

Thus, the crisis of dependency analysis is not due merely to its paucity of empirical referents or to the inadequacy of its operational constructs but, more fundamentally, to its systemic character. It cannot be genuinely salvaged, despite McGovern's attempts, because it is trapped in methodological and intentional asymmetry. Its intention is to generate guilt in developed societies; its methodology fails to make its intended case.

McGovern's valiant attempts to salvage such a decaying apparatus are justifiable only on the premise that the crisis of dependency analysis is a crisis of theory related to some misspecification of the dependency paradigm and its domain assumptions. In that case, it could be resolved either by formulating or isolating a (new) theoretical perspective that is more congruent with its core beliefs. But the crisis of dependency analysis is not merely a crisis of theory, but rather a crisis of paradigm. Hence, it is necessary to reject not only the existing theoretical perspectives of dependency analysis but also the assumptions constituting the paradigm itself.

In conclusion, we may well deduce that the sanest alternative liberation theology could choose would be to examine successful cases of development, rather than to attempt yet another spurious rehabilitation of dependency analysis.

# Notes

1. Fernando Cardoso, "The Consumption of Dependency Theory in the U.S.," *Latin American Research Review,* vol. 12, no. 3, p. 10.

2. Two major studies examining this proposition find that the evidence does not support the contention. See Barbara Stallings, *Economic Dependency in Africa and Latin America* (Beverly Hills: Sage Professional Papers in Comparative Politics, 09-031); and Richard Vengroff, "Neo-Colonialism and Policy Outputs in Africa," *Comparative Political Studies,* vol. 8, no. 2, pp. 234-50.

3. McGovern, p.16.

# It Is Not Easy to Argue with Liberation Theologians

*Arturo Fontaine*

It is not easy to argue with liberation theologians on socioeconomic matters. Their claims are asserted forcefully, but it is not at all clear on what grounds those claims are based. The style of most classical Latin American liberation theology precludes a rational and cool analysis of socioeconomic matters as well as of their connection with the ethical questions at stake. Liberation theology is, of course, changing. I would like to show that no matter where liberation theologians go, they have to depart from their old style. "Socioeconomic matters" refer here to economic and social aspects, but mainly in relation to the ethical analysis of political and economic structures.

The main work I shall consider in this paper, *Nueva Conciencia de la Iglesia en América Latina,*[1] documents, analyzes, and provides commentary on the emergence of a new awareness in Latin America's church. Father Ronaldo Muñoz's investigation analyzes over 300 documents reflecting the views of a great variety of groups and representatives of Christians (bishops, conferences of bishops, local groups, and students) from Mexico to Chile, covering a period from 1965 (after the last council) to 1970. It was during this period that liberation theology established itself in Latin America. With great care and lucidity Father Muñoz unveiled what could be called the set of beliefs underlying the corpus of church documents that express this new awareness. Father Muñoz invites us to look at these documents as a "sign of the Spirit" (p. 175). He does not believe that "only in Antiquity or in the Middle Ages [did] the Church [have] Fathers and witnesses of our Faith."

The author, although clearly committed to this "new awareness" or new mentality, chooses the role of a rather detached witness who registers and organizes a body of beliefs for which he is not responsible. The narrator-commentator of this text about texts is trying hard to be objective. He is showing us Latin America's liberation theology as a "phenomenon" in action; he is documenting the beliefs that are inspiring a pastoral and political practice, not a set of theses discussed by academicians in the cold stone corridors of a theological seminary. Of course, we know that the author holds a doctoral degree in theology from a prestigious German university, that at the time the book was published (1973) he was a professor in the Faculty of Theology of the Catholic University of Chile, and that his book was printed with the explicit support of the Faculty of Theology of the Vatican University. There are two prefaces: one by Bernardio Piñera, former bishop of Temuco and now the secretary and spokesman for the Permanent Committee of Chilean Bishops and Bishop of La Serena, and the other one by Bernhard Walte, professor of theology at the University of Friburg. Both of them enthusiastically praise this work of theology. So much about the book itself.

I have chosen Father Muñoz's book as my main concern in this paper because it is, I think, the best source available on the beliefs that Christians committed to liberation theology do in fact hold and because it documents the appearance of liberation theology on our continent. I am not qualified to examine the theological assumptions of the book. I shall instead discuss only the difficulties that the discussion of the underlying socioeconomic assumptions must surmount. First, I shall summarize the main claims in the documents that Father Muñoz analyzes.

## The Tenets of Liberation Theology

Latin America is in an "inhuman situation," claim the authors of the documents. Insecurity, poverty, hunger, housing shortages, high infant mortality, ignorance, high unemployment, illiteracy, and alienation produced by the educational process itself are some of the indications of the nature of this inhuman situation. At the political level the masses "have little awareness of being an oppressed class." For them "democracy is often a mere word" (p. 47). Problems get worse under "military dictatorships." The "inhuman situation" is, then, identified with underdevelopment (p. 63 and ff.). In Latin America socioeconomic, political, and cultural structures "constitute the main cause of underdevelopment" (p. 67). In particular, the main cause for Latin America's present condition is the capitalist system (p. 68) because it "ignores the value of labor and doesn't respect the dignity of the worker. . . . The difference between what the worker produces and what he needs for his subsistence goes to the hands of the few" (p. 69). Capitalism betrays the content of Christianity (p. 111).

Local capitalism is closely linked to "class struggle at a global scale. . . . The international imperialism of money introduces in the world a true class struggle exploiting entire nations." The "developed

165

world—and particularly the United States—practices institutionalized violence in the underdeveloped world" (p. 84). This is done through national oligarchies. "Ideological imperialism" plays a key role here: "Our countries suffer under a cultural dependence on the United States and Europe which is another form of domination. . . . Educational problems and models imported from the United States and Europe also imply a form of cultural alienation" (p. 86). Latin America is in a situation of "institutionalized violence" because "our capitalist society . . . subordinates human rights to economic results" (p. 108). For example, there is violence against the poor "when he is unemployed, when Justice doesn't listen to him, when his children get sick because of a deficient diet" (p. 108). "We call this violence because it is not an inevitable reality, a problem with no technical solution, but the unjust result of a state of affairs maintained voluntarily" (p. 108).

Latin America is in "a situation of sin" rooted in "individual and collective selfishness, in lack of love, fraternity and solidarity" (p. 110). The values that predominate are "money, individual success, class selfishness, individualist property" (p. 111). In his commentary Father Muñoz interprets this "situation of sin" as expressing a belief in the "internal unity of socioeconomic and religious reality," a relation or unity that "makes possible—within the limits of the awareness with respect to the establishment's oppression of the majorities—a certain negative experience of God" (p. 117). The author suggests that here is implicit a "Christian conception of God . . . a God that is committed to society's concrete history, Who identifies Himself with man and in particular with the oppressed, and that—precisely because of this—is provoked personally by the established violence against the poor masses" (p. 118–19). "The revolutionary imperative," then, is the "fundamental option": what is "at stake is our own relation to God"—"in other words, the meaning or the frustration of our whole lives" (p. 119).

According to the documents "revolutionary violence emerges as a response to institutionalized violence" (p. 233). The documents do not recommend violence: their preference is for "active nonviolence." Experience, however, teaches people that it is not possible to expect that the privileged classes "will yield their position after a peaceful process of moral persuasion" (p. 235). Father Muñoz emphasizes the assertion of the documents that "the important thing in a revolution is not violence or nonviolence, but rather to bring it about with efficacy" (pp. 235–39).

What type of society do these revolutionaries hope for? They want "neither Western capitalism nor Russian collectivism" (p. 297). They believe that although any system is ambivalent "socialism is better suited for the service of men, [because] it accords better with the

Gospels" (p. 298). This socialism will entail "the socialization of the means of production, and of economic, political, and cultural power" (p. 299). It will be "popular," "democratic," "original," "nondogmatic," "nontotalitarian," and "nonbureaucratic." Father Muñoz adds that the documents do not describe in detail the structure of the Socialist society that these writers are advocating. The documents also affirm that there are two groups of clergymen: those who support the powers that be and those whose option is, in fact, in favor of a church that would serve the poor (p. 331).

**The Intellectual Sources of Liberation Theology.** The documents express what could be called a Socialist δοχα, a set of standard Socialist beliefs in Latin America. This web of beliefs constitutes "the mediation" through which the authors of the documents experience their understanding of a Christian revolutionary practice. Father Muñoz thinks that part of the analysis underlying the documents springs from the social sciences as well as from ethical and philosophical assumptions. These matters, therefore, do not belong to the realm of dogma. They have a different epistemological status: with respect to them it will never be possible to achieve a "religious certainty" (p. 79). My comments will deal, then, only with these "contingent" matters, a possibility that Father Muñoz's text itself opens up.

What are the intellectual sources of the documents? Father Muñoz's bibliography is brief. He quotes liberation theologians like Father Gustavo Gutiérrez and Hugo Assmann; sociologists of the theory of dependence school like Father Gonzalo Arroyo S.J., F. H. Cardoso, F. Weffort, and C. Furtado; and the philosopher J. Habermas whose interpretation of Marx seems to interest him. These are, more or less, the same sources of Father Gutiérrez's celebrated book *A Theology of Liberation*.[2]

The Peruvian theologian, in turn, when dealing with socioeconomic matters, refers the reader to Osvaldo Sunkel's well-known work *El Marco Histórico del Proceso de Desarrollo y Subdesarrollo,* first published in 1967 by ILPES in Santiago and reprinted in 1970 by Siglo Veintiuno Editores in Mexico. Another important reference for Father Gutiérrez is F. H. Cardoso and Enzo Faletto's *Dependencia y Desarrollo en América Latina,* first published in 1967, as well as Cardoso's critique of W. W. Rostow's theory in *Cuestiones de Sociología del Desarrollo en América Latina.* Theotonio Dos Santos's "La Crisis de la Teoría del Desarrollo y las Relaciones de Dependencia en América Latina," first published in *Boletín,* Santiago de Chile, in 1968, is another important work for Father Gutiérrez's book. The anthology *Sociología del Desarrollo* published in 1968 in Buenos Aires contains interesting

167

papers on these matters. Yet another work used in Father Gutiérrez's socioeconomic analysis is Celso Furtado's *Obstacles to Development in Latin America,* which was translated into English and published in 1970. He praises Father Gonzalo Arroyo's "good synthesis" of the theory of dependence published in *Mensaje,* October 1968. It is the same article—"Pensamiento Latinoamericano sobre Subdesarrollo y Dependencia Externa"—used by Father Ronaldo Muñoz.

The rise of Latin America's liberation theology was, to a great extent, the result of the pro-Socialist intellectual climate of the period. The political, social, and religious effects of this process of intellectual transmission were experienced very rapidly. As one reads Father Muñoz's synthesis of the documents, one has the feeling that bishops, clergymen, Christian students, and workers are discovering by themselves a neo-Marxist interpretation of history. But one should not forget that Marxism as a doctrine and an intellectual and political network has deep roots in Latin America's cultural life. The theory of dependence school was—and still is—so effective and popular partly because several of its tenets were already familiar through Marx's theory of class exploitation and Lenin's of imperialism. All of them are conspiracy theories of sorts or are at least able to capture the appeal that explanations based on a kind of conspiracy theory do seem to have. The theory of dependence school, then, gave to non-Marxist groups especially an aura of new scientific formulation to old Marxist ideas that had already been assumed in the 1920s by key intellectuals, journalists, trade union leaders, and Socialist politicians. The popularity of liberation theology exemplifies the power of ideas. The movement expresses and amplifies a deep cultural revolution that has taken place in Latin America.

Father Gutiérrez gives us valuable hints with respect to the origin of the "new awareness" that the documents express. Writing about the emergence of this new mentality, he says:

> In the process which has led to this posture, the Latin American Episcopal Council (CELAM) has played a decisive role. Even though when it began in 1955 it was something new among ecclesiastical structures of the time, its activity was confined to traditional models. The change occurred in 1963 under the orientation of Don Manuel Larraín, the Bishop of Talca, Chile. During his presidency there were created the various departments of CELAM, which assumed different pastoral areas. In these departments Bishops and experts collaborated closely. Beginning in 1966, while Dom Avelar Brandao was president, meetings were organized which produced statements—at the time quite surprising. These meetings likewise manifested an initial effort at reflection and commitment.

They were also an effective preparation for Medellín: vocations (Lima, 1966); education (in Catholic universities, Buga, 1967); missions (Melgar, 1968); social action (Itapoán, 1968); and the diaconate (Buenos Aires, 1968).[3]

According to Father Gutiérrez, the key change occurred under the orientation of the Bishop of Talca, Don Manuel Larraín, with the creation of departments where "bishops and experts collaborated closely." The jargon of sociologists supporting the theory of dependence incorporated in the documents illustrates the process of intellectual transmission from "the experts" to the clergymen that took place in the Latin American church. The "mediation" was given by the experts. Eventually, their language, diagnosis, and projects were assumed by the authors of the documents as part of their vision of Christian duties in Latin America.

One of the most impressive traits of Father Muñoz's book is the passionate and anxious search for explanations of and solutions to poverty that comes across as one moves along his categorical, blunt, and bold statements. I cannot agree more that the question of extreme poverty in Latin America is urgent from an ethical point of view. The persuasive way in which Father Muñoz presents this moral, economic, and political challenge will help to deepen our awareness of our responsibilities. The Marxist or neo-Marxist approach and the theory of dependence offer explanations and—if not a detailed project—at least a guide for action. What seems to me the most disturbing factor in this whole debate is that so far intellectuals who believe in the virtues of democracy and open markets have shown an incapacity to communicate their message and establish a fruitful discussion. This seems to be particularly disappointing given the fact that the classical liberal tradition offers an institutional explanation of poverty and solution to it. Liberation theology and liberals share a common view in this sense. And I see a promise of a mutual understanding that might spring from this basic shared intuition.

### The Difficulties of the Discussion

Two years after the publication of *A Theology of Liberation* in Lima and the same year of the publication of Hugo Assmann's *Teología desde la Praxis de la Liberación* in Salamanca and Father Muñoz' book in Santiago, Joseph Ramos published in *Estudios Sociales* an important essay criticizing the economic assumptions of Father Gutiérrez's liberation theology.[4] Since then he has written several papers on this subject.[5] The last and most comprehensive one, "Teología de la Liberación," was published in *Estudios Públicos* in 1983 and deals with the theories of Father Gutiérrez, Dr. Assmann, and Father Muñoz.[6] Unfortunately, Mr. Ramos's work has not received the attention it deserves in our cultural climate. This is rather surprising, especially given the fact that Mr. Ramos is a Christian economist who supports the theological premises of liberation theology but disagrees with the economic premises and remedies favored by these theologians. And this is not an exception. During the years ILPES in Santiago was publishing works crucial for liberation theology, the Faculty of Economics and Business of the Catholic University (where Father Muñoz and Dr. Assmann used to teach on the Faculty of Theology) was an important center of neoclassical economics in Latin America, with a significant number of professors who had studied at the University of Chicago. There was no contact among these three worlds: the world of the economists, the sociologists, and the theologians, most of whom were linked to the same Roman Catholic university. I see that lack of interdisciplinary academic connection at this level in Chile as a sign of the end of that sort of political debate that strengthens democratic institutions without establishing uniformity.

The debate on socioeconomic assumptions of liberation theology has been difficult because philosophical theories and meditations on economic systems have been weak and poor in general in Latin America. Theologians are mainly interested in a moral problem that has to do with the nature and purpose of economic systems. Their criticisms of the ethical values of capitalism, for instance, cannot be answered on purely economic grounds. By and large, philosophers have been unable to create an atmosphere of intellectual discussion that would help to deal with questions of values and morals in relation to socioeconomic institutions. No tools have been offered by Latin American philosophers to focus on such interdisciplinary problems.

On the other hand, the key criticisms of the economic tenets of liberation theology have been these: first, that the status quo that advocates have identified with capitalism is not a good example of the free market system and that therefore criticisms of the prevailing situation do not imply a criticism of capitalism itself; second, that the question of poverty can be addressed better through a free market system complemented by a basic socioeconomic network; third, that the theory of dependence is of little value when one has to face the question of strategies of development; and fourth, that the interventionist prevailing system did in fact offer, at least until the most recent economic crisis, quite significant levels of growth.

A typical ambiguity of the language appears in their notion of "the poor." The poor in fact do not share the same political views. In elections some of them vote for socialism, others for capitalism or neocapitalism. This plurality is seldom recognized except in terms of an "alienation" of a segment of the "exploited class." Therefore, the "true" choice of the people is known a priori by a privileged class: the intellectuals, the clergymen, and the politicians who see themselves as the true representatives of the interests of the poor. No matter what the actual poor of the country say, they know better. And if some intellectuals, clergymen, and politicians have a different view, they are seen as allies of the "exploiters." This paternalism is clearly reminiscent of the sort of epistemological bounds characteristic of that mentality that Milosz called "the captive mind."

Have the views of liberation theologians changed much over the years? Probably their assessment of "bourgeois democracy" is, in general, more positive after the experience of authoritarian regimes where many key "formal rights" have been suppressed or weakened considerably. But the opinions of liberation theologians on socioeconomic matters do not seem to have evolved very far. Father Muñoz, for example, in a book published last year in Chile shortly after Cardinal Ratzinger's famous documents said:

> We have much to learn from Marxism to understand what John Paul II calls the "mechanism" of the capitalist society. What are these mechanisms and how is it that they "produce rich people who are always richer at the expense of the poor who are always poorer"? Then, for us the Christians for whom the misery of the masses of our continent and of our country represent an unavoidable and radical challenge that makes us question the meaning of our lives, to us Christians who have had the opportunity to recognize the rostrum of Christ in these multitudes of impoverished and repressed brothers, to us Marxism has a lot to teach us, in so far as it offers us instruments to understand better the mechanisms of poverty and impoverishment, of dominion and repression. Now, these instruments ought to be submitted to a critical examination from the point of view of a Christian conception of man and history".[7]

The main difficulty is that Father Muñoz does not state clearly his own theory of exploitation with pertinent arguments. "Marxism" is too general. According to the documents, under capitalism "the difference between what the worker produces and what he needs for his subsistence goes to the hands of the few" (p. 69). This could sound like Marx's theory of exploitation as formulated in the first volume of *Kapital*. But, of course, this is hard to believe. Does Father Muñoz support Marx's labor theory of value, for instance? If he does, it would be of utmost interest to know how he manages to refute and avoid the criticisms of that theory that have been around at least since the days of Böhm-Bawerk. And again it would be wrong to suppose that Father Muñoz's position is exceptional. The Brazilian brothers Leonardo and Clodovis Boff have taken a similar attitude.[8]

According to Father Muñoz the poorer are getting poorer in Latin America, while the richer are always getting richer. But this assertion is too vague to be examined from an empirical point of view. As it is, we cannot know how to go about checking its accuracy. For instance, a plausible index of extreme poverty or misery might be infant mortality.[9] But surely this cannot be what Father Muñoz has in mind, because infant mortality has decreased dramatically in most Latin American countries during the past decades. According to the data available, the best-off country in this respect was probably Cuba, where in 1960 35.4 of every 1,000 children born died before they reached their first birthday. In 1979 only 19.1 died. In Peru infant mortality decreased from 92.1 in 1960 to 50.5 in 1978. In Chile, Father Muñoz's country, infant mortality has decreased from 120.3 in 1960 to 31.8 in 1980. (See figure 1 and table 1.)

So, what does Father Muñoz mean by the expression "the rich are always richer at the expense of the poor who are always poorer"? He might mean, for example, that the distribution of income is becoming more uneven; that the real GNP per capita of the poorest 20 percent (or 60 percent?) has been falling (since when?); that relative to the standard of living of the wealthy countries, Latin American countries are worse off than ever; that the standard of living of the poorest 20 percent (or 60 percent or 80 percent) is in real and absolute terms falling, while the richest 10 percent (or 20 percent or 30 percent) are getting that much richer; that in relation to their reasonable expectations the poor are much poorer than they ought to be; and so on. Does Father Muñoz fully realize that such a sentence may have a great variety of possible empirical references from which entirely different kinds of political practices might emerge, including, for instance, "reformism" and "gradualism," and that under quite a few of those possible meanings his sentence would be demonstrably false?

One finds the same pattern in Father Gutiérrez's famous *Theology of Liberation*. For example, he asserts that "the underdevelopment of the poor countries, as an overall social fact, appears in its true light: as the historical by-product of the development of other countries."[10] He does not attempt to prove this: he gives a reference—Osvaldo Sunkel's work.[11] The fact of the matter is that Father Gutiérrez does not explain his specific reasons for believing that dependence is the main cause of Latin America's poverty. I am not demanding original or new theories, only the evidence he selects and reasons he has for accepting a given

FIGURE 1
INFANT MORTALITY IN CHILE, 1925–1983
(deaths per 1,000 live births)

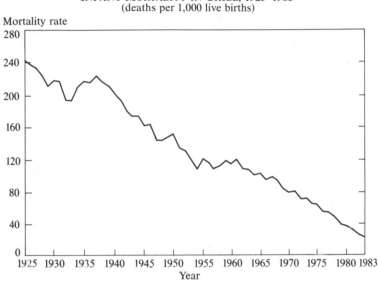

NOTE: Rates correspond to deaths of children less than a year old.
SOURCE: Juan Pablo Illanes, "En Torno a la Renovación del Sector Salud," *Economía y Sociedad,* March 1984, p. 14.

thesis. Although he refers to papers and books written by social scientists, he does not discuss or reproduce the precise arguments that they contain and that he interprets and supports. And while he identifies conclusions that he admires in certain works, he—like Father Muñoz in his references to "Marxism"—does not examine the authors' reasoning. He thereby invokes certain immunity to criticisms of socioeconomic theories as well as to their ethical implications.[12]

A typical ambiquity of the documents is reflected in their use of the concept of capitalism. The present condition in Latin America is capitalism and the result of capitalism. No interesting distinctions are made, for instance, between Brazil's pro-free market policies of the late 1960s and Chile's interventionist welfare state of the same period. In both cases there is capitalism and, therefore, "institutionalized violence." What both countries had then in common was an economic system where private property was predominant. Chile, however, did not have a free market economy because of very high protective tariffs (a legacy of the import-substitution model), permanent and extended price and wage controls, and innumerable regulations.

The documents contain many criticisms of those that favor a reformist and gradualist approach: the "system" as such has to be changed.

## TABLE 1
### LATIN AMERICA: INFANT MORTALITY RATES, 1960–1980
(deaths per 1,000 live births)

| | Year | | | | | Annual Rates of Change[a] | | | |
|---|---|---|---|---|---|---|---|---|---|
| | 1960 | 1965 | 1970 | 1975 | 1980 | 1960–65 | 1965–70 | 1970–75 | 1975–80 |
| Argentina | 62.4 | 56.9 | 58.8 | 44.6[b] | 40.8[c] | −1.8 | +0.7 | −3.4[d] | −8.5[e] |
| Chile | 120.3 | 82.4 | 79.3 | 55.4 | 31.8 | −4.1 | −3.4 | −6.0 | −8.5 |
| Colombia | 99.8 | 69.3 | 70.4 | 55.0 | | −3.5 | −2.9 | −4.8[f] | n.a. |
| Costa Rica | 68.6 | 38.4 | 61.5 | 37.1 | 22.9[d] | +0.2 | −2.3 | −7.9 | −9.6[g] |
| Cuba | 35.4 | 95.4 | 38.3 | 27.3 | 19.1[d] | +1.7 | 0 | −5.7 | −7.5[g] |
| Ecuador | 100.0 | 93.0 | 76.6 | 57.5[b] | 64.4[b] | −1.4 | −3.5 | −3.6[f] | n.a. |
| Paraguay | 90.7 | 74.0 | 93.8 | 84.9 | 91.4[c] | −1.6 | +2.4 | −1.9 | 2.5[e] |
| Peru | 92.1 | 83.6 | 65.1 | 53.8[b] | 50.5[c] | −3.9 | −2.4 | −2.5[f] | −6.1[e] |
| Uruguay | 47.4 | 49.6 | 42.6 | 48.6 | 37.4 | +0.9 | −2.8 | +2.8 | −4.6 |
| Venezuela | 52.9 | 46.4 | 49.2 | 43.7 | 31.8 | −2.4 | +1.2 | −2.2 | −5.4 |

N.A. = not available.

Notes: Rates correspond to deaths of children less than a year old. International comparisons must be carefully considered because of multiple problems that mortality figures may have in the different countries.
a. Calculations made by the author.
b. Corresponding to 1977.
c. Corresponding to 1978.
d. Corresponding to 1979.
e. Corresponding to annual average variation between 1977 and 1978.
f. Corresponding to annual average variation between 1970 and 1977.
g. Corresponding to annual average variation between 1975 and 1979.
SOURCES: Organización Panamericana de la Salud, *Las Condiciones de Salud en las Américas*, 1974, 1978 y 1982; and Tarsicio Castañeda, "Contexto Socioeconómico del Descenso de la Mortalidad Infantil en Chile," in *Estudios Públicos* No. 16, 1984, pp. 5–56.

But what system? The focal point of the attack is private property, because, following a "Marxist" theory of exploitation, it represents the main mechanism of domination. If so, to distinguish between types of capitalism may seem irrelevant. Nevertheless, this would not be the case if liberation theologians wanted to discuss seriously the economic system that ought to replace the status quo. It would then become apparent that more subtle distinctions are needed if they want to avoid new forms of exploitation like, for instance, the monopoly of employment and the centralized control of the resources of the media that might derive from a state capitalism. Again, vague concepts and sweeping statements conspire against clear intellectual persuasion and efficient political action.

On political matters the documents do not condemn all dictatorships, but only "military" dictatorships. The book was published in Chile when the country had a democracy (albeit a "bourgeois" democracy), and there is no indication in the work that this fact makes a really significant difference from the point of view of the thesis of "institutionalized violence." The reason is probably that capitalism "subordinates human rights to economic results" (p. 108). No attempt is made to deal properly with the question and prove the point. On economic matters it is never clear whether the criticism affects the theory of competitive capitalism, its historical applications in Latin America, any possible application of a free market system in Latin America, or the like. On political matters it is not clear to what extent any form of democratic capitalism would entail the subordination of human rights to economic results and the transformation of democracy into "a mere word."

Likewise, the ethical failures of capitalism are simply asserted as self-evident. Who needs a demonstration that the values of capitalism are greed, egoistic individualism, and materialism whereas those of socialism are solidarity, justice, love, and social responsibility? There is no need to mention the possibility of authors who might favor capitalism. What would an ethical defense of capitalism look like? But no, not even out of curiosity does Father Muñoz consider such a conjecture.

And it will not do to say that these are the de facto views of Christian communities or that these are the claims of the poor and that, therefore, they represent a "sign of the Spirit." It is one thing to be exploited, oppressed, and poor, and quite another to be right on socioeconomic, ethical, and political matters. The Christianization of pagan thought is a venerable tradition of Christian churches. The classic example is what Aquinas did with Aristotle's work. To recover the thoughts and beliefs of the people for intellectual examination is also a venerable tradition. Father Muñoz unfortunately departs from those traditions from the moment that he fails to discuss carefully and deeply the arguments that could prove the truth of the documents' tenets.

In some of their latter works both Father Gutiérrez and Father Muñoz insist on labeling liberation theology a form of "spirituality" rather than a doctrine. As opposed to old forms of spirituality, however, it is not individualistic. Their language becomes less secular and socioeconomic and more biblical and prophetic, with much poetical force. Perhaps it signals the recovery of a specifically religious language and the beginning of a gradual separation from particular socioeconomic and political tenets and options. It is not easy to advance in this direction, however, without allowing the "Latin American" peculiarities of liberation theology to become subsumed within its European

175

counterpart, in particular, German political theology.[13] Liberation theology as a form of spirituality might also become more independent of the sphere of influence and control of the Vatican, less inclined to critical analysis and rational discussion, and more prophetic in tone and revolutionary in practice. It is too early to tell: so much will depend on the concepts of social scientists predominating within Christian communities and on the prevailing climate of opinion. Undoubtedly, the debate with the intellectuals who have inspired the political and socioeconomic claims of liberation theology will play a key role in the process of validating new options for Latin Americans who want to commit themselves to the struggle against involuntary poverty. Clearly, several of the authors on whose work theologians of liberation based their tenets have modified their former views.

Spirituality might even give rise to a new kind of fundamentalism. As a matter of fact, I think that there are some fundamentalist traits in the theology of liberation. And, surprisingly, these traits spring from a response to Marx's dictum: "Religion is the opiate of the masses." The response has been to interpret current events as nothing other than sacred history and to blur the distinction between the properly religious and the secular dimension of life in society. Everything—rituals, morals, politics, economics, art—becomes religious and, at the same time, political. It raises the old—and always new—question of defining the realm where reason is separate from faith and of delimiting the area of authority that springs from faith. In spite of allegations to the contrary, the style of most liberation thelogians reflects a tendency to identify the priest with the theologian, the theologian with the social scientist, the social scientist with the politician, the politician with the prophet, and the prophet with the poet. If we do not accept this equation and insist on modern distinctions of roles and types of language, is there room for political-religious prophets?

Liberation theology is of great significance for the future of Latin America. Its supporters have produced powerful manifestoes and created a new revolutionary mystique. Given the vitality of Marxist movements of liberation on the subcontinent, the tactical convergence with church movements is politically explosive. Nevertheless, I am sure of the religious depth of most of those committed to liberation theology as a form of spirituality. I feel that they are exploring a new type of religious devotion. Many of them have given impressive examples of real solidarity with the poor and with those who have suffered persecution. This is the source of their strength and authority. But the cognitive value of their writings on political, economic, and ethico-philosophical matters related to political and economic institutions is close to nil. I am tempted to whisper, "Look! The emperor has no clothes!"

# Notes

1. Ronaldo Muñoz, *Nueva Conciencia de la Iglesia en América Latina* (Santiago, Chile: Ediciones Nueva Universidad, Universidad Católica de Chile, 1973).

2. Gustavo Gutiérrez, *A Theology of Liberation* (New York: Orbis Books, 1973), chap. 6.

3. Gutiérrez, p. 141.

4. Joseph Ramos, "Dependency and Development: An Attempt to Clarify the Issues," in Michael Novak, ed., *Liberation South, Liberation North* (Washington, D.C.: American Enterprise Institute, 1981), pp. 61–67.

5. Ibid., Ramos papers.

6. Joseph Ramos, "Teología de la Liberación," *Estudios Públicos,* N° 10, Otoño, 1983, pp. 51–65.

7. Ronaldo Muñoz, "Soy Teólogo de la Iglesia Católica al Servicio de los Pobres" in *Iglesia, Teología, Política,* Santiago de Chile, CESOC, 1984, p. 152.

8. Leonardo y Clodovis Boff, "Marx, Ni Padre Ni Padrino de la Teología de la Liberación", Ibid. pp. 126–27.

9. Juan Pablo Illanes, "La Mortalidad Infantil como Indice de Desarrollo Social," en *Estudios Públicos* N° 16, 1984.

10. Gustavo Gutiérrez, p. 84. Of course, Sunkel is not the only reference he gives to support his claim.

11. Ibid., p. 84.

12. His article "Teología y Ciencias Sociales" published in *Christus,* Octubre-Diciembre, 1984, however, seems to indicate a change. On the other hand, the writings of Michael Novak are beginning to have influence within Christian circles in Latin America. Also the studies of the Argentinians Alejandro Chafuen and Gabriel Zanotti, who are developing a neothomist defense of the free market system. Maybe the tide will change during the next years.

13. See Juan Luis Segundo, "Capitalism-Socialism: A Theological Crux," in Michael Novak, ed., ibid., p. 23.

# Discussion

ARTHUR McGOVERN, Department of Theology, University of Detroit: You focused on what I have also criticized as a weakness: the absence of analysis. Most people think that liberation theologians do a lot of Marxist or dependency analysis. But when I tried to find those that gave a real analysis, I found very little. The original work of Gutiérrez did have a good bit on development, a chapter or so. Were you quoting from *The Power of the Poor in History* on restricted democracy?

MR. FONTAINE: Yes. There are about twelve pages in that work that have social analysis. Yet Gutiérrez is one of those that speaks the most. In Sobrino, you find nothing.

I agree that, if there is to be analysis, it needs to be spelled out. It's hard for me to tell people, even after reading a lot of liberation theology, exactly what the theologians are saying.

North American audiences, however, ought to understand that different kinds of Marxist analyses lead to different kinds of strategies. I wish that many liberation theologians would explain which strategy they advocate and which analysis they follow and then spell it out.

I see liberation theology as an attempt to articulate a problem and give voice to the poor. And that is a prophetic voice. If some urge that prophecy to move in a certain direction, they should spell out that direction. I am not, however, so unhappy with the rhetoric or the prophetic voice—the Fourier approach—or the Utopian sort of thing, crying out to let people know what the poor are feeling or that there is such a problem as poverty.

I am interested in finding out more about the expression "popular movement" and whether that is current all through Latin America or only in Peru, where they talk about the *movimiento popular.*

MICHAEL JOYCE, President, John M. Olin Foundation: In discussing this fascinating subject of liberation theology, I wish to ask, Where is the theology in liberation theology? How might this discussion have

gone if all of us around the table were self-confessed materialist-secu-
larists? Would the discussion have been any different with that
qualification?

I would like to know how the theological content of liberation
theology defines theology in some unique and distinguishing way.

I see a missing link in the formulation. It seems to me that we are
talking about politics, but politics of a peculiar kind: it is not so much
that liberation politics are ideological politics but that they are not
politics. If "politics" implies the governance of humans, which can be
done only from decisions of legitimate power, what, then, is the role of
the intellectual or perhaps of the liberation theologian?

It seems to me the intellectual must be an adviser of princes or
perhaps, more commonly, the enlightener of the voting public. We must
accept his perspectives, if he is to be of any use or to understand the
nature of the political sphere.

Now, it might be said that this is unsatisfying in some moral sense,
which believers expect; but I find excitement and real moral dignity
aplenty in political life. I think morality is inherent in politics, but one
must always begin from the real situation, from the goals of the political
actors. The question, it seems to me, is how one gets from here to there.

How liberation theology instructs us on that, it seems to me, is
essentially a political question.

HUGO ASSMANN, Universidad Metodista de Pracicaba: The social and
analytical implications of the theology of liberation are not very clear.

I am happy to hear that you believe that, as you see it now,
liberation theology has not so much to do with Marxism. In the strong
dichotomous confrontation in the 1960s and the early 1970s, we felt that
some of the sociological tools available at that time were useful. A few
years later, we also began to see that many of those social, analytical
instruments were not so completely clarified in many respects.

Therefore, many Latin Americans began to say that the essential
thing was not a specific social, analytical mediation. The essential thing
is to realize that mediations—the social analytical ones—may be different, transitory, and not completely fixed in the specific school of
social science. It's really important to have a little bit of tolerance with
the way liberation theologians use the social sciences. It is still a new
approach. In past theological argument, the social sciences were not
taken into account. Some cultural theological aspects of the human
social sciences were taken into account, but economics and the analytical tools of social science were not. So, please be a bit tolerant in
this respect.

Moreover, the time has come to be clear about the following: Marxism does not play as essential a role in Latin American theology as many try to maintain.

It was circumstantial, transitory, and even useful that we appropriated some Marxist tools. In the mainstream of Latin American liberation theology, many theologians have never felt a real link to Marxism. And as for me, in my aggressive language I have changed a lot; in my life in the early 1970s I had adopted some Marxist analytical tools. At the same time, in my books at that time were observations critical of the Soviet model. And these short observations were enough to invite strong attack in the June 1972 issue of the *International Review of the Communist Party*. I was cited as an anti-Soviet. On one side, I am called a Marxist, and on the other side, I am called an anti-Soviet—it is really difficult!

I have a suspicion that we theologians are not yet ready to hear what it means to be deeply involved in practical faith experiences. The power of this phenomenon, felt in our grass-roots communities, is not yet clearly understood. But the phenomenon is there. It does not help to call it a new fundamentalist trend. I feel the phenomenon as spirituality. Please make a little effort to understand it as a real, new phenomenon of renovation in the church, strongly linked to social engagement, without ideological or radical extremism. We have to understand it.

Sometimes I ask myself how we can understand or explain this offensive against the theology of liberation. I begin to analyze the phenomenon of the Vatican. I cannot accept that just this pope will destroy the theology of liberation. There are now in the highest power of the Catholic Church in the Vatican some remnants of the minority of Vatican Council II. This pope was, at that time, a bishop who remained until the last minute on the first schema of ecclesiology, the radical one, against the ecclesiology of the people.

This minority of the council is once more in power. But then I see another tendency, which is very strong. I see it in Chile. There are many big lay movements throughout the world, with power links among them. Opus Dei, for example. And there is a third tendency, quite different, consisting of the Christian charismatics and similar movements; it is a very complex picture. The CELAM (the Latin American Council of Bishops) is surrounded by these kinds of people—Opus Dei, charismatics.

It is not easy in Latin America to publish beautiful editions of reviews. Even in their advertising announcements, we see that they are linked to Opus Dei and others. Then I read about a very strange phenomenon, that the American Enterprise Institute is now deeply interested in theology. It is difficult for me to see why all of these things happen. I only feel that we Latin American theologians of liberation feel ourselves strangely confronted by those powers in a very aggressive way, as if we are really destroying Christianity.

And can you explain why all of this is happening? For me it is really a new sociological mystery why we humble people, without means, without money, in only one country, Brazil—with the more or less official support of many bishops—are tremendously "dangerous." People label us Marxists, whereas we are people deeply interested in spirituality. Is it only that we have made so many mistakes? We accept the critique of our mistakes, our abilities, or our luck in social analytical tools, but please make a distinction between the critiques of us and those of this strange phenomenon of a global attack from the Vatican and from so many institutions with so many means.

JOAN ANDERSON, School of Business Administration, University of San Diego: Dr. Assmann, you're at least ahead of the economists: you may be struggling to bring economics into theology, while economists have yet to find out we even need theology. So we are behind you.

Mr. Fontaine, I'd like to talk about land reform. I agree that the Chilean land reform was a failure and that there are other histories of failures, Bolivia among others. But I would hate to write off the possibility of land reform. I think it is very important, although land reform can certainly fail when it is not done correctly.

Land reform has got to be more than just splitting up land, which in the end, as I understand it, is what happened in Chile. To have meaningful land reform that results in productive farming, agriculture absolutely needs credit. There is no way that agriculture survives anywhere without credit, the United States included.

Therefore, land reform entails more than a system for dividing up the land: it must also include credit and, ideally, technical assistance. You cannot hand land to peasants and expect them to do something with it, if that is all you're giving them. I think that in some cases land reform has been done successfully.

The statistics of farm productivity in Latin America show that the bigger the farm size in general, the less productive it is, especially in terms of the yield per hectare. The medium-sized farms are more efficient than latifundios, and general family farms are more efficient in their productivity per hectare than the median size. Land reform is a very important issue in furthering development.

A lot of people here say we need to move from the ground up. Michael Novak said that. The liberation theologians talk about the base communities and ground-up movements. My experience is with a needs-based development model, which is again a ground-up model in which human capital is built first, with health education and smaller units of production, leading to a market kind of economy.

I tend to be an economic pragmatist, with a basic faith in markets and incentives. For markets to work, however, the wealth needs to be spread, not evenly but reasonably equitably. If wealth is all in a few hands, I don't think markets can really function. I see equitable distribution as a necessary precondition for a market system to operate.

When we talk about splitting things up, we sometimes claim that such a division comes at the cost of efficiency: we will lose efficiency because we lose economies of scale.

In a series of econometric studies in which I have been involved recently, I have found that efficiency in many kinds of industries—apparel, shoes, even electronic assembly—is greater in small-sized plants than in larger ones. My studies and also those of several others have shown similar results, and I think that is very important. In many kinds of plants we will not sacrifice efficiency for smaller units of production.

In general, we've greatly oversold the concept of economies of scale. That is a very important point when we look at what kind of institutions will work. Efficiency is very important, especially in third world countries where many resources are in very short supply.

MR. FONTAINE: Regarding land reform, of course, I am not against every kind of agrarian reform, for every country, and under every condition. That's not my point. In the case of Chile, though, it was a mistake, and not only because of the way in which it was applied.

First, according to studies now available, the proposition that land ownership was concentrated is simply false. Actually, most of the land was well distributed, and the most difficult problem in Chile was the problem of the minifundios already there in the early 1960s.

Since the early nineteenth century, the legal system in Chile had established that, upon the death of an individual, his property was divided equally among the children and that a person was free only to distribute one-fourth of the total estate as he desired. The land, then, was family owned in the nineteenth century, and the process of dissolution was fairly rapid.

The image of a few landowners with huge latifundios is a mistake. Some existed, of course. Some did have huge farms, but they were not relevant in terms of agrarian production or the population living on the farms. It was a political question because of the political influence of this group, but not, I think, an economic question. The wrong statistics were used because a lot of the information on the size of the land is based on the Internal Revenue Service's data. And, of course, the only people who pay taxes are large landowners, while the small landowners never get to the Internal Revenue Service. This point illustrates the difficulty of establishing an efficient credit and support system.

Today, I think there's agreement that in that country at least, the proposition that the land was extremely concentrated was false, although at the time all—including me—believed it was so. Therefore, we must be careful with the data, because accuracy is extremely difficult to come by.

For example, a major statistical inaccuracy occurred because one whole province was never divided legally. Part of the land goes back to Indian titles, which have been legalized. Those Indians were Bolivian and Peruvians, a complication behind the war against Bolivia and Peru. The question of ownership and nationality is tangled from a legal point of view.

If you go there, you know who's the owner. The traditional property rights system has operated there de facto, unsanctioned by the legal system. Therefore the statistics are distorted. The statistics fail to reflect the realities of actual ownership.

As for the question of whether large farms are inefficient, I think that it is hard to tell. To know that, we would have to have a free price system. Most of the prices are fixed, so, of course, people do not invest in wheat if the bread is subsidized. That is why we import a huge amount of our wheat to produce bread, something like 80 percent. The same was true of milk products and wine. The number of controlled products is amazing.

So the degree of efficiency is not clear. It is true that many people had fields that were not producing, but it is questionable whether they should have, given the context of the time in which the economy was operating.

In general, with the price system working properly, is it better to have family farms or large farms? We don't know. It depends a lot on many variables, and I am suspicious that we will not ever know this. My position is to let the market decide.

If it is good to have small farms, we'll have them. The market will distribute land in such a way that we'll find the size that is appropriate. Depending on the region, the crop, the production methods, the land itself, and the comparative advantage, as well as the restrictions on foreign trade operating in other countries and on itself, we might have different sizes.

What we usually find in the literature is that large is good if it is a company, profit-oriented farm, and bad if it is a family farm. But I see an unreasonable bias there. Today, we have very efficient large farms operating and also small ones. So I don't think the point is size.

Third, most people in Latin America today are urban, not agrarian.

This issue, then, really concerns only a small portion of the population, although it is usually transformed into a huge problem in spite of the small proportion of the population involved in agriculture.

The first effect of an agrarian reform in this particular case was to diminish employment in the agrarian areas. The land cannot be given to all the people who work on a particular farm. Large or medium-sized farms might be inefficient, but they also give employment. A lot of indirect unemployment resulted from the reforms. In fact, one of the major causes of unemployment has been agrarian reform during the past years.

In general, fewer than 50 percent of the people working at any specific farm got land. So what happens to the rest? They go to the cities, or they work for the others who got land. How do you manage this process, socially and politically? How do you divide a farm that provided work for a hundred families among fifty people who will remain? How do you do this practically? This is a tremendous political problem that Allende faced in a democratic context, and that could be done only in the context of an authoritarian regime. It would not have been possible in a democratic system, on the large scale in which it was meant to happen, as it did happen under Pinochet.

In addition to a huge problem of unemployment is the problem of the number of minifundistas, who are used to working under a different system and who lack technical agricultural knowledge and the under-standing of the market. The crucial point, it seems to me, is that agrarian reform usually weakens property rights, which is the basic requirement for investment. From Socialists to Libertarians there is widespread agreement on this point in Chile today.

MIHAJLO MIHAJLOV, Radio Free Europe/Radio Liberty: The Commu-nist movement was created not by political or economic science, but by powerful rhetoric. The *Communist Manifesto,* which describes the elitist dimensions of future Communist societies and claims that history will come to an end, is written in religious language. According to the vision of the *Manifesto,* the poor become poorer and the rich richer in capitalist societies.

It was the *Communist Manifesto* that created the Communist movement, not Marx's *Das Kapital:* who reads *Das Kapital?* Perhaps the intellectuals read it, but the Communist movement derived from the rhetorical power of the *Manifesto,* from the religious dimension of Marxism. Marxism, then, is not just an economic movement, but a religious one. But the question remains what type of religion is in question.

I am worried that liberation theology is a movement whose only function is to give religious justification for a Communist society.

All social movements and all revolutions are alike in this respect: people claim that God is on their side and that if a person sides with Che Guevara, for example, for a just society, God will save his soul. This approach is much more dangerous than the economic language of means of production and other such expressions now in the Marxist movement.

At the same time, we were trying to make a link between religious belief and just, free institutions or free markets. But we cannot fight against religious utopianism with arguments for small business institutions.

So the argument is on two absolutely different levels. One level is the religious level of Karl Marx with the *Communist Manifesto* or the theology of liberation, and the other level is this secondary, practical level, which concerns the creation of more business or land reform and the like.

What is most important is individual freedom, because religious totalitarianism can be even more dangerous than secular authoritarianism. This is why I am afraid of this theology of liberation.

As for land reform, I believe that it is not a question of economics but of politics. And it is important, even if the economy suffers from the reforms.

MARK MICHALSKI, World Bank: Mr. Fontaine has suggested that Marxism offers much to learn from. I think that it is one of the things that liberation theology has to examine. I'm reminded of the statement that socialism is a great idea, if only there were no people. That is one thing that liberation theology could learn from this.

Regarding the Vatican's choosing more people from Opus Dei than from the liberation theologians, I think that clearly it has learned from the experience of socialism in Eastern European countries. As they found out in instituting socialism, it does not really provide anything more than an ideal and a myth, and this myth is always something that we aspire for. And since the 1848 *Manifesto,* there has always been the suggestion that we promise something for the next generation and for the future, which is a very appealing and powerful idea because it gives us something to live for.

I can speak from my short experience in Poland about what I remember in the 1950s. My family was very optimistic that the new system would provide everybody with everything that he wanted, not withstanding that everyone had different expectations.

The same was with the Solidarity movement in the 1980s. People again had very high spiritual expectations but lower material living standards. They were living like new people from the beginning, trying to at least.

185

In recent history, except for Albania and Angola, the only countries that are really doing something innovative are the countries implementing more market-oriented practices like Hungary or China. They will try anything if it works.

As for liberation theology, I think it clearly accepts all the Marxist theories. Although some say that Marxism has a practical bearing, I say it has the least practical bearing. Its only practical use is to draw attention to poverty and all the problems of mankind. But it is really a utopian and idealistic theory. We should allow the liberation theologians to try out Marxist theory a couple of years. Perhaps, then, they will experience what they should have learned from the experience of the East European bloc, the countries who went to Marxist extremes themselves.

The pope very much opposes liberation theology because he is a product of a Marxist system and realizes the danger of it. He knows that there is no compatibility between Marxism and Christianity. Although many people believe it exists, they are just misled.

PAUL SIGMUND, Woodrow Wilson Center: The basic question is, "Why are we liberation theologians getting so much attention these days, when we are only trying to pursue our spiritual concerns as we see them?" They are a small group of theologians, although actually 104 is a fair number of theologians in Latin America.

One reason for this attention is that liberation theologians are a threat to the vertical structure of the church, or at least to the pre-Vatican II vertical structure. Those committed to that structure, with a vested interest in it, see liberation theology as a threat.

Second, liberation theologians are a threat to people in positions of economic power in this country and in Latin America. Therefore, an international effort moves against you.

Third, deeply religious people are concerned about the possibility that liberation theology could be a kind of Trojan Horse that leads people to accept a false, materialistic, and class-oriented theory of history and contemporary development, thinking that it is Christian. Such acceptance might lead ultimately to a political structure that would eventually wipe out religion. I have been to Cuba and talked to religious people there; they survive, but under great pressure, with strong discrimination against them. The Communist youth movements even meet on Sunday morning to make sure the children don't go to church.

Some are deeply concerned that what they see as an alliance between liberation theology and Marxism, in which at some future point liberation theologians will be useful fools of the Marxists. Liberation theology might provide a popular appeal that Marxism, in fact, has not had. Although it has had a great appeal for intellectuals in Latin America, it has not had a very widespread popular appeal, except when it has linked itself to trade union movements as it did in Cuba and Chile.

Perhaps it is a mistake to single out any one of these as the reason for the degree of attention. People approach liberation theology from many different positions. Part of the problem with all of this is that social science is not a science: it is a kind of social philosophy, composed of educated guesses, theories, hypotheses, and hunches; it is not a systematic science.

What I find particularly interesting is the link between Scripture and the people and between Scripture and social science. I believe the term "liberation theology" represents an interest in relating theology to social science. The social science that the liberation theologians saw as the dominant social science in the late 1960s and early 1970s was Marxism. Marxism furnished the tools. And, although it is not science, it is one version of society, development, and international economic relations.

I am hopeful that out of this meeting and other continuing dialogues between North and South Americans and among Latin Americans will come some opening toward a kind of pluralism: a pluralism of society, a pluralism of opinions about how society can be changed and transformed in the interest of the poor, and a pluralism of approaches taken by social scientists.

I see the concern with Scripture, with the poor, and with social science as positive. We must look very seriously at alternatives and try to decide which of those can really most appropriately fulfill the preferential option for the poor.

I hope that this meeting, as well as other continuing interchanges of this sort, contributes to that goal.

RODNEY GRUBB, Department of Political Science, St. Olaf College: I would like to continue with the discussion of the social science aspects or elements of analytic philosophy in liberation theology. I am not sure that politics is fraught with morality, but it seems to me that politics may be amoral at times. Politics is the arena in which there is no authoritative allocation of values, and that certainly puts politics in conjunction with liberation theology because whatever social science might say elsewhere, liberation theology has had a tremendous appeal to people. Liberation theology and Ronald Reagan have one thing in common: both create very beautiful visions of the future without filling in the picture of how we get between here and that beautiful picture.

I share some of the vision of the liberation theologians, but I also see a real weakness in the means to the end. I would go a step farther and say that a theological problem is involved with liberation theology.

187

Anybody who has tried to teach a course in the New Testament or the life of Jesus comes to an inescapable conclusion: Jesus had great empathy for the poor. To go from that, however, and to say that the inevitable economic system attached to this concern is socialism is a tremendous leap of faith, and it is not well founded theologically. The New Testament did not know socialism, and, empirically, liberation theology has to show that socialism works to make its case. I don't think that the data are there to prove that it does. And I also think that you don't have to be a Socialist to share Jesus' vision of doing something for the poor.

As we all know, most books on Latin America start with an introduction in which the author states that the continent is not to be taken as a homogeneous whole and that it is very dangerous to generalize about it. They state a commitment not to do so. Of course, then one reads ten chapters or so of generalizations.

This is a very important mythological precaution, however, and I would recommend this practice to avoid being caught with counterexamples, which are very devastating.

Next, I want to make a point about liberation theology. We in Latin America are not in the happy condition that you are here in the states. Here, you have a cultural paradigm that is uniform and generally accepted, whereas in Latin America paradigms battle with each other.

In the nineteenth century, we had the traditional Spanish world view, which was imprinted in the political, social, and economic institutions as well as the liberal paradigm that was established in the United States, France, and Europe in general.

In the twentieth century, we have to add the paradigm of socialism, which has been a very powerful one. We in Latin America have had a battle of ideas or conflicting world visions. This has always made it impossible to find political stability, which you have had here in the United States.

Liberation theology does not really fit into any of these paradigms that I have been talking about. It is not a world view that can be identified with the traditional Hispanic culture. On the contrary, I think that it is in conflict with it.

OSCAR MERTZ, Scientific Attaché, Embassy of Chile: Although I too believe that liberation theology uses political tools of Marxist origin, I do not interpret liberation theology as either Marxist or neo-Marxist: it is explicitly anticapitalist. I see liberation theology as a fourth emerging paradigm, which is in conflict with the previous ones.

This explanation accounts in part for the attention it is getting because people espousing the other paradigms see it as a threat. Socialism and capitalism, in particular, against which there is some reaction or revolt.

Some see modern man's alienation and the misery in today's world as inherent characteristics of our times. This leads me to interpret liberation theology as a fundamentalist movement, perhaps a useful concept for understanding what liberation theology is all about. In its reaction against modernity, this fundamentalism is revolutionary. And it is a revolutionary movement with a tremendous capacity for popular mobilization and violence.

PHYLLIS ZAGANO, Archdiocese of New York: Like others, I've been looking for the theology in liberation theology. Most Americans get their information about liberation theology from the newspapers. As a result, they know nothing about liberation theology and clearly nothing about Marxism. Part of the misunderstanding, therefore, as generated by newspaper-fed intellects, has to do with a confusion of what constitutes Gospel values. That is, some people confuse Gospel values with secular values. And when these Gospel values appear to be imposed from without, the people from the United States feel this constitutes Communist Marxism.

When these Gospel values are generated within, we clearly understand this to be Christianity. The confusion then rests in the perception, perhaps, and not in the reality. Many Americans cannot tell the difference between enforced land reforms or the recommendation of land reforms and the gray, grainy pictures of Soviet tanks running through Hungary in 1956. Because the preponderance of the world cannot tell the difference between Marxism and Christianity, it is incumbent on those who choose to present Christianity as a solution to what appear to be economic problems to present it as Christianity with no confusion.

GEORGE WEIGEL: One important issue here could be termed an expropriation of concern for the poor. Many of the people around this table have direct experience with that issue in inner-city America.

The portrait of the oppressor as painted by liberation theology simply does not fit our experience of ourselves, what we've worked for, or the values we've tried to express in our lives and in our political efforts—any more, I might add, than the Vatican picture of rampant consumerism and the like fits our experience of ourselves. At a personal level, there is a disjunction between portrait and experience here. More significantly, there is a theological problem having to do with who claims the mantle of the Second Vatican Council.

The argument here is not primarily between a return to an a priori, nonhistorical orthodoxy and a Vatican II orientation. The issue is, What dimensions of historical experience will be allowed into material for theological reflection? The main currents here, even those most critical of the various theologies of liberation, do not call for an ahistorical reflection. The notion that to be critical of theologies of liberation is to be abstract, disconnected from history, or somehow disengaged from the issues misses the point. Let's clear that up at once.

Then, at the social and political level, we are not arguing Marxism. Although many of us critical of theologies of liberation are intellectually interested in Marxism as a phenomenon in the history of ideas, we are basically bored by it. The issue in our minds at the social and political level is Leninism. It has to do with the concentration of power. We come to that conclusion for a particular reason: we do not think of freedom only in abstract terms but as institutionalized or mediated reality.

We are not trying to make universalist claims for our particular set of institutions—be they political, economic, or the like. But we also know that social analysis is important. Just as not all of those who cry "Lord, Lord" will inherit the kingdom, so not all of those who cry "freedom, freedom" will have freedom. These ideals must be embodied in structures of common life. Thus, if it is arguably true that some attacks on theologies of liberation are attacking straw men, it seems at least as arguably true that the responses to the attacks are simply confrontations with dimensions of personal, theological, and social-political commentary that exist only as phantoms.

JOHN LANGAN, Woodstock Theological Center: I think that in its initial phases liberation theology presented itself as nonacademic, as practical, as inimical to oppressors, and as calculated to shock and offend. That it succeeded should not come as a surprise.

Liberation theology also seems to have presented itself as a new spiritual way to engage the world. Perhaps such proposals are nearly always suspect in their early stages. If we go back to the thirteenth century and look at the early Franciscans or the philosophy of Aquinas, if we look at the turn of the century and the condemnation of Americanism, or if we look at reactions to someone like Teilhard de Chardin—all of these things elicited an initial aversion and condemnation for being materialistic or undisciplined. Liberation theology, then, can link itself to a long heritage of movements that subsequently became legitimated.

In addition, liberation theology will inevitably have a certain premodern cast to it, for two reasons. First, one of the important functions of religion is to express a kind of discontent with the modern world and with some of the divisions inherent in it. Religion represents a search for a totality of meaning and of value. The poor, it seems to me, are, alas, irreversibly premodern. Of course, individual poor people or particular groups can very well become modernized, but to a very large extent the poor are precisely those people who are most disengaged from the ordinary structures of modern life and who are least exposed to modernizing influences.

Second, liberation theology runs into difficulty because, like a number of very different movements, it builds on certain ambiguities in the ecclesiology of Vatican II, which affirmed certain populist tendencies to be coherent with the continued affirmation of a traditional understanding of the hierarchical church.

Thus the Vatican evinces somewhat similar reactions to certain tendencies in U.S. feminism, to the Dutch church, or to liberation theology. And any challenge to authority or suggestion of a parallel church, such as people's churches in Nicaragua, brings out the heavy artillery of the Roman Catholic church.

Finally, religious fundamentalism is one interpretation of liberation theology. There is bound to be a fundamentalist or premodern pull in it. Moreover, we must not overlook the academic character of some liberation theologians. They earned good degrees with good theological faculties and were exposed to much quite sophisticated European academic theology. As these theologians acquire a broader experience and reflect on it, they will modify their initial interpretations and will make distinctions. Thus, people can have both a religious root and a continually changing intellectual formulation of that experience.

It's interesting that fundamentalism in the North seems to gravitate toward the political right and that those in the North who sympathize with liberation theology are by and large those people who are least sympathetic to fundamentalism in its various forms.

NICK EBERSTADT, Harvard University: First, to Dr. Assmann's list of sociological mysteries, I would like to suggest yet another one. How can people so clearly moved by religious experience entertain such a romantic fascination with states, specifically Marxist-Leninist states, that not only despise the expression of individual, independent religious and spiritual thought, but also attempt, as best they can, to extinguish the independent expression of that thought? Why do the liberation theologians remain so silent about the abuse of religious believers in Marxist-Leninist states?

I have a second observation on a different point. In much of our discussion of land reform, I perceive an obsession with land as a commodity very reminiscent of the obsession with gold as a commodity in mercantilist philosophy. If indeed the purpose of land reform, or any other sort of intervention in agrarian development, is to alleviate poverty or to extend the choices of human beings, a much more practical and constructive way of viewing the role of land might be to think in terms of purchasing power of individuals and households. Over the course of development, land will be an increasingly unimportant commodity.

In industrial nations today agriculture is a very slight fraction of overall economic output, in the United States perhaps 3 or 4 percent and in some of the European nations slightly more. This suggests that as a nation rises in prosperity, agriculture is simply able to offer less and less employment and opportunity for earning income. Indeed, an obsession with land reform can become a trap, leaving people with productivity and purchasing power lower than they might otherwise have if allowed a more flexible development path.

Third, both Arturo Fontaine and Hugo Assmann talked about the need for a system of social communications in Latin American countries and elsewhere. I suggest that one very important system of social communications, which is systematically underappreciated in Latin America and elsewhere, is the price mechanism. In any market economy, in an almost incalculably complex way, the demands, preferences, and values of individuals are expressed through the price mechanism, through supply and demand and through the developments that these propel.

Even though, of course, the free market is not a perfectly efficient allocative mechanism, perhaps if one were interested in improving social communications one way to do so would be to improve the very market system through which the very poor, the very rich, and everyone in between can make manifest their choices and their desires about society.

BARRY LEVINE, Florida International University: An old political philosopher once said that when one decides his politics, he has to decide whether to tolerate fraud to get rid of violence or violence to get rid of fraud.

In your paper, Dr. Assmann, you say that one of the advantages of liberation theology is that now you've been able to change your focus from problems of repression to problems of oppression. And so my question: Are you willing to use repression to get rid of oppression, or are you willing to accept oppression as long as you have no repression?

MR. ASSMANN: The experience of the past fifteen years is very complex. I will mention two different experiences. In Chile immediately after the military coup, for two months I had the opportunity to try to save lives by bringing people to the refugee centers. At that time the so-called Ecumenical Commission for Peace was in operation in Chile. Then two months later, in November, I was expelled, even though I carried a passport of the United Nations.

Six months or so later Pinochet closed the Ecumenical Commission for Peace in Chile. And afterwards was created the famous Vicariat of Solidarity. It's completely clear that the Vicariat of Solidarity in Chile had to work for a long time, especially with problems of repression. Clearly in Chile in the early 1970s and the late 1960s in Brazil the church was for many people the only existing place for the defense of some very basic civil rights. That situation I call repression.

The shift from repression to oppression is linked to the problem of the leftist groups in Latin America, especially in my own country. There are many leftist groups and sects, extraterritorial leftist sects, who until now have not understood that we have moved to a very different situation. The main issue is now not censorship, repression, constant control by the police, or violation of basic civil rights. Even in Chile it's difficult now for the Vicariat of Solidarity to move from the troubles of repression to the larger issues of the problems of the poor.

A wall in Lima, Peru, reads, "The rights of the poor are also human rights." What does it mean to talk about human rights today? In Brazil there exist more than a hundred groups for human rights. If you believe the main purpose of such groups is only to defend people against repression, you haven't much to do now in Brazil. Undernourishment, hunger, misery, unemployment, and the like, however, are real problems—and they are the problems linked to basic human rights that I summarize under the word "oppression." The choice you try to force me to make between oppression and repression is absolutely absurd: if there is repression, we must combat it, but we must not be blind to oppression—and there is a lot of oppression in the world.

# Political Systems and Economic Growth: The Case of Latin America

*Mark Falcoff*

Let me state the thesis of this paper all at once: The economic system that Latin Americans will always choose if fully afforded the opportunity will be a combination of statism and populism. Though both Marxism and free enterprise have important and well-placed advocates, neither appeals to Latin Americans as a whole, and both can be imposed only by repressive and undemocratic regimes. The problem is that to survive any open society must meet certain minimal expectations of economic growth. Statist-populist regimes cannot do this alone, and so they must permit islands of wealth-creation in an environment largely organized for the *distribution* of goods and services. Thus the principal cause of political instability in Latin America is the permanent tension between two imperatives: the need of a parasocialist state for resources and the need of a paracapitalist culture within that state for space to survive and reproduce.

In some ways this dilemma is the same as that which confronts all modern welfare states, most notably in Western Europe. In Latin America, however, the level of urbanization and political development in most countries greatly exceeds the capacity of the economic system to satisfy demands. Historically, the gap has been partially closed by a public sector that is typically financed by huge government subsidies and also by extensive social benefits—sometimes comparable to those available in mature industrial democracies—to a restricted but important urban political clientele. The cost has been underwritten, at least until recently, by printing paper money and by taxing foreign corporations and, less directly, by concessional assistance and foreign loans, either through private banks or multilateral credit institutions. In recent years the flow of these external resources has seriously diminished, which makes the return to democracy in many countries a fragile affair and explains the undercurrent of desperation in the rhetoric of a new generation of political leaders. Nurturing democracy in Latin America—as the United States is frequently urged to do—means to assist in the survival, in some fashion or another, of what many might regard a "premature" welfare state.

## The Limits of the Marxist Option

For many years the conventional wisdom in the United States was that Latin America was inoculated against Marxism by the deeply Catholic beliefs of its population. Given the developments over the past twenty years—both in the church itself and throughout Latin America—nobody would want to make that claim today. It would be an error, however, to rush to the other extreme and assume that the entire continent is teetering on the brink of "one, two, many Nicaraguas." To begin with, there is a difference between anticapitalist sentiment (which is widespread) and Marxist militance (which is not); political constituencies in Latin America seem almost instinctively to understand the difference, and political leaders are quick to emphasize it in private. Vulgar Marxist rhetoric—including notions of surplus value, exploitation, and imperialism—has been in common use since at least the 1920s and has been articulated by such decidedly unradical personalities as Victor Raúl Haya de la Torre, founder of the Peruvian APRA; General Juan Perón; President Victor Paz Estenssoro of Bolivia; economist Raúl Prebisch; the military junta that ruled Peru from 1968 to 1979; and every Mexican president in memory. Indeed, the very ubiquitousness of anticapitalist ideas has drawn much of their sting and has also undercut the revolutionary potential of genuinely Marxist parties and movements. Populist movements—that is, broad coalitions of various social classes united under sometimes incendiary rhetoric—provide the same *frisson* at much lower social and human cost.

It is also important to understand that Marxist movements have had their greatest success when they have abandoned an insurrectionary line to function as populist parties in a more or less open political environment. A case in point is Bolivia, where the Communist party, which had originally opposed the revolution of 1952, nonetheless survived as a viable political force in the following decades by advancing to the maximum the "economicist" demands of the tin miners. The same was true in Chile, where the Communists played a similar role in the copper mines but also in the Congress, where their deputies were always ready to champion the cause of displaced peasants, workers unjustly dismissed from government employment or private industry, or victims of police brutality. So deeply involved had the Chilean party become in the day-to-day business of democratic politics, in fact, that in

195

the late 1960s it experienced a crisis of identity and several schisms on the part of more inflexibly "revolutionary" elements. Nonetheless—and perhaps for that very reason—to the end of the democratic period in Chile (1973) that party remained the strongest of its kind in all Latin America.

The basic problem that Latin Americans have with Marxism as an economic system is that it does not accept the institution of private property or its extension, private endeavor, even on an extremely small scale. It is important to emphasize this point because many outsiders confuse opposition to the inegalitarian distribution of resources or social power in a society with a frontal assault on the principle of ownership. Actually, the desire of Latin Americans—even very poor ones—to exercise some degree of personal control over their lives in this regard should not be underestimated; nor should the number (particularly in peasant societies) who already enjoy the benefits of the market economy. Regimes that attempt to interfere with the small-scale distribution of goods either succumb to massive protests and a vigorous black market (as in Bolivia or Peru) or find it necessary to mount the full apparatus of a totalitarian state (as in Cuba or Nicaragua).

### Obstacles to the Development of Democratic Capitalism

Most Latin American countries could be said to be "capitalist" in the narrowest sense: their legal systems recognize the sanctity of private property; most major industries and landed enterprises are privately owned; the market plays a major role in setting prices and interest rates; the labor force is mobile; housing is individually owned (or subsidized, rather than supplied on a rental basis). The system departs, however, in several ways from that practiced in the United States. First, it is less egalitarian: a smaller percentage of the population owns a larger portion of corporate wealth, and the distribution of income is vastly more asymmetric. Market forces—particularly for basic foodstuffs—are not always allowed to operate. The labor movement is weaker and also less well remunerated. There is extremely limited provision (in some countries, no provision at all) for social security and unemployment insurance, and where it exists it is confined to government employees and members of labor unions, who constitute a minority of the work force. Though public education exists, it is vastly inferior to private education; thus there is a high degree of generational replication across classes, although some social mobility does exist.

Whatever one may think of this system, it is certainly not democratic capitalism as we know it, even when—as is often the case nowadays—it coexists with democratic political structures. Indeed, the relation between Latin American capitalism and Latin American democracy is a nervous one, partly because the private sector in many countries has historically supported authoritarian regimes and partly because the democratic political class has never unambiguously defined its position on the rights and obligations of property. (Needless to say, the two postures are intimately related.) Even in the most modern countries, public life in Latin America is heavily influenced by the ethical values of the precapitalist era—personalism, family and corporate loyalties, *compadrazco*—according to which tradition is preferable to innovation; contracts are limited to persons one knows and trusts; and rapidly acquired private wealth is necessarily the consequence of theft. The most characteristic result is a kind of bourgeois revolution-in-reverse: self-made industrialists become landowners, marry off their daughters to the sons of penniless aristocrats, and, at an age when their counterparts in the United States are plotting corporate takeovers, retire to their estates.

Some may question whether this description is really quite up-to-date. It is true that the number of Latin American businessmen trained in the United States has increased enormously over the past twenty years, and their competence as managers of large-scale enterprises is not to be doubted. Nonetheless, we are speaking here not of roles but of values: when the society magazines in Latin America still fold their local news notes into obsequious photo spreads of the royal families of Great Britain, Spain—even Norway and Sweden—they are telling us that even fairly extensive economic modernization has not fully succeeded in unsettling a profoundly anti-economic mindset.

Almost as great an obstacle to economic growth is the notion that the public sector is inevitably more productive than the private. This is the argument, at any rate, of Latin American politicians, journalists, and intellectuals, seconded by North American churchpeople and academics. On the basis of evidence—whether from the oil industry in Mexico, the copper industry in Chile, the telephone system and the railroads in Argentina, or the tin mines in Bolivia—it is difficult to see how this idea got its start, unless by "productive" something is meant other than the capacity to generate an economic surplus. Nationalized mines and railroads provide any government with an instant source of employment and, therefore, of lasting political support. Not surprisingly, they typically carry an administrative overhead that consumes a disproportionate share of what they produce. They also satisfy the legitimate aspiration to control basic resources, and they prevent foreigners from enriching themselves on the national patrimony. Government interference in the marketplace can also make available certain basic foodstuffs—typically, bread, beans, and cooking oil—to millions

197

of people who would otherwise go without. It cannot, however, provide the incentive for farmers to produce them, which partly explains why PL–480 aid (Food for Peace) plays so large a role in the Latin American policy of the United States.

Governments, politicans, laborers, and consumers are not the only beneficiaries of statist economic policies—so, quite often, are important members of the business community. Indeed, in countries like Argentina and Brazil, it is difficult to say precisely where the line lies between public and private sectors, particularly in the so-called mixed enterprises deemed to be of strategic value or of compelling national interest. Family and political considerations also play a role in the awarding of contracts, the pricing of products, even the configuration of tariff walls to protect a given industry from foreign competition. I refer here not to corruption in the ordinary sense of the term but to serious, systematic interference with normal market mechanisms. Inasmuch as this interference is accepted in many Latin American countries as part of the capitalist game, it is not surprising that people associate the system with privilege rather than with opportunity.

The major obstacle to the development of democratic capitalism in Latin America is, however, fear of empowering ordinary people. Property enfranchises; lack of property renders one dependent. The entire hierarchical structure of Latin American political and social life rests upon this fact and produces some peculiar paradoxes. Advocates of land reform typically oppose the awarding of fee simple titles to the peasantry, ostensibly because they believe collective exploitation of holdings is more efficient, but more fundamentally because they fear that enfranchisement will lead to exaggerated individualism, the primacy of private agendas, and the loss of revolutionary ardor (all of which is true). Governments prefer not to part altogether with the ultimate political resource—the capacity to offer employment. Modern banking, which introduces an element of impersonality to credit decisions, is subversive to the political hegemony of ruling parties. And of course in countries with large Indian populations, "white" ruling elites fear that enfranchisement will undercut their control of native populations; that is in part why Church-sponsored cooperatives have met with such bitter resistance in Central America and Colombia.

Having said all of this, I must step back and look at Latin American economic systems as they appear to ordinary people. First, they are *advertised* as capitalist by both their advocates and their opponents. (Actually, the former place emphasis upon the term "property," which need not be capitalist at all.) Second, the fruits of the system are distributed in a very (sometimes radically) inegalitarian fashion. Third, the system is incomplete: that is, it lacks the capacity to ensure anything approaching full employment. Fourth, the "safety net" is limited, so that unemployment is a horrendous catastrophe. Fifth, because job opportunities are limited, unions are weaker and are able to deliver less from private employers than from public firms, particularly when they are affiliated with the ruling party. Finally, the state is naturally seen as an equalizer that intervenes to tilt the private economy more nearly in the direction of the public weal. That all sorts of counterproductive trends are generated in the process does not fully undercut the compelling logic of the statist-populist commitment of the vast majority of Latin Americans.

### Can Hybrid Sytems Work Indefinitely?

This question seems wholly gratuitous since the statist-populist model has already been in existence some sixty years. As noted at the beginning of this essay, however, during most of that time it has survived through inflationary monetary policies or, indirectly, by the infusion of external resources. In the foreseeable future, neither course will be viable. It is now generally recognized that inflation is the most serious obstacle to economic growth, and a reluctance to recur automatically to the printing press is growing. Foreign private investment—from which governments have derived a large and reliable tax base—is moving out of Latin America to Canada or the Pacific Basin; and neither Western European nor Japanese capital seems poised to replace it. Concessional assistance will probably continue to be available to some of the Central American countries (El Salvador; Honduras; Costa Rica; and, from some sources, Nicaragua) but not to the larger economies in which there are nonetheless great numbers of people in dire straits—Peru, Colombia, Chile, Brazil, even Argentina. Nor is there an easy solution to the debt crisis, which involves service on some $360 billion in foreign obligations. I do not wish to go too deeply into an issue that deserves a paper of its own; but it should be obvious that, even assuming the best possible case for Latin America—that the entire debt is capitalized by the Western governments and Japan—the region's credit standing will take some time to recover fully. Probably some arrangements will stretch out the debt over many more years, and some countries will adopt the Peruvian practice of partial moratoriums keyed to their balance of trade. However the matter is ultimately sorted out, it will never be possible to return to the situation that prevailed until 1973, in which most Latin American countries could obtain as much credit as they desired.

This situation places particularly acute pressures on the newly democratic governments of Central and South America, which must all at once manage a return to the rule of law and satisfy economic expectations pent-up over long periods of authoritarian rule. For the first time in many years, Latin American democracies have no choice but to reexamine the imperatives of wealth creation, not with a view to becoming democratic capitalist societies (which will probably never happen) but merely to sustain their statist-populist model over the longer term. Moreover, given the present international context, they may have to go further than in the past and, for example, lift subsidies on certain articles of prime necessity, cut the deficits of state enterprises, and revise foreign investment codes. President Alfonsin has been doing precisely this in Argentina; and, in spite of predictions of devastating political fallout, by making these hard decisions, he seems so far to have enhanced public confidence.

One can easily imagine, nonetheless, how such reforms might undercut the stability of these countries before they have a chance to work. Much also depends upon commodity prices, interest rates, and other developments out of the control of any Latin American government. But one thing is clear: these reforms are the only way to save these societies as reasonably open and responsive political systems. If this effort fails, one can anticipate the worst of both worlds—authoritarian political systems combined with permanent economic regression. It behooves policy makers in Europe and the United States to view this dilemma with sympathy and generosity. Likewise, it is incumbent upon Latin American economists and public figures to reflect upon the need to maintain the balance between public and private spheres so that this point of no return is never passed.

# Discussion

DAVID BECKMAN, Universidad Metodista de Piracicaba: I found the paper outrageous because it is so remote from my experience of what is happening in Latin America. Of course there are gross economic inefficiencies, as there are in almost any country. But I thought the argument was that Latin America as a whole would experience negative economic growth if it were not for the inflow of foreign resources. It seems to me the second paragraph of Mark's paper is saying that the level of urbanization and political development in most countries greatly exceeds the capacity of the economic system to satisfy demands. The result is a highly active role for the state, the cost of which has been underwritten, at least until recently, by various kinds of foreign investment.

I don't have a lot of data at hand, but I have looked at the World Bank's *World Development Report* and have picked out some data that just do not square with this kind of stereotype of Latin America. One thing, for example, is the share of central government expenditure in national income. Of sixteen Latin American countries, there are, at least according to these statistics, ten countries where the share of central government expenditure is lower than in the United States, including a couple of large countries, and six countries where the share of public or central government expenditure is higher. These data, it seems to me, do not support the vision of a grossly bloated public sector. I also looked at some figures on gross domestic investment as a share of gross national product for a sample of thirteen Latin American countries, including all the big ones. For the years 1973 to 1978, those thirteen countries invested at roughly 22 percent of their national income; that is, their domestic investment was roughly 22 percent of their national income.

The United States invests about 17 percent of its income, a comparison inviting the argument that these countries are not simply eating up more than they are consuming. If they invest over 20 percent and receive just 5 percent on that investment, that amount itself would be a rate of economic growth of about 1 percent a year. Because these are relatively capital-scarce countries, the average rate of return on invest-

201

ment is considerably higher than in the industrial countries. There is no question that their own domestic investment during that period would have generated some economic growth.

For the same period 1973 to 1978, the same thirteen countries had an average current account deficit of 4 percent of GNP a year; that is, the total capital inflow was on the order of 4 percent a year. For those same countries during that same period, average growth was about 5 percent a year. It's just not the case that all of that capital wasn't enough to account for the economic growth that they achieved.

Mark suggested in an earlier discussion that some of the stereotypes that strike me as almost bizarre are based largely on the experience of the Southern Cone. To test that notion, I looked at the data, and in fact Argentina and Chile for the period 1965 to 1983 had rates of economic growth lower than ten Latin American countries and roughly comparable to four small Latin American countries. These figures support the argument that Argentina and Chile have had exceptionally unfortunate economic experiences over the last twenty years and may explain why these stereotypes strike me as so exaggerated: my experience of Latin America is with areas where the economic situation is not quite so grim.

NICK EBERSTADT, Harvard University: I would like to speak to some of the possible misapprehensions of economic fact and of economic theory that might encourage the stereotype that mismanagement is not largely responsible for Latin America's economic problems. The World Bank's *World Development Report 1985* has done a great service to the world in pulling together many disparate and diverse economic statistics. It may have done less of a service to the world than is first apparent by often mixing together apples and oranges, so to speak, that is, pulling together numbers from different accounts that should not be in the same categories.

One thing, for example, that seems to be a problem in the *World Development Report* accounts is the typing of fraction of government expenditure versus GNP as a whole. The handling of parastatals is also a problem. Sometimes parastatals are counted as part of government expenditure; sometimes they are not. Not counting them yields a systematically distorted view of how little a role government has been playing in the overall economic picture within nations.

A word about investment: investment is rather a magic word in the modern world. Whatever one wishes to call investment is something one thinks is good and is usually a program the government supports and wishes to spend money on. It does not at all necessarily follow that anything that is labeled investment generates productive returns.

If something does not generate productive returns after having been labeled investment, very likely it is going to end up costing money and will have to be continually sustained. Many of the white elephant projects in Latin America certainly would seem to follow this kind of notion.

I think it unusual to argue that external finance has not played a great role in Latin America's overconsumption. The debt crisis itself simply seems to indicate that an unsustainable amount of money has been borrowed that currently cannot be paid back because the returns earned on it have not been sufficient to cover service payments. I do not really see how one can deny that the pattern of development has been unsustainable and that external resources have been critical.

MR. FALCOFF: I just want to make two comments. One is that the years 1973 to 1978 were years of a tremendous kind of credit bonanza, and I think the development that was achieved in those years would not have been possible without it.

The other is that I think it is no accident that Argentina and Chile—also Uruguay, I suspect, though I have not got the figures in front of me—should be the countries suffering from this syndrome precisely because they were the most open and—particularly in the case of Chile and Uruguay—were until 1973 and 1974 the most participative political cultures. I expect, for example, that in countries like El Salvador and Guatemala, which historically have not had, to put it mildly, much political participation, the size of the state and the public sector would be much smaller. What I was trying to point to in the paper was that the growth of participation and of democracy in Latin America will probably spread a condition that I call permanent tension. This tension is so evident in Argentina and Chile precisely because of the high degree of political participation. Although Argentina didn't have democratic government during all this period, it still had all kinds of pressures arising from a very well-organized and politically powerful labor movement, much more powerful than probably any other labor movement in Latin America.

Regarding stereotypes, the intellectual history of a Latin American specialist follows a certain progression. First, one encounters the subject of stereotypes; then of course one enters phase two—no, the stereotypes are wrong. Phase three is next—you know something, those stereotypes had something going for them in the first place. Maybe they were overstated and did not have enough nuances, but they started for a reason, and the reason is that they have a lot of truth to them.

Whether or not my broad-brush portrait of the industrialist who becomes a landowner and retires to his estates at age fifty-five is totally true, I would not write as I did, believe me, at this stage of my career—now twenty years into this business—if I could have found another way of doing it. Every so often in Latin America I am again reminded that there is really not that much new under the sun. I would like to believe there is, but I do not.

MR. BECKMAN: Regarding Nick's earlier points, the World Bank data on central government expenditure are collected according to common definitions. But there are problems with the data because state and local government expenditure wouldn't be included, especially in large countries. We might then expect, for example, the total public sector of Brazil to be considerably understated in size. The data therefore are not great.

My sense is that in most countries parastatals are in fact included; I may be wrong. Nevertheless, I do not think that the data support the claim that Latin America generally has a smaller state sector than the United States or anything like that, but the data at least raise questions about sweeping statements regarding state-dominated economies.

It is also true that not all investment pays off and that there are problems with what is called investment. Nevertheless, from the same accounts for roughly the same period investment in Latin America on average paid off quite handsomely. I am not arguing that some foreign debt was not used to finance consumption, though the occurrence of a debt crisis does not necessarily mean that most foreign investment was wasted. In the same year that the debt crisis broke internationally, 60,000 U.S. companies went bankrupt. We have just gone through the longest, most severe recession in 50 years. Interest rates remain at their highest levels in approximately 200 years. All kinds of enterprises that depend on borrowed capital have had a devil of a time. The simple fact that there has been a debt crisis does not therefore prove that foreign investment has been used primarily to finance consumption.

Regarding Mark's comments, I picked the years 1973 to 1978 partly because the data were available but also because those were the years of the credit bonanza. During those years it is very interesting to note that despite the substantial inflow of foreign investment, the rate of that foreign investment was less than the rate of economic growth.

Clearly, the increase in the income of these countries was not entirely due to foreign investment, as if foreign investment were simply underwriting the cost of wasteful consumption.

I think your stereotypes do have something to them, but what a way to obtain truth—by throwing out gross stereotypes and publishing them!

MR. FALCOFF: I did not wish to say and do not believe that I said that foreign investment finances wasteful consumption. Of course, it depends on what is meant by wasteful consumption. I do not think employment is wasteful consumption. A lot of employment or social security benefits and other kinds of benefits come from foreign credit or foreign investment. I certainly did not mean to suggest in this paper that the Latin Americans are going out and having a good time on borrowed money. They are not having a good time at all.

What I am suggesting is that the infusion of foreign resources has an absolutely critical role, and that is where we disagree, I think. To the degree that we have open political orders, foreign resources are going to be even more critical. In a very undemocratic society, say, Paraguay, such resources do not really come into the picture; they may be desirable but are not socially and politically necessary with so many other ways of controlling a society so that pressures don't surface. But in the complex democratic systems that we now have again in Argentina and Uruguay, that we certainly will have in Brazil, and that we hope to have one day in Chile, the role of foreign resources will be the lubricant, so to speak, that will cushion all those friction points and make it possible for the system to work.

ARTHUR McGOVERN, Department of Theology, University of Detroit: You seemed to be saying that the welfare state in most Latin American countries is limited, so I am concerned about what is meant by wasteful consumption. Certainly there do not seem to be major expenses for what we would consider transfer programs. Social security is not widespread, nor is health care.

What is the extent of the welfare state? And where is the wasteful consumption?

MR. FALCOFF: First, I am glad I already have said that I do not believe employment is wasteful consumption. I have in mind a welfare state that exists in a slightly different form. Take a company like Argentine Railroads, or the Bolivian YPF, which is the state oil monopoly, or the state mining company in Bolivia. These agencies employ two, three, or four times as many people as is really necessary to run them, and that is a form of welfare state.

Regarding wasteful consumption, I was thinking of the period from 1973 to about 1981 when there was an enormous amount of foreign travel in the countries of the cone, and also Brazil. I wish I had some statistics on this. The form that welfare takes in Latin America is employment in government or parastatals. I think Ambassador Ortis told me that Argentina has more employees for Argentine Railroads than we have for Amtrak even though Argentina has a much smaller system. And that is really a form of wasteful consumption.

Most of the modern countries have such things as social security funds, but they are small. Government employment is the form that welfare typically takes. If I may come back to David's point, when I think about private business activity in Latin America, several things occur to me. First, I think of a national business class—and here I'm generalizing for twenty countries—that is not particularly adventurous or entrepreneurial. Not that these businessmen couldn't be good entrepreneurs, but I am describing them as a class in terms of their values and the way they operate. They are very attuned to the trends of international business in their country. They regard the willingness of foreign capital to invest as a sign of confidence in the economic order and follow this very carefully. Governments eagerly seek foreign investment partly to support a climate of business confidence that they hope will encourage local businessmen to invest more, because there has been a tradition, now more accelerated than ever, of sending resources abroad. The role of foreign capital or foreign credit, therefore, is not merely economic but psychological.

The other thing is that if you've distorted my argument, let me try to distort your argument for a minute and say that it is just inconceivable. You seem to be arguing that the Latin Americans really have been doing quite all right in economic growth. Foreign capital was helpful in some cases, even necessary, but we should not overrate its importance; Latin Americans have the capacity to produce sustained economic growth on their own. Is that what you're saying or is that really my distortion of what you're saying?

MR. BECKMAN: I do not think the evidence shows that without foreign investment there would have been negative economic growth. The negative economic growth that Latin Americans have suffered the last couple of years has been due to extraordinary exertions to meet their international obligations in very difficult times and to regain credit-worthiness.

If you have really substantial capital outflows as you had in 1984, then it is hard to maintain economic growth. But without capital inflows, I think that it will be very tough for Latin Americans to have the kind of growth that they've had in the past. The inflows have been important. What I am saying, however, is that these are not grossly wasteful, worthless societies kept afloat only by gringo money.

MR. FALCOFF: I certainly was not trying to say that at all. They are not grossly wasteful. In fact, I do not know who is more wasteful in some ways than we are. What I was trying to say is that if we're concerned with democracy and development, which I think everyone in this room is, we have to think about how democracy will survive, about what preconditions are needed to nurture it and make it work. And how can development be encouraged so that democracy will survive? Without development, it simply will not survive.

What I then tried to say is, let's face facts; the new order will be neither Marxist nor free enterprise. It will be a combination of public and private in which, however, there will always have to be an important balance. At the American Enterprise Institute, that is considered a controversial statement, though perhaps not with Michael Novak. I don't know exactly what the proper mix will be, but if we start from the assumption that there is going to be a very dicey balance, then we can answer all the other questions about how to reconcile the imperatives of democracy and development. If that doesn't come through in the paper, then obviously I need to rewrite it.

MR. NOVAK: I would like to raise two questions for later discussion. First, if we think that Latin America will need at least the larger dimensions of capitalist institutions to produce the growth necessary for democracy, what business institutions might we want to recommend that are now either absent or weak in most Latin American societies? What skills can be transferred, that is, taught, so that increasing numbers of people can participate?

It is the case, I think, that people universally are born with the potential for immense commercial skills, but those skills have to be learned. Such skills have technical aspects that don't just drop out of the sky, but they are quite accessible to transferral.

Adam Smith talked about the universal propensity to truck and barter, and I think there are some other universal propensities—to create and invent, for example—that given the proper institutional setting would flower in millions more people than is now possible. I would therefore like to encourage thought about what institutional structures would generate business activity, especially at the bottom of the economic scale.

The second question has to do with the income inequalities we have talked about. What can one do to encourage the great modern transformation of riches to capital that was John Stuart Mill's crucial point in the *Principles of Political Economy*?

During his lifetime or the lifetime of his father, Mill said he saw in Britain a transformation as more and more families moved from wealth, which meant building castles, holding great parties, and maintaining private armies, to productive investment, which meant job creation and new goods and services to an extent Britain had never before known.

207

When the wealthy moved from being wealthy to being capitalists, a new type of society came into being, a society in his view much more promising for the common good and much more promising for democracy as well.

What can be done at the upper scale to move the wealthy of Latin America to greater investment in productive goods and services? It seems an outrage sometimes that many of the basic elements of life are not produced in the countries of Latin America.

Brazil does seem to have everything from vacuum cleaners to refrigerators or whatever; somebody in Brazil is making them, and somebody in Brazil can service them. Based on what I've heard, Brazil's economy is much more self-contained than many of the others of Latin America.

What could be done to encourage the wealthy, instead of consuming their wealth, to invest it, thus creating jobs and producing goods and services that the countries otherwise would not see? For both ends of the socioeconomic scale, it seems to me, we need to think about institutions. And this is the practical focus I had originally hoped for in this conference. It sometimes takes a while to get there; the presuppositions have to be cleared out first.

LESLIE LENKOWSKY, Institute for Educational Affairs: I also wondered, Mark, why your paper was so controversial.

MR. FALCOFF: Now we have learned that it really is not.

MR. LENKOWSKY: I also agree that it is a brilliant paper, but for someone whose specialty is not Latin America—I have been studying the history of the welfare states in Europe and North America—what you have set forth here is a fairly familiar argument that touches upon a theme that we have been dealing with since the conference began. And that is the relationship between politics and economic development.

If I could just probably further distort what you're trying to say, I think your argument is that mass democracy will lead to economic disaster, indeed is leading toward economic disaster in a number of these countries. As the publics are mobilized, the governing classes respond by providing more and more through the public sector, thereby spending more on consumption than investment and incurring all that debt.

This theme goes way back in the history of the European welfare states. Macaulay used to worry that with the extension of the franchise, democracy was going to be all sail and no anchor. Great debates in the late nineteenth century in Britain about whether or not the working class should be given the right to vote revolved around similar themes.

208

As Mark and some of my colleagues at AEI know, my particular interest in life is examining why the negative income tax—an idea that is beloved by virtually every economist I have ever met—is such a disaster politically. I have a little book coming out on that later this year.

I would like to share a small anecdote about one of the efforts to enact the negative income tax in the United States.

MR. NOVAK: Les, I think you ought to explain for some the negative income tax.

MR. LENKOWSKY: The idea is to get rid of all or most of the income transfer programs coming through the welfare system and replace them with a single cash payment through the tax system. People below a certain level of income would receive money, and others above that level would pay money, that is, taxes. It seemed a neat, efficient, and rational idea, and though about a dozen and a half countries looked at it between the end of the 1960s and a decade later, none, to my knowledge, ever enacted it.

In the United States one effort to move toward a negative income tax came in the form of the family assistance plan proposed by President Nixon in 1969. And it was almost single handedly defeated by Senator Russell Long of Louisiana.

At one point I had a long interview with him, and I said, "Senator Long, what was it that worried you about the family assistance plan?" And he said to me that he felt it would mean an end to democracy if it were enacted.

I said, "Oh?" He said, "Well, you see, in my state, Louisiana, if the plan had come into effect at the benefit level proposed, which was something around half to two-thirds of the poverty line, the benefit for somebody without any other income, roughly 20 percent of the state of Louisiana would be receiving benefits." That was correct. And he said, "Now, how am I, as their representative, going to resist them when they ask for higher benefits?"

He went on to say that because of the nature of income distribution and because of the way a negative income tax works, increasing the benefit level means that more people will get benefits. And he concluded by saying the only way out of this cycle would be a coup. We would have to get rid of representative democracy or sooner or later benefits would go so high they would bankrupt the country.

It seems to me that is the same form that your argument has been taking, Mark, and it is a concern that has always accompanied the development of democracy. We have referred to it here from the start. We have discussed with Peter Berger the relationship between political participation and economic development. It has certainly been a theme in our discussions of liberation theology. I just want to propose where we might come out on this. Democracy is fine, but not if it brings down the country, though that is one alternative. Mark, it seems to me you're suggesting a second kind of alternative, which is a familiar conservative theme: Tell the elites to shape up; quit making foolish decisions; figure out how to run an economy wisely; and so on. The same message was also implied in Peter Berger's response, I think.

Historically there is a third approach. If democratization is going to come, as I suspect for better or worse it is, are there ways to tie the interests of the newly enfranchised masses to those institutions that will make for the overall health of the economy and society? This was, of course, the notion that Disraeli used to argue for, with some success, that is, the phenomenon of the working-class Tory. The idea was that the newly enfranchised working-class voters could nonetheless have Tory values and vote for Tory candidates coming to office, giving more stability to British politics than those who worried about the enfranchisement of the working class feared there would be.

I think this ties into what Michael has just said about the conference's practical focus. There is a need to come up with interesting ways of getting the broad spectrum of voters to exercise the degree of self-restraint necessary for a viable democracy.

PETER SKERRY, Brookings Institution: May I just make a brief response to that? I admit that like most people I have this idea in my head of how the world should work, even though it does not always. Extrapolating from the history of Western Europe and the United States, we have a very idealized notion, as you have just reminded me, about our wonderful economic development. The working class is enfranchised, everything just falls neatly into place, and this is what we want to see everywhere. But according to Trotsky's law of combined development, in some countries—the Latin American countries, for example—things just do not turn out that neatly. In fact, the pieces probably never did fall quite as neatly into place in our own history and Europe's history as we think. We are therefore faced with an interesting dilemma if we believe both in democracy and in development. We have a lot of problems, we and our Latin American friends. How do we sort them out?

As for mass democracy leading to economic disaster, I think that is Senator Long's view, not necessarily mine, because nonparticipation does not necessarily ensure against economic disaster. I can think of quite a few nonparticipatory states, including the Soviet Union, where economic disaster is quite well advanced.

With respect to your options, it seems to me the second option is actually the one that is happening in Latin America now. It is probably the biggest unreported story. Maybe if I had included it, my own paper would have been somewhat less vituperative. There is a sea change in the elites that has not yet become quite visible on the horizon. But I think that is partly responsible for what is happening. The third option that you talk about, Les, is the direction I want for Latin America, and what I want for every society. Now let me now talk a little about this sea change. I will pick three countries—El Salvador, Argentina, and Chile.

El Salvador is a country in which the public sector was never very large, and of course its political system was radically nonparticipatory. Naturally, anyone who considered himself or herself an advocate of change would favor some sort of mixed economy. Interestingly, since Duarte has been in office the Christian Democrats in El Salvador are beginning to recognize the desirability of a mixed economy. Such a recognition would have been, I believe, quite unthinkable five or six years ago. I do not know whether or not this is because of the heavy penetration of the U.S. government and U.S. society in El Salvador. The country has become very close to us in a lot of ways, but it is also true that in the past five or six years the Christian Democratic party in El Salvador has really begun to reexamine a lot of its assumptions about communitarianism and the relationship between community and property.

Argentina, in my view, has a public sector somewhat larger than the figure in the World Bank's *World Development Report.* But President Alfonsín is saying privately and now publicly that there are certain tough decisions that have to be made and that he is making them. Interestingly, there is a certain willingness to recognize this situation, and support for Alfonsín is solidifying. I've talked to the Peronists, and even they say we are going to have to do something about a public sector that is way out of hand.

Although the situation in Chile is of course a little more complex, I think one thing remains from the experience of the Allende years. There is now a much greater consensus, even among socialists, that the Allende approach of expanding the public sector, nationalizing it as much as he did and printing unbacked paper money to finance it, is not the way to go.

In fact, Arturo Fontaine's journal, *Estudios Publicos,* has a very interesting article for those of you who read Spanish. It deserves to be translated into English, and maybe we can do something about that. Written by Benevente of the Catholic University, the article discusses all the different trends in the Chilean Socialist party. It is fascinating to read what Chilean socialists, who have been quite revolutionary in the past, are saying both in exile and in Chile about economic systems and the need to have a more mature and realistic (*realistic* is probably the word they would use) attitude toward the role of property, capital, and development.

WILLIAM GLADE, Director, Institute of Latin American Studies, University of Texas: I think, Mark, that your paper comes very close to where I would be in assessing the prospects in Latin America, but in a somewhat more negative tone; that is, your reading of the situation is rather more negative than mine under almost the same set of circumstances on which we agree.

It seems to me that the survival of a balance of power between the public and private sectors, which you see happening, is not altogether a bad thing. That balance, one could argue, has served Latin America rather well. The system is much more resilient politically and even economically in the long run than I thought some years ago.

But this system has experienced enormous stress, rapid urbanization, mounting demands, and accelerated industrialization, in some ways with really astonishing grace. Despite all of the political trauma, the structural elements of the system are fairly undisturbed.

We therefore have a system that has withstood the crises of the latter 1950s and early 1960s when everybody was afraid that Castroism was going to sweep Latin America. It has survived the military interventions, and I think it stands a fairly good chance of surviving even the current economic crisis, which, as Dave has pointed out, is global and extraordinarily severe.

But I think it may well survive with greater economic efficiency and prospects. And in this sense the current crisis, for all of its devastating effects, human and otherwise, may be in the long run a rather salutary experience.

The crisis has forced more realistic policies upon the public sector, if not necessarily through a sense of the limitations of intervention, at least through a greater appreciation that intervention itself must be handled carefully. There is in country after country a much greater willingness to consider how to make, say, the parastatals efficient, not necessarily to abolish them. There is far more concern today with parastatal efficiency than there was fifteen or twenty years ago or perhaps at any time in the past. There is also a much greater appreciation of the crucial need for realism in the price structure; the kinds of subsidies to urban consumers that have been historic in Latin America are now increasingly recognized to be antieconomic in their effects on the rural sector.

There is a movement away from political price structures toward market pricing with the express expectation that this will yield a more productive environment for rural producers, whether they be small producers, co-ops, or whatever. They have all been penalized by the kinds of price structures that have been quite common. There is also an increasing appreciation of the usefulness of real or positive interest rates, even in countries where they are not evident yet, as opposed to the negative interest rates that have been fairly common in the wildly inflationary period of the immediate past and even before that.

The pricing of public services is becoming much more realistic and productive in its effects on resource allocations. Above all, there is a much greater appreciation than ever before of the need for realistic pricing of foreign exchange. I think we can anticipate that the public sector will continue to be large and certainly not devoid of anti-economic impact. We have this situation in our own country, and for a variety of reasons I think it may continue for a while longer in Latin America.

On the whole I think the public sector will be an even stronger source of support for the economy in the future than it has been in the past, thanks in part to the current crisis, which forces a rethinking of public policy design.

I think you're also a bit pessimistic about the private sector entrepreneurs. It may well be that they are running off to their estates or reading the movie magazines or whatever. Perhaps they do that here on the sly. [Laughter.]

Be that as it may, I think we can look at what is going on in the private sector, at least in some of the major countries and in some of the smaller ones too, and take hope that there has been, as in the public sector, a lot of learning by doing. The entrepreneurial-managerial capabilities are considerably greater than they were certainly when the Alliance for Progress got started, for example, and when Frank Brandenburg wrote his book about private enterprise in Latin America.

With more stable monetary situations, better interest rate policies, and, above all, suitable foreign exchange pricing, we will see a flowering of private sector entrepreneurship in a number of countries. We have seen this in two very opposite cases in Latin America under very different circumstances. Earlier than most countries, Brazil moved to better foreign exchange rate policies and began to experience a remarkable diversification of nontraditional exports. Its manufacturing exports, a diversity of products that withstands international competition, have spread into foreign markets such as the United States, Africa, the Middle East, and elsewhere. One doesn't need too much imagination to see that Mexico is poised—certainly IBM sees it—for considerable export success in the manufacturing area, given suitable exchange rate policies. Without the latter, Mexico and many other countries have been penalized in the past.

Finally, I think the opposite case is Chile. I always dislike trying to find beauty in the Chilean experience. In recent times it is rather like poking among the ashes to see what survived the conflagration. And yet if we look, we see even there a basis for hope. One would have supposed for a variety of reasons that the experience of the 1970s would just about have wiped out the manufacturing sector in Chile. I am referring to the hot-house growth, in any standard economic sense a wholly artificial product, that resulted from the policies of the 1920s on.

Chile was subject to wrenching twists of national policy in the 1970s. And yet in spite of all of that and the double jeopardy of having been exposed to extreme foreign competition from imports by the overvalued exchange rate, the manufacturing sector in Chile made some astonishing adjustments to avoid being wiped out. Although it certainly isn't strong and right now isn't flourishing, it's still there. Product lines and so on were readjusted, which suggests much more entrepreneurial and managerial agility than one might have expected in that extreme case.

I think there is much reason to hope that the balance not only will develop as you foresee but will be rather more productive in the future than it has been in the past.

FRED TURNER, Department of Political Science, University of Connecticut: I would like to tie Mark's paper in one or two ways to our discussion in the first three days of the conference and to make a particular plea. I see Mark's paper as essentially descriptive rather than prescriptive. But after his paper and after our conference, I think that one of the best directions for some of us here may be toward making detailed, analytical, forward-looking, prescriptive statements for individual countries.

Let me relate this to what I see as an underlying theme of the conference. I mention it in the context of a discussion last night about Arturo's paper with Paul and Barbara Sigmund. I made a statement, referring to the last sentence of Arturo's paper about the emperor and his clothes, that those who believe that emperors should wear clothes should go into the clothing business; that is, they should carefully design royal vestments. An underlying and a largely unspoken conference theme that has come up over and over again is the degree of specificity in designs for programmatic change. One of the criticisms, which I think may in retrospect be quite unfair toward liberation theology, has been about this issue of specificity.

Some of us as long ago as the 1960s wrote with great enthusiasm about Christian democracy as an energizer, not necessarily as a whole set of prescriptions that would work everywhere, but a religious per-

214

spective that would helpfully galvanize and energize the masses of people in Latin America. If we were so willing to do that in an earlier generation for Christian democracy, why can we not view liberation theology with the same commitment and with a similar absence of detailed specificity?

The specificity issue comes up in relation to Marxism, too. Father McGovern noted in his paper and in his presentation that it's rather exciting intellectually that Marx himself would have fit more with the modernization paradigm. One of my most treasured memories of this conference will be the chance to have listened to, and then have lunched with, Professor Assmann to understand how, as he told us yesterday, he is not so ready now to use Marxist categories as he was twelve and fifteen years ago, to have heard the story of how he was intellectually persecuted by Soviet journals worldwide for taking an apparently anti-Soviet stance.

Although Marxism figures in our discussions in quite contrasting ways as it does in Arturo's paper, nevertheless one thing that it is very natural to criticize in classical Marxism is the absence of specificity. In Arturo's paper, the great criticism is that Chilean liberation theologists have not been more specific. That is the original Marx rather than the reinterpreted Marx. Marx provided a critique of capitalism, not a blueprint for socialism. There was no blueprint for socialism until well into this century, and critics would say there is no effective blueprint for socialism even at the end of the twentieth century.

Once again the issue as I see it is specificity. If we want more specificity and think it is useful, then the question is, how do we develop more appropriate paradigms? Perhaps what we really want is competition—a marketplace of competing ideas and of competing, more detailed institutional structures.

I expect there is a good deal of support around this table for Peter Berger's suggestion, that the more appropriate paradigms will be capitalist in some sense. But my own plea is that we need people with different orientations to develop their own national paradigms in far more detail.

After reading Arturo's paper, listening to his presentation, and talking with him at two meals here, I second Paul Sigmund's comment in the meeting yesterday that Arturo may be in one of the best positions to provide a new paradigm from his own perspective.

Having a poet for a son, I am impressed by poets who can do many things. In fact, I remind you that Henry Fielding could write *Tom Jones* and head the London police and reform the London police. Sometimes poets are in the best position to bring creativity and a fresh outlook to what we need.

215

Some people might feel that reading Michael Novak is the answer. The closest to a conversion experience that I have seen in the last year was the euphoria of a visiting Venezuelan economics professor who came to lunch at our faculty club day after day having read more chapters of *The Spirit of Democratic Capitalism*—truly a convert.

I understand that this book is now in Latin America in its third edition, and that is fine as far as it goes. If we are to take the analysis in Mark's paper into account here, though, this is not enough. We will never get enough converts for that. What we may need most are a series of plans for national development that may lead us toward a general theory based on the experiences of the countries.

It is hard enough to trace development and democracy in Brazil or in Argentina or in El Salvador. Perhaps we should not think now about the overarching global or even hemispheric paradigm but about national development and related political and democratic strategies. After we get a series of more effectively competing national paradigms, we can then start thinking in larger terms.

HUGO ASSMANN, Universidad Metodista de Piracicaba: I am very happy that the paper and presentation of Mr. Falcoff touch on the essential questions. In Latin America we now have to recognize the whole issue of parastatals. Experience is different from country to country, however, so it is difficult to generalize.

In Brazil we have the phenomenon of the leftist parties wanting less statism rather than more. There are more than 520 state or public enterprises in Brazil, and around 28 or 30 have been already sold back to the private sector. And the new government intends to sell around 300 of the 520 enterprises. No private capital can support the enormous burden of overemployment in those state enterprises.

The example Mark gave of the tin mines in Chile is very clear. If the cost of production of a kilo of tin in Bolivia is $16 and the market price only $5, that does not mean that the production price has to be $16. It could be less. There are so many miners there. We have the same situation in the state enterprises of Brazil. And private capital cannot afford that. I expect we therefore will necessarily have new kinds of joint ventures between the private and public sectors because the current system cannot be dismantled quickly. Mark introduced a new concept of productivity to include productivity in employment and social security and so on. Productivity cannot be defined only as the output of products. One obstacle for reprivatization is that normally the salaries in the state enterprises are higher than the salaries in the private factories.

Is it possible that the diversification of Brazilian exports has a lot to do with this big state apparatus? The diversification did not happen, in my opinion, only through initiatives from the private sector. The public sector has created the possibilities of diversifying exports.

Another point: the public sector has created technology and appropriated it. How this technology will be transmitted to the private sector, that is, to the small factories and other small enterprises, I cannot see. In Brazil there's really an indigenous technology created through the state, not just a technology coming in from the outside.

It is understandable that Brazil has become an important competitor in the electronic market and will not allow that market to be controlled by the Japanese or by IBM, and so on. Brazil really has developed a lot of technology internally in aviation, and is selling airplanes and computer components in many places.

The reprivatization of technology is very difficult. And discussing the private initiatives of three creative nations is sometimes very difficult because we have to think of intermediate solutions in relation to the state.

In conclusion, one of the most difficult challenges for Brazil would be to democratize the welfare apparatus without the intervention of the state, since welfare at present is truly controlled by the state through overemployment on a large scale. Social security, health care, and even education are tremendously controlled by the state. How can Brazil dismantle this whole apparatus and at the same time ensure that social benefits are not destroyed? Please comment on these issues.

MR. FALCOFF: First, I thank you very much for enriching this discussion by telling us very specifically about what is in many ways the most important country in South America, particularly regarding these issues. Your comments underline a couple of things. First, what is needed is a new social pact. Someone called it a paradigm. There's a recognition that some kind of new social pact is needed, though I don't know what it will look like.

Second, I went out of my way not to idealize the private sector; if I feel that strong antieconomic biases exist in the parastatals, they must also exist in the private sector. So I am glad that I did that.

You also underline another point—that there is a logic to the public sector that may serve other agendas. It does not happen to serve the agenda of putting all the ink in the black, but it may serve other agendas, be they employment, national security, national sovereignty, and so on.

As for exports, both Brazil and Argentina are significant exporters of military hardware. I do not know anything about your state military factories; but I will tell you about the ones in Argentina that I do know about. First, they have been very successful with the Pucara counterinsurgency aircraft. The directorate general of military factories in Argentina is, however, one of the biggest causes of the deficit.

A close examination of their budget reveals how highly paid their executives are, most of whom are retired generals. The DGFP is therefore used as a kind of gilded retirement for the military. One other thing that needs to be studied in the case of Argentina is how the military state, as I call it, has expanded into all kinds of areas during the 1970s. A shoe factory might be owned by the military, or a winery. Why would the military need a winery? Well, they have to have wine for their soldiers, so they have to have a winery!

Some of these things were acquired through the expropriation of politically undesirable personalities, and some were acquired by takeovers, sweetheart contracts, and the purchase of stock options under very curious circumstances. I am sure the government is looking into this now. I do not think anybody in Argentina knows the full extent to which the public sector is or was until 1981 controlled by the military. It won't be reflected in the defense budget.

Again relying on the countries I know well, I want to mention one last thing about Argentina. The atomic program is one of the most expensive items in its budget, but does not figure in the national accounts for reasons of national security. This is reserved information, but people at the World Bank are supposed to know what it amounts to, and it is a very big item. I was told by a friend of mine at the bank in 1981 that the program budget was about $1.5 billion for 1980, which struck me as huge. It was hard to believe that figure, but that is the figure he gave me.

Thus, the demilitarization of Brazil, Argentina, and Uruguay is probably going to have strong implications for decreasing the size of the public sector right away.

In my paper I also mentioned empowerment as an issue and fear of empowerment by government and politicians on the left and right in Latin America. I would like to ask Dr. Assmann whether he thinks that because Brazil is now a democracy, the whole environment in which liberation theology is taking place is going to be a quite different one.

In the past, as Dr. Assmann said last night, the church was the only haven for certain kinds of protest and social thinking, and so it took on a new identity. Now we have a new context, and I wonder if you would tell me what you think of two or three possibilities. Don't you think that the possibility of politics as usual in an open environment is necessarily going to deprive liberation theology of some of its past mystique, that the process of participating in an open environment might demystify it? Would you speculate on what might happen to liberation theology as it ceases to be a means of protest with its added spiritual mystique within a dictatorship, and moves into an open environment where many different forces compete for people's attention and support? We hear about watered-down Marxism. What about watered-down revolutionary Christianity? How do you see this developing?

MR. ASSMANN: There is a kind of anxiety among the Christian communities now, even among the theologians, because of the feeling that something about the context of the past has changed completely and that, as you have stated correctly, one of the essential points of the past mystique is being lost. This kind of liberation mystique cannot continue now as it did in the context of repression. Then there was a kind of survival mentality, the survival mentality of an extreme situation. At the same time it was and is a tremendous accumulation of energy, of solidarity, of new human relations, and of new forms of organization. The old forms of leftism in political groups are over. They have not much to give to these people who have experience with restless communities. Power for them means something different from the old Leninist conception of the party, whereby a central committee and a group of people with ideas go in and dominate the rest of the people.

The only official statement regarding discipline coming from the Catholic bishops to the grass-roots Christian communities was two months before the elections of November 15, 1982. Before then there were a lot of documents from the bishops applauding the grass-roots communities.

The possible economic activity of these communities is a new issue. Until now the primacy of the political and of the pastoral dimensions was the only thing about which we really were aware. But now we sense a new context. The political parties, the new forms of trade unionism, and many other kinds of popular movements are assuming the kind of political role the grass-roots communities had. Will the communities' mission be voided by this? I think not.

But this perception is perhaps not the perception of many people or many political organizations. I will just say how my own party sees it. Our constituencies of the workers' party are to a great extent the constituencies of the grass-roots communities. Many of the elected people in my party are coming from the grass-roots communities and from the new trade unionism.

My party's program very clearly holds that all forms of popular organization, of economic cooperation, and of religious discussion have to be treated at their own level. Was that included just as a tactic in the party program? No, there is a new awareness. We will go through a time of perhaps five or more years when political discussion will always be

219

very superficial, even if very vociferous. We need more profound discussions, and that is where the grass-roots communities have really accumulated experience.

The economic usefulness of the grass-roots communities has been an unwritten chapter until now. I hope there will be energies that can be directed to economic initiatives beyond the level of survival, because at the level of survival we already have a lot of experience.

HENRY NORMAN; Volunteers in Technical Assistance: I would like to go back to Michael's invitation to cite some actual examples of grass-roots development of industries, but first I would like to point out that there is not a tremendous amount of interest on the part of most developing world governments in rural enterprises or even in small enterprises. Most of them are interested in export industries so that they can gain hard currency.

Another factor is that the international donor agencies, such as the United Nations and the World Bank, have to work through governments. And you therefore have a diversion of resources away from the development of small industries and rural industry.

I have worked in Marxist countries and non-Marxist countries and in one country, Afghanistan, that went from being a Marxist country to a communist country. Everywhere there was very little interest in the development of rural industry or small industry. I have talked to any number of government people in various countries, pointing out to them that in this country the Fortune 500 companies have not produced a single new net job in the past five years; that all of the entrepreneurial explosion has come from small and medium companies in this country. I encouraged them to think of building from the bottom up.

There are two countries that are doing this, and we are working closely with them. The model I would like to cite to you is the Center for Entrepreneurial Development in India. Those at the Center have taken the theory that entrepreneurs are not born, but can be created. They have modified that a bit to develop an entrepreneurial profile. They have a whole series of testing devices. They simply put ads in the papers asking people if they are interested in starting their own businesses. When people respond, they are given examinations and a choice of classes they may take.

People go through a period of training during which they may receive counseling on the kinds of businesses that they are specifically interested in. The Center tries to do market studies and tries to determine if indeed a business is a viable option for the person who is being trained. At the conclusion of the training the Center will lend persons small sums of capital to set up businesses. This is an Indian organization—a parastatal—not a foreign-aid kind of operation. Their spinoff is an industrial consulting organization, which does consulting for the entrepreneurs who are now on their own; in addition, it consults with larger Indian companies and tries to bring in foreign technology to be exploited by the Indian organization.

Last year we entered into an agreement with *Gujarat Industrial & Technical Consultancy Organization* and with the U.S. Small Business Administration whereby we gave a conference in Boston for 100 American companies and explained to them the advantages of doing business in India. Nine months have passed since that time; last month an American company signed a joint venture agreement with an Indian company, and five more American companies are negotiating with Indian companies.

Last month we had a conference in Seattle for the People's Republic of China, and 142 American companies came to that meeting. We are now in discussions with Chinese government agencies on the development of a low-cost modernization program for Chinese industry. We are talking about a $400,000 industry—no small economic question.

We think that when a government is interested and gives priority to rural or small industry, development is possible—even on a major scale.

The other day I mentioned that Korea had built from the top down; what I meant was that they have vertical organization. The Korean government did a superb job of cooperating with American research and development institutions to bring in the technology and information that helped it set up large industries.

But the government drove so hard for exports that these industries were vertically organized; it starved the small industry of capital. Now it is turning that around. It is trying to build up small industries by making capital available to them and is using research and development activities to bring in technology as well as to develop indigenous technology.

There are information and resources available if the host country or developing country gives priority to the development of rural and small industry. And I think that the absence of these industries in some countries is very much due to government policies and government-induced indifference to such development.

MR. NOVAK: Could you say a word, Henry, about another phenomenon I heard you mention privately; namely, that in those countries that are politically more developed than economically, one who gets to a local village with a new venture typically encounters resistance from the strongest local politician, worried about the threat from some new venture.

MR. NORMAN: I think this is simply a microcosm of what I am talking about with regard to the governments. There is a resistance to a new power center. I regret, for example, having missed the session yesterday, but I was talking to the Johnson and Johnson Company about their interest in doing some things in Zambia. We had proposed that we develop an existing women's group and work with them—since women do 80 percent of the agriculture in Africa. Scholarships go to the males; when the males come back, of course the last thing in the world they want to do is to go out and farm. They want to stay in the capital city and become agricultural bureaucrats.

We have proposed recruiting female agricultural technicians in this country and sending a female technician to Zambia. Of course the men would not be interested in working with her. We would set up a combination program. We would increase agricultural production with women who do the farming, particularly by introducing new seeds and new labor-saving machinery or tools that we have helped develop. We would also do nutrition education and, probably most important of all, would help set up small rural industries to do food processing because nutrition is such a critical problem in Africa now.

When the women start making money, then the position of women will very rapidly improve in Africa. Our whole strategy is to try to improve nutrition, to improve agricultural production, and to create wealth through micro-industries for food processing so that food is not wasted.

The University of Lusaka has done a study and has determined that half of all the food produced by peasants on small farms is lost through pests, climate, and so on. If you could just cut that in half, I think you'd have a greater availability of food than any agricultural program I've seen.

The reason I suggested this example is that the woman who heads the program is related to the president of the country. We would not dare to go just anywhere and propose this because of the resistance to creating a power center that has money and skills.

MR. NOVAK: Are you doing anything in Bangladesh?

MR. NORMAN: No. We have been asked by the Bangladesh government to do there what we are doing in India.

May I make just one more point? Regarding parastatal industries, in the Bahamas there is a very large parastatal or state-owned farm that has been losing money for a long period of time. We got together with a multinational agricultural group and developed a project whereby they would gradually take the farm private. We would work with the displaced workers on farming the unused land. When a major industry is going private and consequently has to fire a great many of the workers, it can try to put displaced workers into the kinds of activities that would nourish the industry.

MR. EBERSTADT: I would like to follow up on Henry Norman's comments about small enterprises and parastatals. One of the real virtues of Mark's paper is that it very skillfully described the political base for a nexus of bad policies that seem to affect in varying degrees on entire continent.

The signs of the pathology are slow growth, international financial dislocation, pronounced unemployment, and exacerbated poverty. One of the significant ways in which these problems are related to each other concerns government policies specifically, uneconomic and highly restrictive foreign exchange controls, bifurcated credit policies, uneconomic subsidies, far-reaching and restrictive price controls, and unwise state investment policies.

What do these policies do besides exacerbate the problems I previously mentioned? What they do, it seems to me, is to create various sorts of barriers to social mobility between sectors for individuals.

These barriers to social mobility are a very important aspect of inequality that we are not always sensitive to, but they have far-reaching consequences in their effects on attitudes, motivation, and incentives. I see a link between policies that create barriers to social mobility on the one hand and a preoccupation with the distribution of (but not accountability for) power on the other hand. There is much talk in Latin American circles about group interests but very little talk about individual rights.

I wonder whether Mark or others would care to comment on the extent to which empowering the poor necessarily involves some sort of reconception or reassertion of individual rights and on the extent to which individual rights in Latin America can be promoted by changes in the legal system.

MR. FALCOFF: I have two things to say about that. It is not at all odd that in Latin America people think in terms of sectoral rights rather than individual rights. If you look at the history of the region, you will see that the only concessions people have been able to exact from the system have been through sectoral conflict or what they call conquests.

Latin Americans use the metaphor of war in which you seize terrain and consolidate a conquest. Sometimes you lose your conquest, as a barber in the Hotel Careda in Chile explained to me while shaving my beard with a straight razor recently. I was very much in favor of restoring his conquest.

If one looks at the history of the region, this perspective is not too surprising. As I alluded in my paper, all kinds of vested interests of all kinds of groups keep the game this way. In these societies there's a disjunction between the part of the community that is in the modern economy and the part that is not, which is the desperately poor in many countries. Still I do not think it's too surprising that there has been a tacit agreement that this is the way the social pact should be forged. If one starts to do something on a one-to-one basis, then one calls into question the whole relationship between the people inside the social pact and the people outside the social pact, which of course is the vast majority in most countries. The idea of individual rights is thus tremendously subversive; both conservatives and reformers have chosen to go the sectoral route. And for all I know, it has been the best route for stability and for social progress, though it has not much helped to bring into the system all those people that are outside it. This issue is interesting; it also shows why the political culture of the United States in some ways is very much more radical than any in Latin America, though there is sectoral conflict in the United States as well.

ARTURO FONTAINE: Part of David's problem with the paper was due to some general concepts that could be made more precise. One of them is the "welfare state." Others are "democratic capitalism," "populism," and "statism." Since all these concepts have a wide variety of possible interpretations, their meanings are vague. And then we have the suggestion, which I'm sure was not intended, but that somehow the development of the welfare state has been paid for by American investment or loans. That suggestion is risky since, in fact, the welfare state developed prior to and independent of the cheap loans of the period we're discussing. There is therefore no causal connection. It is true, however, that a great deal of the money coming in during the very brief period of cheap money because of the oil glut was by and large inefficiently used. Perhaps the real question is, Why were the institutional structures in place prior to the arrival of this money so badly prepared to make good use of it?

I think there are cases where the degree of mismanagement of this money has been exaggerated. Obviously the key element is the extremely high interest rates that we've had. No one predicted them; they would have been very difficult to predict. One has to face this element because it's a major factor.

Regarding the welfare state, in Latin America a number of things must be considered. One of them is what could be called the area of the public good—funding for education, health, and the arts and sciences—areas traditionally taken care of directly by the state, usually by state institutions. In America these areas, though privately funded, become part of the welfare state, too, through the kind of subsidy provided by tax exemptions. These institutions wouldn't be possible otherwise, of course. Latin American culture, by contrast, depends directly on the state—an important and unchanged historical fact.

Another part of the welfare state, transfer programs for health care and social security, is in most of the countries of South America, at least, very developed and actually reaches an enormous variety of groups. It is not the case, though, that every worker has social security or health security. The system doesn't work to the extent it does here, but that is simply poverty.

These programs are very extensive and quite sophisticated, I think, in the way they function, at least in some of these countries. Of course there are inefficiencies, but inefficiencies also exist here.

Another part of the welfare state concerns regulations and interventions—distortions of the price mechanism, high tariffs, and so on. And yet another area, state-owned enterprises, has usually been badly managed, overexpanded, and overemployed, as Dr. Assmann has pointed out, and for a while was thought by many on the left as well as on the right to be a great solution. The idea of nationalization was supported on different sides of the political spectrum.

Now, by and large, the situation has changed. It is a major change one can see in the economy—a widespread agreement that transferring an enterprise to the public sector or establishing some kind of cooperative management for the enterprise simply doesn't work. The latter alternative still has some appeal but is the more unfair. If the wealth being transferred is assumed to be so important that no private company should have it, it is perhaps even more unfair to transfer this wealth to people who happen to have been hired there at a certain time and who then acquire a monopoly on the management of a key sector of the economy that they didn't create. The situation would be different for someone who actually created an enterprise. But simply giving the management to the people who happen to work in an industry makes a difference in quality of power. A lawyer, an engineer, or a worker in a large industry would unjustifiably have much more power than their counterparts in a small industry.

There is also a consensus, which Bill Glade mentioned, on the tremendous importance of realistic foreign exchange rates. Most countries have had bad experiences in moving away from the traditional

225

position of relying on the price structure, on positive interest rates, and on other standard, orthodox measures that are not as revolutionary or shocking today as they were awhile ago.

I'm even more encouraged with what Bill said about the entrepreneurial capacity of Latin America, which I believe we were discussing in connection with Peter Berger's paper. It's always very difficult to measure entrepreneurial capacity when the institutions do not exist that would allow that capacity to express itself. We never know whether we are talking about the rational decision maker simply doing what has to be done, given the circumstances, to maximize income, power, influence, what have you, or whether we have some independent variable at work here. Why do Chileans, Brazilians, or Argentinians like to work as bureaucrats of large corporations or state-owned enterprises? Well, there is an easy explanation: high incomes. They are simply maximizing the options they have. A deeper question is why certain countries design institutions of one sort or another. That is for me the most difficult cultural question still to be answered. Perhaps the capacity to design free institutions is more crucial than the lack of entrepreneurial capacity. What made the South Koreans establish the institutions they did? A number of hypotheses could be made for the economic area. Why did they not do the same things in the more important political area?

These kinds of important questions still have to be addressed. And the positive recognition of entrepreneurial capacity that I agree has been shown during these years ought also to encourage us to respect the traditional organization of these countries.

Part of the lesson from the Japanese experience is that one ought to respect the traditional ways in which people establish working relationships. There are extraordinary values in Latin culture. Latin Americans have a high regard for sharing and for family relations, and they understand the business enterprise in a very human way. Some people attack these values as remnants of feudalism. But I think the example of Japan shows that there can be many good things about feudalism. There can be great productivity even within certain traditional social structures, provided of course they are forced to be competitive in an open environment.

I would like to see a growing consensus on two specific proposals. The first is to get rid of inefficient state-owned industries and use this opportunity to open up new possibilities by distributing stocks and creating a capital market of small stockholders using the state enterprise. We have a historical opportunity to distribute property without crisis, starting with the state-owned companies that lack legitimacy today. This would be a way of empowering individuals.

The second is to design and implement a safety network for the very poor, those on the socioeconomic floor, so to speak. This idea has been criticized as impossible. We would achieve a great deal if we could direct our transfer programs to establish a preference for the very poor, and if we really made an effort to see that all our taxes for transfers would at least reach this group. Many other more theoretical questions about an even distribution of wealth from different sectors of the society could be postponed for a while, so that we could advance in this area. We already agree in many respects about how to do this. The ultimate challenge is to liberate the creative energies now held in check in Latin American societies not only by regulations but also by certain ideas.

Finally, the issue of development and in a sense wealth is basically a function of the expectations of the decisions of the society's elites. People who trust the elites to make rational decisions invest and become wealthy in one way or the other. But when people do not expect the elites to make rational decisions, poverty is more likely. The issue is not natural resources; it is institutions. But institutions are ultimately simply vehicles for organizing the decision-making of a society.

No matter where we stand and how wide our differences have been and are, certain notions are beginning to emerge. One is that no matter who is in power, those who are out of power will be able to survive. The other is that the decision-making process will be more rational. A lot needs to be done to emphasize the rational decision-making process in all areas of the society, particularly in the cultural area. The cultural element might be crucial. Anthony Downs, an authority on this issue, is here, so I hesitate to comment further.

But for me the great question is, How do we tie the notion of self-interest to the cultural values, which at times can become part of a group's self-interest. The intellectuals, it seems to me, need to redefine their notions of self-interest. Then the pressure groups that have been suppressing the energies of society might, by facing certain specific and concrete problems, bring about dramatic changes.

MR. FALCOFF: I just have two comments. First, what you said about tradition was, of course, the whole point of the paper. Maybe I should have embraced tradition more joyously than I did, but that was certainly the point. Your comment about the Japanese is an interesting metaphor, but it is also a puzzling one, because the Japanese manage to have it both ways—to keep tradition and to develop. I wish we could find a way to do this in other countries.

I have asked many Japanese economists and social scientists about this, and they always throw up their hands and say we Japanese do not know how we did it, so we cannot even tell anyone else. And that is too bad, for obviously Japan would be the ideal paradigm for third world countries.

My second comment is about rationality. I brood about it a lot, thinking that maybe people do things because to them those things make sense. The problem is I do not like what they do. I am therefore constantly trying to figure out ways to discover a new rationality that would cause people to act rationally the way I want them to act. But, anyway, I think that rationality is a real problem. We approach the notion of development with the idea that there's a certain kind of rational economic conduct that, once observed and followed, would then maximize everything.

Unfortunately one does have to admit that perhaps what people are doing, as you mentioned a minute ago about those seeking jobs in parastatals, obeys a logic that makes a lot of sense in terms of maximizing the available options. I guess this brings us back to the chicken-and-egg argument. How do you transform institutions so that they impose a new and better rationality?

MR. NOVAK: That is a very good comment with which to close. The whole secret of political economy has to do precisely with setting up a system for people, whether for a virtuous or a nonvirtuous people, that on the one hand arranges incentives and punishments in such a way as to preclude the worst abuses (the checks and balances idea) and on the other hand promotes maximum creativity and makes behavior that seems quite rational and responsible to individuals also work to the public good. That is the whole secret of designing institutions and is why the design proves to be so crucial.

# Appendix

*During the conference, the question of Latin American debts lurked constantly in the background. Two excellent articles germane to several of our discussions appeared. With the permission of their original publishers, we herein reprint them.*

## The Return of the Debt Crisis

### *Tom Bethell*

Two years ago there was a nine-month publicity campaign directing our attention to the international debt crisis. In the end it achieved its purpose. The Reagan administration reversed itself and supported an $8.4 billion expansion of the International Monetary Fund's lending authority. But it was a close shave because the necessary legislation passed the House of Representatives by only six votes. It was opposed both by leftists who saw the potential for nationalization in a banking collapse and by rightists who saw that continued foreign lending is the only thing that keeps international socialism afloat.

At that time the foreign debt totaled about $800 billion. Today it is approaching $1 trillion, and what we are hearing, unless I am mistaken, is the lull before the next storm. The problems that existed two years ago not only have not been corrected. They have been aggravated by the IMF's loan conditions, which impose a regime of austerity on indebted countries. The wrong belts get tightened. The people rather than their rulers are expected to suffer. (The current wave of austerity economics emanates not just from the IMF but reflects the consensus of professional economists in the United States and Western Europe.)

#### Dollars, Dollars, Dollars

The countries with the largest external debt are Mexico and Brazil, both owing about $100 billion. Then comes Argentina with close to $50 billion. The person most conspicuously agitated about Latin American debt ($360 billion) is Fidel Castro, who vacillates between advocating

229

outright repudiation of the debt and suggesting that the U.S. government bail out the creditor banks. Here we can see that he is torn
between a desire to punish capitalists on the one hand, and on the other
to encourage the useful-idiot bankers to keep the loans flowing so that
the international socialist elites can continue to live comfortably off the
Western surplus.

It won't be long before influential voices in the United States are
heard echoing Castro's latter sentiment. The rationale will be that the
emerging democracies of Latin America are fragile, and unless we keep
shipping them dollars they will slip back into darkness and dictatorship.
"Most of Latin America's democratic leadership continue to warn that
the United States must act more aggressively to help resolve the continent's economic crisis, or face the loss of the continent's rare embrace
of moderate democratic politics," writes Jackson Diehl, who recently
completed three years as the *Washington Post*'s South America corre-
spondent. "In the simplest terms, that means more U.S. dollars—more
investment in Latin American industries, more favorable terms for
Latin American exports to the United States, and, above all, more help
paying off the banks."

This recommendation is self-defeating, but the bankers will heart-
ily endorse it nonetheless. The problem (for the bankers) is that democ-
atically elected leaders are more self-confident than autocrats and are
much more inclined to respond to the popular sentiment in their countries to rid themselves of the IMF and Yanqui-imposed austerity and
debt. By contrast, the old military dictators were more insecure, less
beholden to the people, and far more responsive to their patrons and
supporters abroad. Democracy is more likely to bring the debt crisis to
a head than to resolve it.

As things stand, the bankers have a problem. Big slices of third
world debt are recorded on the "asset" side of their balance sheets.
What this means is that such institutions as Citicorp, Chase Manhattan,
and BankAmerica contain in their well-guarded vaults pieces of paper
bearing the signatures of foreign government officials (some of them
retired and living in Switzerland), ten-figure sums with dollar signs
attached, and a promise that these debts will be repaid in U.S. dollars
by a certain date. These pieces of paper are called "assets" because
they are also supposed to yield their possesors a stream of interest
payments. On the "liability" side of the ledger they have deposits, on
which of course they must pay interest out.

The problem is that most of the countries owing these huge sums
are in such bad financial shape that they can hardly pay the interest, let
alone the principal. As John Kenneth Galbraith noted recently, bad

debts are now called "nonperforming assets." A whole new euphemistic terminology is growing up and around banking, hiding from view the poor judgment of loan officers. Thus "nonperforming" loans are frequently "rolled over." In such cases interest payments have not been received, and so the bankers pay themselves the interest and quietly add that amount to the principal. Sometimes the IMF will chip in with a "loan" to one of the indebted countries, which promptly mails it back in the form of overdue interest payments to the various banks. In such cases one can best visualize the money going from IMF headquarters on Nineteenth Street, N.W., in Washington, to Wall Street in New York City.

### Ortega's Credit

Obviously this is a game that can't be kept going forever, or at least without fresh infusions from the U.S. taxpayers to the banks, via Congress and the IMF. And here we may hope that Congress will balk. On July 17 the second largest bank in the country, BankAmerica, unexpectedly declared a second-quarter loss of $338 million, a development that "surprised even top executives at the bank holding company," according to *Barron's*. A team of investigators from the U.S. Comptroller of the Currency discovered some nonperforming assets, apparently, and told the bank to set aside an additional $527 million as a "loan-loss reserve."

The big New York banks have now established among themselves a secondary market for their international debt, trading it back and forth at a discount. The size of the discounts, as the *New York Times* put it in understated fashion, "provides tangible evidence that many Third World loans are not worth their face value." Nicaraguan debt trades at 10 percent of face value, according to the *Times* story, Bolivian debt at 20 percent, and Peruvian debt at half face value.

If correct, these figures suggest that bankers remain an incorrigibly optimistic breed. It is hard to imagine who would want to pay 50 cents for a dollar's worth of Peruvian debt. According to *The Economist,* Peruvian creditors "have not received a red cent of interest on their $11 billion in the past six months." (Actually, Peru's foreign debt is closer to $14 billion.) And according to recent congressional testimony by Christine Bogdanowicz-Bindert, a senior vice president of Shearson Lehman, "Interestingly, Peru also moved its international reserves out of U.S. banks to forestall any attempts by U.S. creditor banks to attach its assets." She added: "Surprisingly, the banks have so far remained quiet. They have declared no defaults."

It would also be surprising if Nicaraguan debt is worth a tenth of its face value. Daniel Ortega has repeated Castro's call for a repudiation of debt and has made it as plain as can be that Nicaraguan debt is not going to be repaid. Bolivia is likewise in default and declared in May 1984 that it would pay no further interest to its creditor banks.

In its detailed story on BankAmerica's second-quarter loss, the *Wall Street Journal* noted the bank's assessment of a group of debtor nations "to which the bank wishes it had never lent money and won't soon again. The latter category would include Paraguay, Nigeria, Bolivia, and Nicaragua." Clearly we have come a long way from the time when bankers used to say that it was reassuring to lend money to countries "because countries can't go bankrupt."

When the international debt crisis is discussed people sometimes ask, What happens to the money when it goes abroad? As it happened, on the same day that the *Wall Street Journal* reported BankAmerica's woes, an adjacent story on the "Imperiled Continent" of Africa illustrated the point that when governments accept responsibility for managing investment, then no one is responsible, and *investment* is thereby converted into *consumption*.

"Joseph Wayas, Nigeria's former speaker of the house preferred to spend," reported Lee Lescaze and Steve Mufson. "One contractor remembers being summoned to draw plans when the speaker wanted a new house. The house had to have: a separate apartment for each of four wives, a separate room for each of ten children (the speaker was the father of six but was planning ahead), a special room for the speaker's three hundred pairs of shoes and for the full-time shoe shiner. Finally, the speaker wanted a room for his 108 suits. From his closet he plucked a pin-stripe suit that he boasted cost $25,000. Each stripe was made of gold thread. He told the contractor he kept identical suits in his London and New York homes."

The two reporters added the following coda: "Like the speaker, many Africans who have grown rich in government have taken large parts of their fortunes abroad. A group of African central bankers estimated last year that between $4 billion and $6 billion left Nigeria during the four years of the civilian regime that was overthrown in 1983." (Nigeria's external debt is in the region of $17 to $20 billion.) Apropos the final point, one can only comment that anyone with money in a country ruled by people like that would be well advised to send the money abroad as soon as possible.

The bankers, development experts, government officials, and above all the professional economists do not understand the key difference between successful, functioning economies (the United States, Japan, and perhaps a dozen others) and the unsuccessful ones, including all the Socialist countries, almost all the African ones, and all those subjected to Islamic law. I refer to property rights.

Claiming that property rights are crucial to economic success has now reached something approaching the status of a taboo, especially among the development economists and international bureaucrats who attend conferences and cocktail parties with their Soviet-bloc counterparts and have been intellectually Finlandized. You won't hear much discussion of property rights in the corridors of the World Bank or the IMF; nor are such rights among the loan conditions imposed by any lending agency. "Property rights," you see, are "ideological." To bring up the topic is an embarrassment in polite society. So it is not brought up. Nor is it ever discussed in the news media, as far as I can tell. In addition property rights are not quantifiable, and for some decades now economists have tried to pretend that economics is one of the physical sciences—dealing with things that can be expressed in graphs and equations.

I can only suggest how important is the notion of property, and how serious the failure to comprehend it, by an analogy. Suppose that a certain country has a drought; its inhabitants are dying of thirst. News of this reaches the United States, whose compassionate citizens dispatch cargo ships filled with water. Upon arrival the aid officials pour the water directly onto the parched earth—not realizing that there must first be in place appropriate receptacles if the inhabitants are to be helped.

The refusal of most contemporary economists to acknowledge the importance of property rights is of the same order of magnitude. To most economists, poor countries are simply short of money. So the officials gather up a shipload of dollars and dump them on the bare soil, unprotected by the foundations of property. The dollars disappear into the ground—one way or another they "evaporate"—and then they reappear later in Swiss bank accounts and New York co-ops.

### Law and Property

Property rights depend on the prior establishment of the rule of law (rules applicable to all, not some commanding others). Over time—and it does take time, which is one of the things the development experts always try to circumvent—the rule of law will yield the security of ownership, individual decision making, the acceptance of personal responsibility for the success or failure of one's decisions, and the ability of owners both to appreciate the value of what they own and to realize that value by exchange. These are the fundamental conditions of economic behavior. They are absent in all societies subjected to the arbitrary rule of autocrats and to the commands of central planners. The fundamental point that some economies have foundations while most do not is not understood by the loan officers of New York banks. They do not understand it because they are most unlikely to have ever heard the subject discussed in meetings. Or when they were in college.

The economics profession is now dominated by people who missed their true calling as accountants. They think of a nation's economy as something contained wholly within a ledger. Some such economies are thought of as "sound" because they are in balance. That is the only recommendation that most economists now have to offer. Budgets should be balanced. Trade should be balanced. To that end taxes should no doubt be higher. Belts in general should be tighter.

Is it any wonder that foreigners, who can look at prosperous America and without too much difficulty conclude that it *must* have been established on greater and more generous principles than mere bookkeeping (namely, the rule of law), should despise us now for having no better ideas to export than mere accountancy and equilibrium—to be attained by encouraging the people to undergo greater hardship?

Giving "loans" to foreign officials—who supposedly will buy something called "development" with the money—in fact precludes the emergence of the rule of law, hence a property base. Government employment becomes an opportunity for plunder and a subsequent getaway. Useful production is an arduous matter and people will only make the effort if there is no alternative. Foreign aid, the World Bank, the IMF, and the fraudulent employment offered by the numerous UN agencies ensure that the educated elites abroad never have to make this effort. Their corruption is guaranteed by multilateral (which is to say mostly American) money.

The donors of this feckless capital cannot easily penalize the recipients for its dissipation into personal consumption. Certainly World Bank officials and U.S. bankers cannot lay a finger on anyone. In the maze of government bureaus—whether at home or abroad—responsibility for decisions is itself shifted and dissipated, just like the original capital, until in the end the blame lies with some nondescript umbrella agency of government, whose head (the aid donors will be reassured) has now been replaced. The aid donors will deceive themselves into thinking that this is a "structural change" and will recommend another loan.

Think by contrast of the U.S. builder who has bought a site and obtained a bank loan to develop it. For him the clock is running. His time is short. He must meet his payments. The only way he can is by building something that is more valuable than the site and the materials and labor that go into developing it. Productivity, efficiency, and effort, which come easily to no man, are thrust upon him by the exigencies of his potential failure.

As long as counterproductive bank lending and multilateral "assistance" continue, the "lesser developed countries" are going to stay that way. In fact their condition will deteriorate, as it has done in the two years since the last debt scare. By contrast a third world default now would be salutary. The welfare states would be forced to make it on their own, which is the only way that prosperity can be attained. At the same time our own economists and development experts might learn a useful lesson about the fundamentals of economic life.

At the present time, however, we are far from any such understanding. A. W. Clausen, the president of the World Bank and before that the president of BankAmerica, wrote in a 1983 *New York Times* Op-Ed piece ("To Help Developing Countries Sustain Growth") that "the first step is to get the problem right. Debts are not the main problem. They are a symptom. The real problem is lack of growth. Unless sound investment continues, there will be insufficient growth to service the debts. The debts can be managed but only if growth is sustained."

You can see the way he is thinking. Aid from accredited sources is to be called "sound investment" and that in turn is the source of growth. There is a "world economy" and its parts are basically fungible and of course "interconnected." Clausen's model is really that of the circulation of the blood. As long as "liquidity" is pumped through the veins of foreign economies, why then they will "grow." And Washington, Clausen clearly believes, is the heart. If the heart stops beating, then the "capital flows" will cease. And then the banks won't get their money back. Let's face it, they're not going to anyway, except no doubt from South Korea and Taiwan.

Clausen merely reflects the current consensus. What is more disturbing is that there are increasing signs among U.S. elites not merely of a failure to comprehend the principles of society and government that made America great, but an actual hostility to those principles. Domestic politics make it difficult for these elites to implement a revisionist agenda at home. In foreign policy, however, they encounter little resistance. But that is another story.

# Where the Latin American Loans Went

## Larry A. Sjaastad

Many a hand has been wrung over the problems that foreign debts pose for Latin American countries. The five largest borrowers—Brazil, Mexico, Argentina, Chile, and Venezuela—have accumulated foreign debts that total almost $300 billion. The burdens have become so onerous, many commentators say, that some means must be found to reduce the interest rates or forgive substantial portions of the debt, which amounts to the same thing.

Certainly debt service puts uncomfortable constraints on the governments of the debtor nations. Moreover, no one questions that the cost of the debt service is greatly magnified by the combination of high interest rates and falling prices for the commodities that Latin American countries export.

However, other important facts usually are left out of discussions of the debt crisis. The figures that frequently appear in the press refer to *gross* debt, about 80 percent of which is owed by the governments, rather than *net* indebtedness (gross debt minus foreign assets) of the borrowing countries. One-third of the borrowed money went to finance the flight of private capital out of the debtor countries; individuals in Argentina, Mexico, and elsewhere used the funds to buy investments in places like New York, Miami, and Geneva. When these foreign investments by residents of the major debtor countries are taken into account, the picture changes quite dramatically. What emerges is an internal deficit problem rather than an external debt problem. What also emerges is the potential for the greatest ripoff of the twentieth century.

The evidence that the borrowed money was used to finance capital flight comes from balance of payments statistics. Large foreign borrowing, which shows up in the balance of payments as a capital inflow, normally causes or is caused by a commensurately large trade deficit. Not so in most Latin American countries. Instead of sending the borrowed dollars back to pay for capital equipment and consumer goods, individuals in Latin America shipped them out to pay for foreign investments. The one big exception is Chile; its residents did use the foreign borrowings to pay for imports and have not acquired many foreign assets.

236

Consider the following data, all of which come from a study by the U.S. Federal Reserve. Argentina's foreign debt grew $9 billion in 1980, a typical year in the period of the heaviest borrowing, while foreign investments by Argentine residents rose $6.7 billion—nearly 75 percent of the increase in debt. That same year Mexico's foreign debt jumped $16.4 billion, and assets held abroad by Mexicans increased $7.1 billion. Brazil's foreign debt rose $11.2 billion in 1980, and Brazilians managed to move $1.8 billion abroad despite very tight exchange controls. Venezuela's debt rose a mere $3.2 billion in 1980, but her residents acquired $4.7 billion in foreign assets that year. For the entire period since the debt explosion began in 1973, residents of these four countries have acquired nearly $100 billion in foreign assets.

Even those figures fail to reveal the full extent of foreign assets owned by the debtor countries. The figures refer only to the funds actually placed abroad and do not reflect the growth of the investments. Since most of those investments were made in the late 1970s and 1980s, it is reasonable to assume that they have earned returns of at least 10 percent a year on average.

If the earnings have not been repatriated—and neither balance of payments data nor the obvious incentives for tax evasion give any reason to believe they were—the foreign assets owned by residents of Argentina, Brazil, Mexico, and Venezuela have reached the magnificent sum of $146 billion. While the gross foreign debt of these four countries is estimated to be $272 billion, their net foreign debt is $126 billion. With the interest rate on that debt averaging 10 percent, net interest payments amount to only $12.6 billion a year—hardly an onerous burden for a group of countries with a gross national product over $500 billion and annual exports of $70 billion.

So what is all the fuss about? Why is country after country marched kicking and screaming to the International Monetary Fund to have its fiscal backside abused? The answer is that the foreign assets are privately owned, while the foreign debts (which made the accumulation of foreign assets possible) are owed by the governments. The government of Argentina, for example, must make the payments on nearly all of the country's $45 billion of foreign debt, with no help from the $31.5 billion of foreign assets owned by Argentine residents.

Herein lies the potential for the great ripoff. The foreign liabilities of the debtor countries are largely sovereign debt, subject to default or repudiation if the governments cannot or choose not to pay. The foreign assets, on the other hand, are quite private. If, say, Argentina defaults, U.S. banks cannot seize the deposits of Argentine citizens.

One might well ask how this sorry situation came to pass. The modus operandi was simple enough. With the exception of Chile, most of the borrowing by Latin American countries was done to finance government deficits. The governments quickly transformed the dollars into pesos, cruzeiros, and bolívares at their central banks and used the currency for their general expenditures, including the enormous losses of government-owned businesses. Savvy residents of the borrowing countries, correctly sensing an early demise of this order, borrowed the pesos, cruzeiros, and bolívares and converted them back into dollars. They used the dollars to buy foreign assets that would be safe from confiscation when the inevitable reckoning came. When the existing order did in fact break down—dramatically so in Argentina and Mexico—those peso borrowings were either forgiven outright or washed away by inflation.

At the core of the issue, then, is an internal fiscal problem. The governments of the major Latin American countries are heavily indebted to foreign banks and can raise the resources to service that debt only with great difficulty. Ample resources exist in the form of foreign assets, but those assets remain beyond the reach of government. When President Alfonsín calls for foreign aid to "save democracy in Argentina," he does so because he cannot persuade Argentines to pay for it themselves. Argentines with foreign assets apparently value financial security more highly than political freedom.

Some Latin American governments are doing better than others in servicing their external debt. Of the five major debtors, Chile is in the worst shape by far; interest alone amounts to 10 percent of its gross national product. Nonetheless, Chile is meeting its obligations. Argentna is at the other end of the spectrum. The interest on its foreign debt is 4 percent of GNP. However, Argentina's budget deficit is approaching 20 percent of GNP while Chile's is about 4.5 percent of GNP. (The figure for Argentina, which is much higher than the published numbers, was cited by Argentine Congressman Alvaro Alsogaray in a discussion at the University of Chicago in October and includes the deficit of the central bank.) A deficit as large as Argentina's clearly precludes any serious approach to the foreign debt issue.

I do not mean to condemn individual Argentines, Brazilians, Mexicans, and Venezuelans who have accumulated such enormous foreign assets. Most of them simply pursued their self-interest and acted within the laws of their countries. But one surely will be excused for a certain irritation with the foolish munificence of U.S. banks and the governments of the debtor countries in promoting those self-interests. The banks gave the money to the governments, and they dumped it in the streets, and the people picked it up and took it to New York.

238